Inflation and Social Conflict

By the same author

The Modern Business Enterprise (ed.) (Penguin, 1972)

Inflation and Social Conflict

A Sociology of Economic Life in Advanced Societies

Michael Gilbert

Lecturer in Interdisciplinary Studies
University of Kent at Canterbury

WHEATSHEAF BOOKS

First published in Great Britain in 1986 by
WHEATSHEAF BOOKS LTD
A MEMBER OF THE HARVESTER PRESS GROUP
Publisher: John Spiers
16 Ship Street, Brighton, Sussex

British Library Cataloguing in Publication Data
Gilbert, Michael
 Inflation and social conflict.
 1. Inflation (Finance)——Social aspects
 I. Title
 332.4'1   HG229

 ISBN 0–7108–0238–2
 ISBN 0–7108–0243–9 Pbk

Typeset in 11 on 12 point Linotron Times
Printed and bound in Great Britain by
Biddles Ltd, Guildford and King's Lynn

THE HARVESTER PRESS PUBLISHING GROUP
The Harvester Group comprises Harvester Press Ltd (chiefly
publishing literature, fiction, philosophy, psychology, and science
and trade books); Harvester Press Microform Publications Ltd
(publishing in microform previously unpublished archives, scarce
printed sources, and indexes to these collections); Wheatsheaf
Books Ltd (chiefly publishing in economics, international politics,
sociology, women's studies, and related social sciences).

For My Parents

Contents

Tables and Figures

TABLES

FIGURES

Preface

In this study I present an analysis of the ways in which sociological factors contribute to the processes whereby inflationary pressures are generated and magnified. Naturally, this involves some consideration of the circumstances in which inflation can be reduced. It also implies that, in general terms, inflation is a 'bad' thing; something which we should try to reduce or eliminate. However, a caveat is in order. Lest the reader should feel that this means that I regard control of inflation as the paramount priority, I should make explicit that this is not the case. Indeed, one of the implications of parts of this study, in particular Chapters 3 and 8, is that attempts to eradicate inflation can impose social and economic costs that far outweigh those produced by the inflation they are intended to eliminate. Unfortunately, those that suffer the costs of the cure are often far less able to voice their discontent than those groups who benefit.

I first became interested in this area of study as a result of a seminar given in my university in the mid–1970s by a visiting American professor. As I disagreed profoundly with his views, it might be best if he remained anonymous. However, should he read this and recognise himself, I hope he derives some satisfaction from being the initial stimulus of my efforts.

Subsequently my work has received much impetus from the comments made by colleagues, friends and students – the categories are not mutually exclusive. So many have been of assistance that it would be invidious to single out individuals. However, it should be said that many of them will be all too little aware of how much benefit and encouragement I have derived from their advice and support over a number of years.

Needless to say, none of them bears any responsibility for the shortcomings that remain in this work.

The theoretical basis of this study has already been published elsewhere (Gilbert, 1981). Parts of Chapters 1 and 2 are heavily based on this earlier account. I am grateful to Edward Elgar for his support and encouragement over the last few years in getting me to extend the earlier analysis to the comparative study that forms the core of this work.

Last, but by no means least, I should mention the small group of secretarial staff who performed the miraculous transformation of a messy manuscript into a polished typescript. My thanks go to Jean, Jo, Linda, Val and Viv.

MICHAEL GILBERT
Canterbury, October 1985

1 Introduction

There can be little doubt of the significance attached to inflation by social scientists in recent years.[1] The rise of consumer prices in the post-war years in western countries has brought inflation to the centre of attention. This rise was already of substantial proportions by the early 1970s, but the oil price explosion of 1973–74 pushed average levels of inflation into double figures in 1974 and 1975, a process that recurred in 1980 and 1981 as a result of the second major price increase in the late 1970s (see Table 1.1).

It is hardly surprising that this resurgence of inflation triggered off renewed academic attention. After all, it had dramatic implications for western governments. They found that concern with inflation replaced growth or unemployment as the key factor in the political business cycle whereby success or failure in gaining re-election was thought to be predicated on the outcomes of economic management (Mumper and Uslaner, 1982; Holmes, 1985). Nowhere was this more marked than in the United Kingdom. Control of inflation became the central objective of the 1979 Thatcher administration, being valued both as an end in itself and as the primary means by which other desirable economic objectives such as growth and rising employment could be engendered. Indeed, such was the primacy attached to the goal of curbing inflation that the hitherto paramount aim of maintaining full employment was excluded from formal statements of government objectives (Pliatsky, 1982, p. 176, quoted in Holmes, 1985, pp. 33–4).

Yet what could not be so readily predicted was that academic interest should no longer be confined to the disciplines

1

of economics, and to a lesser extent that of industrial relations, but should now extend to more behavioural disciplines such as sociology and politics. For the 1970s and 1980s have seen a burgeoning of works discussing the sociology, politics or political economy of inflation as indicated, for example, by those by Fox (1974), Hirsch and Goldthorpe (1978), Medley (1982) and Lindberg and Maier (1985). Where once the study of inflation was an intellectual desert, now several species of flower bloom.

What factors can account for this broadening of academic concern? Apart from the obvious comment that all disciplines have an in-built mechanism to colonise or cultivate new territories, particularly when, as in the present climate, it may be politically advantageous to stress the useful or pragmatic applications of one's expertise, two possibilities can be suggested. First, although higher inflation has become widespread in recent years, none the less there are significant variations in the rates experienced by different countries. A cursory glance at Table 1.1 indicates both the wide dispersion of inflation rates in 1974 and 1975 and the differing speed with which inflation rates fell in subsequent years. As Keohane (1984) suggests, there may be international mechanisms that transmit inflationary pressures from one country to another but countries appear to have differential capacities for absorbing or damping down these pressures. Furthermore, there appears to be no obvious connection between variations in inflation rates and differences in economic and technological variables such as the rate of growth, the share of international trade in domestic production or consumption, or the level of industrialisation. This suggests that non-economic factors might be of some significance. Hence the growth of interest by other social scientists in showing, for example, how the nature of the political system, the structure and form of industrial conflict or the broad cultural values of society might play a role not simply in generating inflationary pressures but in damping or magnifying exogenously-produced pressures.

Much the same conclusion might be reached by a different route. Those traditionally concerned with producing accounts of inflation have themselves begun to introduce socio-political

Table 1.1 Consumer prices: percentage changes from previous years, 1970–84 (selected OECD countries)

	1970	1971	1972	1973	1974	1975	1976	1977	1978	1979	1980	1981	1982	1983	1984
Australia	3.9	6.1	5.8	9.5	15.1	15.1	13.5	12.3	7.9	9.1	10.2	9.6	11.1	10.1	4.0
Austria	4.4	4.7	6.3	7.6	9.5	8.4	7.3	5.5	3.6	3.7	6.4	6.8	5.4	3.3	5.6
Belgium	3.9	4.3	5.5	7.0	12.7	12.8	9.2	7.1	4.5	4.5	6.6	7.6	8.7	7.7	6.3
Canada	3.4	2.8	4.8	7.6	10.9	10.8	7.5	8.0	8.9	9.2	10.2	12.5	10.8	5.9	4.3
Denmark	5.8	5.8	6.6	9.3	15.3	9.6	9.0	11.1	10.0	9.6	12.3	11.7	10.1	10.9	6.3
France	5.2	5.5	6.2	7.3	13.7	11.8	9.6	9.4	9.1	10.8	13.6	13.4	11.8	9.6	7.4
Germany	3.4	5.3	5.5	6.9	7.0	6.0	4.5	3.7	2.7	4.1	5.5	5.9	5.3	3.3	2.4
Italy	5.0	4.8	5.7	10.8	19.1	17.0	16.8	17.0	12.1	14.8	21.2	17.8	16.6	14.6	10.8
Japan	7.7	6.1	4.5	11.7	24.5	11.8	9.3	8.1	3.8	3.6	8.0	4.9	2.7	1.9	2.2
Sweden	7.0	7.4	6.0	6.7	9.9	9.8	10.3	11.4	10.0	7.2	13.7	12.1	13.6	8.9	8.0
United kingdom	6.4	9.4	7.1	9.2	16.0	24.2	16.5	15.8	8.3	13.4	18.0	11.9	8.6	4.6	5.0
United States	5.9	4.3	3.3	6.2	11.0	9.1	5.8	6.5	7.7	11.3	13.5	10.4	6.1	3.2	4.3
Weighted average all 24 OECD countries	5.6	5.3	4.7	7.8	13.4	11.3	8.6	8.8	7.9	9.8	12.9	10.5	7.8	5.3	5.3

Source: OECD (1985), Table R10, p. 165.

and socio-psychological variables into what hitherto have been narrowly conceived economic discussions. Illustrative examples include the work of Wootton (1954 and 1974), Clegg (1971), Jackson, *et al.* (1972), Baxter (1973), Jones (1973), Brittan (1977), Rowthorn (1977), Scitovsky (1978), Rosenberg and Weisskopf (1981) and Tylecote (1981). In the concluding section of this chapter I shall examine in detail how economic analyses of inflation have generated an interest in the contribution of other disciplines, particularly sociology, in accounting for inflation.

FROM ECONOMICS TO SOCIOLOGY

Economic explanations of inflation abound. A recent survey by Hudson (1982) mentions no fewer than seven theoretical stances, most of which he then uses in his own attempt to provide a synthesis. For ease of exposition two broad explanatory models will be discussed: those termed 'cost–push' and 'excess demand'. Both approaches have a number of variants. The monetarist theories will be subsumed under the latter heading. However, particular attention will be devoted to a variant of the 'excess demand' model that may be termed 'excessive democracy'.

(a) Cost–Push Theories
Cost–push models of inflation stress the role of an increase in the price of a factor of production in generating inflation. Factors of production include labour, capital goods, intermediate products and raw materials. Thus, rises in wages or the prices of goods and commodities used in the production process lead to further price rises, unless they are offset by some increase in productivity occasioned by more economical use of productive resources. Such models normally assume that the cost increases are passed on fairly automatically in the form of higher prices either because the costs or production of all firms in the industry are similarly affected or because the level of competition is such that firms are effectively 'price-makers' rather than 'price-takers' (Galbraith, 1969, Chs. 16–19).

In most versions of this model rising wages normally occupy a crucial position. Often they are taken to be the starting-point of cost–push inflation, but in some cases they have a transmission role as they result from a reaction to some other increase in prices thereby generating not a 'wage–price' but a 'price–wage–price' spiral. In the former version wage-receivers are thought to be pressing for a wage increase either to keep up with another group of employees, or to attain some higher desired standard of living, or simply to gain an accustomed or taken-for-granted increase in money wages. In the latter case they may be trying to maintain a level of living standards in the face of rising prices, such as those of oil-based goods in 1973–74, or rising taxes, as in Britain in the late 1960s and early 1970s (Jackson, Turner and Wilkinson, 1972). In both versions, organised labour is thought to have the power to force through its claim for higher money wages even though these claims are in defiance of the 'economic facts of life'.[2] Thus claims are pursued which are not warranted by changes in productivity in the firm concerned and thereby result in rising prices, assuming, as above, that the firm can pass on its rising costs. Alternatively, the deflationary impact of higher taxes or price increases caused by devaluation or rising import prices is mitigated as employees strive to maintain their real living standards.[3]

These mechanisms can be specified more closely. Wages may rise significantly in industries where productivity is rising relatively rapidly. This may occur either because firms can afford higher wages or because the higher wages are themselves linked directly to higher productivity. However, if employees in other industries or firms, where productivity is not rising so quickly, demand and attain similar increases, then this is likely to have inflationary implications. Such wage claims may be based on the view that those performing similar work tasks or utilising similar skills or qualifications ought to receive similar rewards, or that customary differentials between those performing different tasks or having different skills ought to be maintained (Wootton, 1954; Jones, 1973, Ch. 2; Behrend, 1973). In Sweden, the notion of equivalent wage increases for those performing similar work regardless of underlying changes in productivity has been formally built into the wage-bargaining system (Edgren, Faxén and Odhner, 1973).

Of course, it is open to question whether wage claims based on comparabilities or differentials reflect genuine normative beliefs or are simply rationalisations for pursuing instrumental claims. But one way or another, values of fairness or materialism form part of the analysis. Again, the likelihood of such claims being made may depend not simply on the values held by particular groups of employees, but also on the structure of bargaining and the form of union organisation. Decentralised bargaining units and non-industrial unions are likely to facilitate such claims as both tend to increase the range of comparisons that can be made and therefore the chance of some sense of deprivation being experienced. Thus, 'relative deprivation' may be a function of institutional arrangements. Furthermore, as the pattern of expectations and beliefs about pay increases may not be consistent, successful demands for higher wages by some groups may trigger off other demands elsewhere. Again, the structure of bargaining units and union organisation will have implications for this process.[4]

Attempts to compensate for or keep ahead of rising prices or taxes also reflect similar mechanisms: expectations about customary living standards or a more acquisitive or materialistic orientation. Again the institutional setting may have implications for the level of demands. Moderation is less rational if the behaviour of other wage groups is unknown and their restraint uncertain, for one risks being left behind by both their wage increases and the subsequent price increases they induce.[5] As Lange (1984) has pointed out, the situation is akin to the Prisoner's Dilemma game both because one is penalised for showing restraint or cooperation with an incomes policy when others do not behave similarly, and because if other groups do moderate their wage demands with consequential beneficial effects on inflation one gains an advantage through one's own lack of restraint: the 'free-rider' argument.[6] Accordingly, decentralised, fragmented bargaining systems are more conducive to the pursuit of sizeable claims.

Of course, the mere pursuit of wage claims is not of itself

sufficient. What is of importance is that organised labour has the power to pursue successfully such claims. Arguably, in the post-war period such power has increased. In some cases particular groups have a monopoly control over the supply of a particular sort of labour through the use of craft or professional qualifications. More generally, the increased interdependence of economic production gives a greater degree of functional significance to any group of employees performing a specific task within the division of labour and hence increases the bargaining power of such groups of workers.[7] Lastly, the higher levels of employment that pertained until the mid–1970s gave labour power in general a greater scarcity value. Conversely, particularly in oligopolistic situations, management has little reason to contest strongly vigorously prosecuted wage claims. This is partially because the costs can be passed on in the form of higher prices but also because resistance that leads to industrial conflict in the absence of similar behaviour by other oligopolistic competitors might mean not just a short-term loss of production but a long-term loss of customers (Galbraith, 1969; Scitovsky, 1978).[8] Tylecote (1981) has produced a more general 'bargaining theory of wages' which he relates both to the structure and organisation of unions and management. In particular, he points out that the existence of cohesive employers' associations engaging in collective bargaining leads to a tougher bargaining stance by management because strike costs are likely to affect everybody. Thus the power of organised labour may be offset in some cases more than others.

Clearly, the development of 'cost–push' analyses of inflation involves a significant departure from a purely economic analysis. Wages, and thereby prices, do not result simply from the interplay of market forces and the adjustment by actors within markets to changes in supply and demand conditions. In addition, they reflect the norms, reference groups, aspirations and notions of fairness of these actors. Furthermore, specific outcomes of market processes, and in particular labour markets, depend on actual cultural and institutional arrangements and their associated power relationships. Left to itself a capitalist market system does not automatically reach a stable position. Nothing in this should be of any great surprise to sociologists. The lack of any authoritative or normative basis to the structure of income and wealth distribution has long been held to be potentially destabilising. Only if the potentially conflictful claims of different groups and classes can be held in abeyance or if one group has sufficient power to dominate others will stability occur. Thus, sociologists have maintained that as a capitalist economy develops various stresses and conflicts emerge particularly over the distribution of scarce and valued resources. Lack of order is taken to be a key characteristic rather than an aberrant feature of such economies.

The economic cures for 'cost–push' inflation reflect this analysis. They try to impose order on an anonomic situation. The most common solution is some sort of incomes policy aimed primarily at controlling wage increases.[9] Wages are not simply to be determined by the playing-out of market forces but are to be subjected to some external authority. This may take a variety of forms. In some cases expectations and aspirations are to be held in check by the constraints of the policy. Preferably, such policies should be principled either in terms of equity considerations such as equal pay for equal work or special treatment for the low-paid, or those of economic rationality such as different pay for different skills or higher rewards corresponding to increased productivity.[10] Other solutions focus on changing the power of organised labour. If its claims cannot be limited then its ability to pursue successfully these claims must be reduced. Mechanisms include legal restrictions on union activities, restrictions on the system of wage-bargaining and changes in labour market conditions by increasing the level of unemployment or mitigating monopoly powers by limiting 'closed-shop' provisions.[11] A further possibility is to increase competition in product markets, thereby limiting the ability of firms to transfer wage increases automatically into price increases and so stiffen the resistance of employers to pressures to raise wages.

In sociological terms these solutions fall into three categories. First, some are attempts to alter the economistic values and expectations of employees. Next, some involve trying to restrain the pursuit of such values by the use of moral/normative mechanisms. Finally, there are attempts to alter the power relationships between different groups and classes with conflicting interests. As will be seen shortly, the solutions to 'excess-demand' inflation are somewhat similar.

(b) Excess-Demand Theories

The emphasis here is on the level of demand relative to supply in an economy. If demand exceeds supply there are shortages and queues. As a result the prices of scarce commodities are bid up. This includes the possibility of wages being bid upwards if labour in general or in terms of particular skills is in short supply. In theory, the prices of relatively scarce goods and services will be increased until supply and demand are brought into equilibrium. In practice, stability may never be reached if producers or consumers seek to protect themselves against expected price increases and themselves raise prices in anticipation of this, or even if they just react to past increases.

The actual mechanisms whereby 'excess demand' occurs vary. The processes described from a micro-economic point of view in the section above on 'cost–push' can in macro-economic terms produce 'excess demand'. Higher wages, which are not offset by higher productivity, increase effective demand relative to supply (unless the surplus earnings are saved) for various goods and services. Unless their production can be increased or augmented by imports, some sort of 'excess demand' with the consequences described above will result. Thus wage inflation has dual implications for price inflation. Of course, normally these wage and price increases will need to be accommodated by government expansion of the monetary supply. Indeed, monetarists would claim that both 'excess demand' and 'cost–push' inflation are caused by a failure of governments to pursue a proper monetary policy.

From this point of view excessive wage increases only arise as a result of governments 'printing too much money' or trying to run an economy at too high a level of demand, that is, above the 'natural rate' of unemployment.[12] The latter means that the demand for labour will be too high, thereby facilitating wage increases as employers bid against one another for this scarce commodity as well as provoking shortages in other commodities such as capital and consumer goods. The former means that the government is unwilling to finance its own expenditures by raising taxes or the price it charges for the goods and services that it provides. It therefore prints money to finance its own activities, thereby producing the 'too much money chasing too few goods' syndrome. The excess money supply both produces excess demand and lubricates the economic system by providing the cash flow for higher wages and prices.

One solution to 'excess demand' inflation is to raise supply, hence the recent emphasis on 'supply-side' economics. This involves trying to increase output and productivity and making labour more flexible and mobile, thus lowering the 'natural rate' of unemployment. However, usually the solution is to deflate – or as some would put it, to disinflate – the economy.[13] In monetarist terms the government must reduce the money supply by a combination of correcting its own budgetary requirements by cutting expenditure and/or increasing its revenue, and carrying out a restrictive credit policy, usually involving high interest rates, for the private sector. If supply cannot be adjusted to meet demand, then demand must be adjusted to meet supply.

It might be argued that this Micawberish solution is simply a technical matter of economic judgement that is of no sociological import. However, there are two immediate objections to this. First, if organised labour is pressing for high wages, as discussed in section (a) above, then a deflation or reduction of money supply will not act initially to restrain increases in wages and prices but will mainly reduce the levels of production and employment. It is true that deflationary policies will in general lower the power of organised labour, but none the less, it is likely to resist strongly these policies particularly if it is reacting to past price increases or to taxation changes which are being used as part of the deflationary package. Furthermore, some labour and product markets may be so monopolistic that wages and prices can continue to be raised irrespective of modest deflations. Hence, rather than unemployment being traded off against inflation, a 'stagflation' of both rising unemployment and inflation can occur. Some producers faced by falling demand for their products will simply raise the 'mark-up' on their costs thereby increasing prices in order to generate the same volume of profits on a smaller volume of sales. Thus unemployment and inflation can rise together (Wachtel and Adelsheim, 1978).

Put in this way the practicality of the policy does depend on some of the considerations discussed earlier, and its implementation may take on aspects of a class struggle or at least an interest group struggle between those who stay in employment and those who become unemployed. This distributional conflict might be heightened by the particular deflationary mechanisms used. For example, cuts in public expenditure focusing on either reducing the employment of public sector employees or cutting welfare expenditures to particular groups have very different distributional implications from policies of general credit restriction. In a very real sense 'excess demand' inflation may result from a conflict of interests between different groups such as workers, capitalists, transfer-payment recipients and other beneficiaries of government programmes whose aspirations and power collectively generate excess claims on the economic resources of a society (Rosenberg and Weisskopf, 1981).

Second, governments may find it extremely difficult to cut government expenditure in areas which appear to be of functional significance for the maintenance of a capitalist economy. This point has been well made by Marxian writers such as O'Connor (1973). He distinguishes between the functions of accumulation and legitimation. The state has to facilitate the maintenance of profitable capitalist accumulation and try to maintain or create social harmony. The former involves expenditures that indirectly assist the profitability of private enterprise; the latter various sorts of welfare expenditure. These points will be developed in a later section. It is sufficient to note here that the 'economic' cures are subject to constraints which in part appear to have a 'social' nature. This is particularly likely to be the case if cutting welfare expenditure threatens the social cohesion of capitalist society.

The issue of legitimacy has been raised in a different form by Brittan (1977, 1978) and Jay (1976), who comment on 'excessive democracy' as a factor promoting inflation.

(c) Excessive Democracy

Brittan suggests that in western democracies governments are too accessible to pressures from various interest groups. Competition between political élites in elections held at fairly short intervals means that parties have to be responsive to outside pressures. These strains are exacerbated if the government is generally held to be accountable for dealing with or curing various economic and societal problems. Failure to deal with them threatens the future chance of electoral success of the government because its effectiveness and therefore its legitimacy is laid open to doubt. Perversely, potential governments actually heighten expectations about their performance in office by bidding against other political parties in terms of management of the economy and provision of social services.[14]

In general terms, unemployment and inflation are the two most important items of economic management for which governments are held accountable. For example, Hibbs (1979) notes that in the USA since 1972 at least 70 per cent of the electorate view these two items as the most important problem facing the government. To be sure, which is viewed as the greater problem may depend on immediate experience, but it appears to be taken for granted that governments are responsible for both. Certainly in post-war Britain successive governments until, as noted above, the 1979 Thatcher administration, have assumed responsibility for both. Furthermore, it is arguable that it is the perceived responsibility for maintaining full employment that has generated excess demand inflation, as Keynesian budget deficits have been repeatedly used to try to reduce unemployment and promote pre-electoral prosperity. However, Holmes (1982, 1985) has argued that British governments need not have been so concerned about reducing unemployment in order to maintain electoral credibility. He points out that everybody is affected by rising inflation whilst only the unemployed are affected by unemployment. Hence, success in coping with inflation is likely to be of greater electoral benefit than reductions in unemployment. However, Holmes relies disproportionately on the 1983 electoral success of the Thatcher administration to provide support for his view. This success appears to have depended as much on non-economic factors such as the Falklands War and the weakness of the main opposition party as on the 'political business cycle'.[15]

Also, as Husbands (1985) points out, the unemployment issue may be salient not simply to those who are unemployed at any particular point of time but to those who have been unemployed recently, who face worsening employment prospects, or who are closely connected to those in such positions. Hence direct concern with unemployment at a personal level, rather than as a general national problem experienced by others, is likely to be very high when unemployment has stayed at levels in excess of 10 per cent for a number of years.[16]

If coping with unemployment is the most general manifestation of the problem of excessive democracy then it is reinforced by the specific demands of various interest groups. Demands which are in turn reinforced by the threat of loss of electoral and financial support if they are not satisfied. In response to these pressures, and in order to sustain an electoral popularity, governments may need to maintain or increase expenditure in just the sorts of area indicated by O'Connor: industrial infrastructure, industrial aid, welfare and education. Furthermore, as raising taxes or the price of governmental goods and services are not likely to be popular, these measures are likely to be avoided.

Brittan quite specifically relates this discussion not simply to the structure of political institutions and the resultant need for political parties to compete for electoral support, but also to what he terms the excessive expectations of the population as a whole. People expect the government to perform too many functions: in effect, they overload the political system with their demands for successful economic management and enhanced economic prosperity and social welfare.[17] Furthermore, Brittan claims that self-interested groups aggressively pursuing their interests make government resistance difficult. In particular he singles out trade unions as being able successfully to push governments into following full employment policies which are both directly inflationary (excess demand) and further sustain the power of organised labour to claim higher wages and to pressure governments, thus perpetuating the cycle.

Brittan's arguments may be conveniently summarised thus:

The growth of expectations imposes demands for different kinds of public spending and intervention which are incompatible both with each other and with the tax burden that people are willing to bear. At the same time, in their pursuit of 'full employment' without currency collapse, governments are tempted to intervene directly in the determination of pre-tax incomes. But these attempts come to grief when they come up against the demands of different groups for incompatible relative shares. (Brittan, 1977, p. 249)

Governments in this situation face a very awkward dilemma. The more they act to meet successfully the demands placed on them, the more likely they are to legitimate and heighten the expectations underlying these demands. Instead of the wage–price spiral we seem to have an expectations–achievement spiral! Brittan's solutions rest on a combination of depoliticising some economic decisions; damping down expectations or desires for distributional justice; and reducing the power of interest groups, particularly organised labour. In general, these solutions bear considerable resemblance to the cures for 'cost–push' inflation. However, they are to be applied at macro rather than micro levels and involve the further stage of trying to separate the polity, that is the governmental system, from social and economic pressures.

SOCIOLOGY AND INFLATION

This brief review of economic theories of inflation has shown how what starts as a narrowly defined economic analysis is developed to include various non-economic factors. Constantly, reference is made to the norms and values of various groups of income-receivers and to the aspirations and expectations that they have. Furthermore the power they have to pursue these claims either at the micro level of wage or price determination or at the macro level of affecting the overall level of demand in the economy often assumes crucial significance. Not all these factors fall specifically within the sphere of sociological analysis. For example, social psychologists such as Behrend (1973) have much to say about standards of comparison and reference groups used in formulating wage targets whilst political scientists have contributed to discussions on the capacity of the state to withstand inflationary pressures (Anderson, 1978; Olson, 1975). However, in recent years a distinctively sociological contribution has emerged.

This contribution differs radically in one important regard from mainstream economic analysis. For although economic analysis has developed to include non-economic factors it tends to regard them as peripheral elements which in some way distort the core mechanisms of a liberal capitalist economy or cause it to malfunction. Thus income-receivers are represented as having unrealistically high expectations or as disregarding the 'laws' of economic life. Perhaps they are too forceful with their claims or have too much monopoly power. Possibly, governments are too exposed to their pressures. Somehow a picture is presented of a normal economic world in which inflation would not occur if only people behaved properly or at least if those whose behaviour upsets the system could either have their power reduced or their access to and influence over governmental decision-makers limited.

Many sociologists would agree with some of the details of this analysis. In particular, they would also stress the role of organised labour in pressing for higher wages and the competing pressures on national governments to leave their budgets unbalanced. However, they would also dispute that these are abnormal elements whose presence distorts the functioning of a capitalist market economy. Rather, the contrary argument is put forward that they are integral to the development of a capitalist market economy and as such are not disturbances that can be corrected by the appropriate combination of good-will, common sense and institutional reform.[18] Instead, the sociological argument puts strong emphasis on the core materialistic values of capitalist societies: what MacPherson (1962) has termed 'possessive individualism'. As these values of economism and acquisitiveness gain ground amongst all social groups, so excess demand and inflationary wage pressures are likely to result unless the pursuit of these values is restrained or the power to pursue them is limited. Thus, sociological analysis puts distributional conflict between competing groups of income-receivers at the centre of the stage as an element that arises from the nature of the liberal capitalist economy. Inflation is seen as a 'natural' consequence of the development of capitalist market economies where self-interested individuals and groups have sufficient power to pursue their distributional claims.

This view is also accepted by some radical or Marxian economists (Rowthorn, 1977; Rosenberg and Weisskopf, 1981). It surfaces in a different form in other Marxian critiques, but again the emphasis is on inflation being a natural or normal feature of the development of a capitalist market economy. The concern of these writers is with the need of governments, or the 'state apparatus', to spend heavily to maintain the capitalist economy or to put off the 'crisis of capitalism'. Expenditures fall into two areas: those concerned to maintain the profitability of capitalist accumulation in the face of the tendency of the rate of profit to fall; and those concerned to legitimate the capitalist economy. The former comprise essentially governments carrying out various investment activities that the private sector would not otherwise perform, subsidising other investment programmes and, through various expenditure programmes, particularly on defence or aerospace, providing effective demand for profitable capitalist production. The latter is normally taken to be welfare state expenditure that allegedly assuages discontent that might otherwise occur. The central point of the argument is that these 'necessary' expenditures tend to rise and are not offset by increased government revenues: hence the 'fiscal crisis of the state' (O'Connor, 1973).

On the surface, this approach appears to be very similar to that of Brittan's 'excessive democracy'. But whereas there the emphasis was on governments being exposed to too many pressures for expenditure from the electorate at large or from specific interest groups, here the focus is on the state acting as an 'agent of capital' and recognising tasks of economic and political management that are necessary for the maintenance and survival of the capitalist economy (Habermas, 1976; Offe, 1975, 1984, Ch. 1). These functionalist explanations have a teleological nature whereby government actions are explained in terms of how they are 'necessary' reactions to crises of the capitalist economy. As such it is difficult to see

how they really account for which particular forms government expenditure takes particularly as often expenditure
which is discussed as being necessary to meet functional
problems of capitalism is in turn held to lead to a deepening
crisis. This is not to say that governmental decision-makers do
not react to particular contingencies such as declining investment or pressures for welfare expenditure, but rather to
argue that proper investigation requires historical study of
each structural situation and analysis of the ways in which key
actors perceive and react to these constraints.[19]

In Chapter 2 the analysis of inflationary pressures by contemporary sociologists will be examined in some detail. Their
accounts will be used as the basis of a sociological model of
inflation. The sociological implications of inflation on, for
example, social integration and social inequality will not be
discussed except in so far as they feed back on the processes
whereby inflationary pressures are generated or transmitted.
The model of inflation will then be used to see whether it can
help to account for variations in the experience of inflation
in different western capitalist countries. Studies of four
countries; the UK, USA, West Germany and Sweden will
form the subject-matter of Chapters 3–6.

For several reasons the case-study approach has been
preferred to that of cross-sectional analysis using a greater
number of countries. First, even in cross-sectional studies the
number of countries for which there is relatively reliable data
is still small, normally about twenty, and this is not really
enough for the sort of correlational statistical techniques that
are used. Next, many of the key concepts are extremely
difficult to operationalise effectively. This is partially because, as with the issue of the power of organised labour,
several different measures such as union density, strike activity
and the number of years labour-oriented parties have participated in government have to be combined, but also because
official statistics are often collected in different ways making
accurate comparisons difficult. Strike statistics are an obvious
example. This problem of operationalisation often leads to a
further difficulty as apparently exceptional or deviant cases
appear in particular countries or at particular times. These
exceptions then have to be explained away if the statistical

analysis is to retain credibility.[20] Last, the model developed in Chapter 2 stresses the interrelationship of a number of factors. The case-study approach gives greater scope for a qualitative and historical study that can show the interplay of these factors. The reasons for choosing the particular countries that have been studied will be elucidated at the end of Chapter 2.

The Marxian analysis referred to above will not form part of the development of the sociological model. However, in Chapter 7 it will be utilised to explain how inflationary pressures are coped with in East European countries, Poland being selected for the most detailed analysis. The contrast with the western case studies should help to highlight how capitalist economics generate and cope with inflation.

In the final chapter the sociological model of inflation is reassessed in the light of the case studies. No attempt is made to provide a 'sociological' cure for inflation but indications are given as to what social and political circumstances are most likely to be propitious for coping with inflationary pressures.

2 A Sociological Model of Inflation

We have already noted that whereas economists tend to view inflation as arising from some malfunctioning of capitalist market economies, sociologists tend to view it as being a natural or inherent feature of such economies. Nowhere is this put more clearly than by Goldthorpe (1978, p. 195):

For the sociologist, however, the natural tendency is to look for quite specific connections between inflation, as experienced in capitalist societies, and the market economy; and in fact to regard inflation as being the particular manifestation, within a given historical context, of the social divisions and conflicts which such an economy tends *always* to generate. (My emphasis)

Goldthorpe, like Fox (1974, Ch. 8), takes for granted that values of economism and acquisitiveness are widespread in contemporary western societies. Indeed, Goldthorpe argues explicitly that these values have long been present in capitalist societies, and probably even preceded them (Goldthorpe, 1978, pp. 200–1). However, Goldthorpe claims that the significant development in recent years has been a change in the way that these values have been pursued. Thus Goldthorpe argues that it is not that these values have intensified and become more widespread, but rather that restraints on their pursuit have abated and that the structure of power is such that more groups of income-receivers are able to prosecute their claims. The result is a vigorous distributional conflict where the vigour owes little to any rise in aspirations or 'revolution of rising expectations' but more to the willingness and ability of a multiplicity of wage and salary-earners to exploit their market position to the full.

Goldthorpe provides the empirical basis of his argument from recent British experience. However, he does indicate that Britain may be the prototype for other capitalist societies:

The suggestion I would venture is that secular changes in the form of stratification evident in British society may be taken as the most developed manifestation of tendencies, or potentialities, which are in fact generally present in the societies of the advanced capitalist world – a speculation that I would then naturally wish to link with the position of some pre-eminence which Britain today also holds in inflationary 'league tables'. (Goldthorpe, 1978, p. 197)

These changes in the stratification system are those that both reduce the restraint and enhance the power of large groups of employees.

First, Goldthorpe points to the 'decay of the status order'. He argues that in the past, the status order provided a consensual set of values about the relative worth of different groups of people. It thus helped to legitimate the class inequalities of pay and authority that derive from market relationships in the capitalist economy. However, Goldthorpe suggests that the status order belongs to the pre-capitalist origins of British society and its underlying values and beliefs are increasingly being eroded as the capitalist economy develops. In particular, he indicates that 'urbanisation and the greater physical mobility of the population, which are concomitants of industrialism *per se*, largely eliminate the local status group structure in which a status order tends to be manifested in its most concrete relational form' (Goldthorpe, 1978, p. 199). In addition, the growing commercialisation of exchange relationships, that is the spread of the cash nexus to new areas, undermines exchanges based upon mutually accepted notions of obligations and responsibilities. Furthermore, he asserts that as status comes more to depend on achievements in market exchange and less on entitlements of birth or on localised interactions, the whole notion of social superiority becomes problematic.

Goldthorpe goes on to suggest that this undermining of the status order removes one of the main restraints on the pushfulness of individuals or groups in market relationships. For the existing market-based inequalities can no longer be legitimated by reference to norms of social superiority which are widely accepted. Thus it is open to groups of employees to assert whatever market power they have to maximise, or at least enhance, their rewards. Indeed, as Fox (1974) has forcefully argued, workers may simply be aping other groups such as employers and professionals in exploiting their market power to the full.

Second, Goldthorpe refers to the 'realization of citizenship'. In particular he suggests that citizenship rights now include a widely accepted notion of the right to work. Thus contemporary governments are held responsible for maintaining full employment and will reap the electoral consequences of failure so to do. Apart from loss of electoral support, Goldthorpe also points to the likely loss of trade union cooperation that would make economic management more difficult as a further possible consequence of a government allowing unemployment to rise. Now, it must be said that recent British experience suggests that high unemployment may be tolerated by the electorate, particularly if it tends to be geographically and socially concentrated. Governments may appeal to the self-interest of those who are in employment or are self-employed to attain electoral success. However, Goldthorpe's argument has a more general validity. The widening of the political franchise and the development of state-run social welfare systems may jointly serve to increase the range of obligations and expectations that governments feel they have to meet. In this context, the difficulties experienced by the Thatcher administration, elected twice on a commitment to reducing public expenditure, in actually reducing social expenditures may be significant.

Last, Goldthorpe points to the 'emergence of a mature working class'. By this Goldthorpe means that the objective power of the working class has developed, as opposed to any question of norms and expectations that might govern its use of such powers. As evidence for this maturation Goldthorpe argues that the British working class has become more stable. The transition from rural, agrarian economy to urban, industrial production is long over. The working class is largely self-recruiting, that is to say it is the offspring of people who themselves formed part of the urban, industrial proletariat.

As such it is both more attuned to its material circumstances and has been able to develop organisational institutions to advance its position, in particular trade unions. Goldthorpe implies that even if the working class is not, in Marxist terms, a self-conscious class, it is a series of sectional groups with the ideological and organisational capacity to further their position. Maturation, as an historical process, has led to the development of power which can and is used to disrupt the workings of the integrated capitalist economy.

Taken together these changes in the stratification order provide the opportunity and means for distributional conflict to provoke rises in inflation. The increased 'pushfulness' of the mature working class results in inflationary pressures both at the micro and macro levels. At the micro level it takes the form of cost–push inflation whilst at the macro level governments are pressured to maintain full employment thereby facilitating excess demand inflation.[1] Indeed, Goldthorpe goes as far as to suggest that governments may be content to allow high levels of demand and their associated inflationary pressures as a means of warding off social conflict. For if they were to follow monetarist doctrines and deflate the economy the resulting unemployment would stir up social unrest, and possibly lead to a serious class-based challenge to political authority:

a monetarist policy would appear designed to sharpen the social conflict stemming from the unpersuasive character of market criteria . . . and, at the same time to structure this conflict on broad class lines, bringing organized labour into direct confrontation with government in defence of its achieved bases of power and security. In turn, then, the serious danger, from government's point of view, would arise of the crisis of legitimacy now existing in the sphere of distribution being extended into that of political authority also. (Goldthorpe, 1978, p. 209)[2]

Furthermore, distributional conflict heightens the sectionalism of the working class as, effectively, they compete with one another: conflict may both be contained within the economic sphere and used to fragment the working class (Crouch, 1978).

In essence, Goldthorpe's argument is that capitalism is a socio-economic system which produces a structure of inequality that results from the interplay of market forces. The structure of inequality is no longer legitimated by any consensual set of values. As such, individuals and groups feel free to use whatever market power and advantages they possess to further their materialistic interests and improve their socioeconomic condition. The maturation of the working class means that organised labour has the power to generate and transmit inflationary pressures, even though their short-term ability to raise money wages through threatening or carrying out industrial action is subsequently offset by rising prices. Similarly, their ability to maintain governmental commitment to full-employment policies has the cost of rising inflation. Thus, inflation occurs because capitalist market economies are essentially anomic societies in which self-interested individuals and groups have sufficient power to produce inflation as a result of their distributional conflict.

Fox (1974) and Crouch (1978) also put distributional conflict at the centre of their accounts of inflation. However, Crouch raises a series of other issues that are also of relevance. First, he is far more explicit than Goldthorpe about the power of business arising from increased industrial concentration. This has two important implications. On the one hand, it provides fertile ground for unionisation as unions usually find it easier to organise recruitment in large-scale plants. On the other hand, the rise in oligopoly facilitates the wage–price spiral aspect of cost–push inflation as producers find it easier to pass on higher wage costs as price increases. Thus, Crouch is much more explicit than Goldthorpe in indicating how capitalist development leads to roughly equally-matched power blocs opposing one another with both organised labour and large-scale business able to use their power to push up prices, of wages or goods, to gain a short-term advantage.

However, Crouch is also much more explicit than Goldthorpe in discussing whether there are circumstances in which groups of income-receivers might exercise restraint in the pursuit of their claims. Basically, he argues that restraint is more likely under two sets of circumstances. First, if the workforce, and in particular their leaders, can trust that restraint in the short term will be reflected ultimately in higher living standards and social welfare because of higher production and output. Crouch (1980) develops the point more fully by specifying that restraint in the pursuit of wages is more likely to occur in societies where employers invest a high proportion of profits in domestic industry rather than distributing them in dividends or investing them abroad, because organised labour knows that long-term growth is more assured. In societies such as Japan, Sweden and Germany where this 'high trust' dynamic occurs, union leaders are more likely to cooperate in formal and informal incomes policies. Furthermore, they are more likely to carry their members in support of such policies, for their members too will be more trustful because past experience has shown that current sacrifices will yield future benefits.[3] This could be a very important mechanism for explaining why some societies appear to be more able to withstand exogenously-produced inflationary pressures, such as those generated by the 1973–74 oil price rise, than others. 'High trust' societies may be better placed to make short-term adjustments, such as a freeze or small fall in real wages, that limit the development of inflation. In addition, the greater industrial harmony engendered in such societies, as wage settlements are less likely to involve overt industrial strife, is likely to facilitate increased production. Thus higher living standards and increased social welfare benefits are doubly assured: both because of higher investment and through more fruitful use of productive resources.

Crouch also suggests that increased participation in government by the leaders of organised labour is likely to lend itself to restraint. His argument is that this will extend their concern from narrow issues of self-interest to broader questions of economic management. Crouch recognises that this will bring with it the potential problems of leaders losing the support of their members who are distanced from them and may not share their broadened concerns. Although Crouch does not fully develop the argument he appears to see increased participation not simply as another way of engendering 'trust' relationships, but also as a way of tackling the problems raised by Olson (1965) of 'collective goods' and 'free-riders'. If union leaders are more involved in governmental decision-making then they are more likely to recognise that what might be good from the point of view of one sectional group, namely higher money wages, may be bad when applied across the board because it generates higher inflation and loss of international competitiveness. Furthermore, a consensually agreed policy with the active involvement of representatives of organised labour lessens the probability that there will be 'free-riders' who push their own demands whilst benefiting from the restraint shown by others. Accordingly, Crouch suggests that corporatist modes of interest organisation, where interest groups are directly involved in governmental decision-making, are more conducive to wage restraint than pluralist modes, where interests remain autonomous and contend with one another in sectional terms.

In a more recent paper Crouch has extended his earlier analysis. He concludes: 'once economic actors have become organized, the socio-political content most likely to be consistent with relative freedom from economic distortions will be one which encourages co-ordination of action and centralization of organization rather than one which tries to reproduce among organized interests situations analogous to a free market' (Crouch, 1985, p. 137). Here Crouch is referring not simply to the involvement or incorporation of organised group interests into the governmental apparatus, but also to the organisation of these group interests into their own collective bodies. Much the same conclusion is reached by Paloheimo (1984). He too suggests that where interest groups are autonomous, decentralised and compete with one another (the liberal or pluralist situation), distributive conflict is likely to be significant. But where they are incorporated and organised in centralised federal structures (the corporatist model), then distributive conflict is likely to be limited. Thus, Paloheimo argues that broad, encompassing labour federations are more conducive to the promotion both of industrial harmony and of lower inflation than small section unions. His main reason is that they are more likely to be concerned with the collective Olsonian goal of growth than simply redistributing income in their favour. It is not surprising that in his one explicit discussion of inflation, Olson (1975) suggests too that unified union structures are likely to have less inflationary implications than fragmented sectional unions.

Paloheimo tests his theory by a cross-sectional study in which industrial militancy, measured by labour dispute activity, is correlated with the way in which interest groups are organised. Unfortunately, Paloheimo's classification of countries by the degree of economic consensus between government and organised groups introduces an element of tautology. For it is hardly surprising that where consensus is high, conflict is low. There is a further problem in Paloheimo's methodology which arises from his use of labour dispute activity as an indicator of industrial militancy which, in turn, is a proxy for the degree of distributional conflict. Although strikes may often indicate underlying conflict, the threat of strike activity is also indicative of conflict. In many cases this threat is sufficient to force concessions from employers. Thus actual labour dispute activity may be a poor indicator of the extent of distributional conflict. However, Paloheimo's work is important in raising a series of questions about how far the power of organised labour as measured by unionisation, centralisation and access to the governmental process forces policy concessions, such as commitment to full employment and a growing social wage, in return for which restraint is offered in the industrial arena. We shall return shortly to a fuller consideration of variations in the power of organised labour.

Before doing so, brief mention should be made of the work of Lindberg (1982). He too sees inflation as resulting from distributional conflict, but he stresses also that institutional arrangements may lead to a moderation of claims for greater social and economic rewards. He suggests that high information and high (group) participation societies are more likely to resist inflationary pressures whether they are produced exogenously or endogenously. He defines information as:

The extent to which there is among members of all major groupings whose relative income shares are at stake a symmetrically distributed capacity to perceive how variations in prices, employment, and real income affect their interests (and those of others?), and to organise to articulate demands based on these interests. (Lindberg, 1982, p. 33)

Whereas group participation refers to:

The extent to which common interest groupings, with the power to press (successfully) for a larger nominal share of the incremental social surplus, symmetrically and continuously participate in the decision-processes that determine macroeconomic target variables and instrument variables. (Lindberg, 1982, p. 34)

Lindberg is suggesting explicitly that in countries where interest groups are highly organised, then the greater their shared information about the consequences of their activities and the greater their involvement in decision-making then the more likely they are to recognise the broader implications of their distributional conflict, for example, for raising inflation or lowering employment and output, and thus adopt consensual policies to mitigate these effects. As with Crouch and Paloheimo, Lindberg is arguing that where cooperative processes have developed with centralised unions (and employer federations) directly involved in economic policy formulation then the combination of information and participation is likely to enhance inflation-stabilisation and growth-maximisation policies. International variation in inflation rates may then be at least partially explicable in terms of historical variations in the development of interest group organisation and involvement with government.

However, this discussion assumes that organised labour has already become sufficiently powerful to press forcefully its claims, both at the micro and macro levels. It is only in this context that the questions of whether or under what circumstances that power will or will not be used become relevant. In other words, the preceding discussion assumes that the dominance of capital has been threatened and possibly matched. At the micro level of the workplace organised labour can press for wage claims that can generate or help transmit inflation. At the macro level of economic decision-making governments pursue expansionary and inflationary pressures both to buy the cooperation of powerful unions and to buy electoral support. Again, it is possible that there can be significant national variations in the power of organised labour or in the power and willingness of business interests to resist it.

As regards the micro level one widely accepted indicator of organised labour's power is the density of unionisation.

However, as can be seen from Table 2.1 this shows significant variations in western countries. Furthermore, in some countries union organisations are split on religious and/or ideological grounds. For example, in France there are major union confederations which are communist, socialist or Catholic. Union power at the workplace is also affected by whether or not there is a closed shop, thereby giving the union a monopoly of power.

Table 2.1:   Union densities and splits in the labour movement in eighteen OECD countries, 1900–76

	Before World War I %	*Inter-war* %	*1946–60* %	*1961–76* %	*Union split*
Australia	30	37	52	48	
Austria	6	43	54	56	
Belgium	5	28	42	52	Political, religious
Canada	8	12	25	27	
Denmark	16	34	48	50	
Finland	5	8	30	47	Political, religious
France	7	12	25	27	Political, religious
Germany	16	46	36	34	
Ireland	—	15	33	40	
Italy	11	19	27	18	Political, religious
Japan	—	20	26	28	Major
Netherlands	16	27	31	33	Religious
New Zealand	17	25	44	39	
Norway	6	19	47	44	
Sweden	11	30	65	76	
Switzerland	6	15	25	22	Religious
UK	15	29	43	44	
USA	8	10	27	26	

Source: Korpi (1983), Table 3.2, p. 32, Table 3.6, p. 40.

But union density and organisation is only one side of the coin. In some countries employers may be better situated to resist the demands of organised labour. Tylecote (1981) has pointed out that where employers' associations are strong there may be greater resistance to wage demands. This might also happen if managers are more directly accountable to shareholder interests and thereby cannot readily buy a quiet life by conceding wage demands.[4] Furthermore, Tylecote has also pointed out that large multi-plant companies are better able to withstand pressures in any one plant, because production may be kept going elsewhere. This highlights a central problem of labour organisation. As production tends to be increasingly multi-plant and multi-national in nature, even if union densities are high in a particular country or region of the country, that power may be of little avail if employers are not dependent on a particular source of labour. Yet the problems of agreeing collective action amongst groups of workers in different countries are difficult enough even when union density is high let alone when, as is often the case, the relevant groups of workers are in poorly unionised developing countries such as Taiwan and Singapore.

In more general terms the question of organised labour's power at the workplace can be related to the question of dualism (Goldthorpe, 1984). There may be some sections of the economy where organised labour is strong and able to press for significant wage claims. But these may coexist with areas where labour is not unionised and where it has little leverage. For example, workers in small firms which either compete with one another in the production of consumer goods or produce capital goods or intermediate goods for large or giant firms are in a vulnerable position. Whatever power they possess to disrupt production is mitigated by the fact that their companies are in a weak or dependent commercial position. Their power is affected by their employer's market situation. Even within a large company, some workers may have a weak position if they do not perform some key activity and/or are easily replaceable. Unionisation may to some extent enhance their position but only if their union can control the supply of labour by use of a closed shop or entry qualifications. However, where labour is readily replaceable because work tasks have been deskilled these conditions are not likely to prevail.

This dualism of labour market conditions between those in secure, well-paid jobs with the potential of industrial muscle arising from the monopoly or control of functionally important

and indispensable activities as opposed to those whose positions are precarious because of their dispensability or the
weak position of their employers is also affected by broader
factors. Clearly, the legislative framework provided by
governments is of crucial importance because this affects the
legality of particular forms of industrial action as well as the
vulnerability of groups of workers to fines and compensation
payments for breaches of employment and commercial contract. More generally, governments can choose whether or
not to legislate for various worker rights in such areas as
minimum wages, conditions of employment, information disclosure, employment protection and worker participation
in managerial decision-making bodies. Furthermore, the
government's attitude towards unemployment has important
implications for workplace bargaining in so far as high unemployment generally weakens the position of organised
labour and low unemployment strengthens it.

The role government has in influencing workplace power
relationships directly, as well as indirectly through affecting
the level of employment and demand, means that worker
power at the macro level has also to be considered. A variety
of writers have pointed to national variations in the influence
of organised labour on the government (Korpi and Shalev,
1979; Korpi, 1983; Cameron, 1984). They tend to use similar
measures as indicators of union power. In particular, they
point to the existence of links between union confederations
and a labour-based political party, to the absence of cleavage
between left-wing parties, to the proportion of manual
workers supporting that party as well as to the electoral
success and participation in Cabinet-formation of those
labour parties. Again, considerable national variations are
shown in Table 2.2.

The writers tend to agree that where the power of organised labour is high as measured by the electoral success and
participation in Cabinet of a party allied to their interests,
then they are able to gain pay-offs in the form of expansionary
policies, enhanced social welfare provisions, and a set of
legislative rights advancing and protecting the worker's
employment position. Where this has happened organised
labour has been able to offset the dominance of capital's

position and has the basis either of controlling the state apparatus with a view to developing a socialist society (Korpi, 1983) or of bargaining its restraint and moderation for future policy concessions (Crouch, 1985).

Table 2.2: Working-class influence on government in eighteen OECD countries, 1946–76

	Left votes as % of electorate	Weighted cabinet share	Proportion of time with left representation in cabinet	Party split
Australia	44	Medium	Low	
Austria	45	Medium	High	
Belgium	32	Medium	Medium	Minor
Canada	11	Low	Low	
Denmark	39	Medium	Medium	
Finland	39	Medium	Medium	Major
France	32	Low	Low	Major
Germany	31	Low	Medium	
Ireland	9	Low	Medium	
Italy	34	Low	Medium	Major
Japan	28	Low	Low	Major
Netherlands	31	Low	Medium	Minor
New Zealand	41	Medium	Medium	
Norway	41	High	High	Minor
Sweden	43	High	High	
Switzerland	18	Low	High	
UK	35	Medium	Medium	
USA	1	Low	Low	

Source: Korpi (1983), Table 3.6, p. 40.

A SOCIOLOGICAL MODEL OF INFLATION

The discussion above has ranged over a variety of factors. It is now opportune to identify more formally those analytical variables that underpin sociological accounts of inflation. The model contains four elements, two normative and two structural. The normative elements refer first to the existence and strength of economistic values, and secondly to the extent to which there are normative systems restraining the pursuit of such values. The structural elements refer first to the structure of power amongst groups of income-receivers, and secondly to the productive capacity of the socio-economic system.

The argument, in brief, is that a high inflation is more likely if economistic values of calculative self-interested advantage are widespread and strongly held, and if normative systems that might restrain the pursuit of such goals are weak and less pervasive. As regards the structural elements, high inflation is more likely if power is widely dispersed amongst different groups or individuals so that they are able to affect the prices of the goods and services (including labour power) that they sell or influence the pattern and scale of government expenditure in their favour. Again, high inflation is more likely if the productive capacity of the system is relatively low. Conversely, stable prices are likely to be facilitated by low economism, high normative restraint, power restricted to a few groups and possessed by buyers rather than sellers and high productive capacity.

In effect, the model accounts for inflation, other things being equal, as the consequence of unrestrained distributional conflict between different groups whose total demands or aspirations are greater than the capacity of the economy. It can produce either 'cost–push' or 'excess demand' inflation. Indeed, in terms of the model, both are really variants of excess demand distinguished by whether their effects occur first at the micro level when the sellers of goods and services directly force up prices, or at the macro level when the total intended expeditures of consumers, investors and government is excessive. Of course, 'other things being equal' has to be stressed. The model only attempts to predict tendencies which can be offset by other circumstances. The model is not an attempt at sociological imperialism. Countries which operate under different economic circumstances will be affected by them. Thus, for example, the degree of openness of an economy to international trade may make it more or less vulnerable to importing rising prices, particularly of commodities, though this in turn may reflect a world-wide relative scarcity of these goods. In addition, the extent of international trade both reflects the self-sufficiency of the domestic economy and, by providing other potential suppliers, affects the structure of power in domestic markets. However, the converse point is also true, our sociological factors should be important in determining why countries with similar economic and technological features do not always have similar inflation rates: they are, in a sense, the explicit or implicit 'other things being equal' of economic models.

One last general point should be made before examining the elements of the sociological model in greater detail. At this stage the model only identifies a number of analytical factors. It is essentially a-historical as it does not explain how or why these factors came to have a particular form in a particular society. Hence the importance of historical studies of individual societies which can assess why, for example, normative restraints are as strong or weak as they are currently and possibly, thereby, the stability of such restraints.

(a) Normatively Prescribed Goals of Action

The goals of action of actors within a socio-economic system may be more or less economistic. That is to say, the values associated with possessive individualism may be more or less widespread. These values do not refer simply to the ends of action but also to the rational calculation underlying their attainment. Thus economism has both a materialistic and an instrumental dimension. These values would appear to be most consonant with a capitalist economy because the logic of capitalism is that of market exchange between self-interested actors who enter into such exchanges on the basis of rational calculations of advantage. Contracts specify the rights and obligations of parties to an exchange, and people try to enter contracts which offer the most favourable balance of rewards to costs, and of benefits to be gained against duties to be performed (Fox, 1974, Ch. 4; Gilbert, 1978, pp. 343–6).

However, the assertion that these orientations are most consonant with the logic of capitalism tells us little about how widespread and pervasive they are in actuality. Presumably, there may be empirical variations between different societies as to their presence and strength. As we have seen, Gold-thorpe (1978) assumes that materialist values probably pre-ceded capitalist development in the UK but argues that they have become more pronounced in recent years. His argument also implies that other capitalist countries are likely to follow suit. However, Inglehart (1977) suggests that materialistic values may vary with the objective level of material advance-ment. Inglehart's argument depends heavily on the seminal paper by Maslow (1943) in which he distinguished a hierarchy of needs and tried to demonstrate that the higher-level needs of esteem and self-actualisation only become of importance if the lower-level needs relating to physical well-being are satis-fied. In a similar manner Inglehart argues that high levels of material living standards may lead to the sating of material needs and a consequential switch to post-materialistic values. In a sense, Inglehart is saying that economic well-being may come to be taken for granted and greater stress may be given to hitherto latent values which are qualitatively different – for example, those of environmental concern and intrinsic job satisfaction.

Inglehart's thesis suggests that economism may vary curvi-linearly with the level of material advancement of a country. As economic development gathers pace, economistic striving may increase in pervasiveness and intensity because appetites are whetted by rising prosperity in a revolution of rising expectations. But at more advanced levels of development and prosperity, economism may decline because appetites are now satisfied and concern with material factors slackens. Thus there may be national differences in the extent and strength of economism that reflects differences in the level of material prosperity. Furthermore, there may be class differ-ences within a country that reflect differences in class well-being.[5]

In his more recent work, Inglehart (1981) has stressed that the balance between materialism and post-materialism may depend on both long-term generational factors and short-term exigencies. Thus, on the one hand, he emphasises that the circumstances in which people are brought up socialises them into values which are more or less materialistic. Here he pays particular attention to the level of economic prosperity during the formative years in shaping values. Yet, on the other hand, immediate economic difficulties occasioned by a slow-down in the rate of growth or a rise in inflation (or the two combined in a stagflation) can cause all generational cohorts to swing towards materialistic values as their economic well-being is relatively threatened. From this point of view it may be that changes in the rate of growth are as important as absolute income levels. For people may come to expect rises in living standards and take them for granted and therefore feel more threatened when such rises do not occur. This view is quite consistent with the work of Soskice (1978), who argues that the rise in industrial militancy as measured by strike activity in West European countries in the late 1960s was directly linked to the increased frustration experienced by workers as inflation rose and the rate of real wage growth slowed. In a similar vein Jackson *et al.* (1972) have stressed how the combination of inflation and the growing burden of direct taxes affected real wages in the UK and caused increased pressure on pay levels. Thus economism may be related to short-term as well as long-term economic advancement.

(b) Normative Restraints

Whereas the first normative element concerns the content of individual values in terms of goals (materialistic) and mode of attainment (rational calculation), the second element concerns the existence of any authoritative normative system that might restrain the pursuit of such goals. The difference is akin to the Durkheimian distinction between egoism and anomie: the former pertaining to the content of values, the latter to a system of regulation of the pursuit of such values.[6] The distinction is important, for people may or may not have economistic values, but even if they do they may be restrained by normative means from using whatever power and resources they have to achieve them. Goals cannot be equated directly with action.

Authoritative normative systems may take two forms: a transcendental value system which dominates or incorporates individual values: or a set of rules that governs how people may strive to achieve their goals. Both imply some superior authority whose values are internalised by individuals. The main examples of the former are traditional status orders and nationalism. As the earlier discussion of Goldthorpe demonstrated, a traditional status order legitimates a structure of inequality. Individuals and groups know and accept their position, not because their appetites are sated but because their position is prescribed by the status order. In theory, however, the status order is untenable with the assumptions underlying a capitalist market economy. In a market economy rewards derive from the interplay of market forces, whereas in status society they derive from position (rank) in society. In the former case, the structure of rewards is essentially unprincipled or anomic, in the latter case it is essentially authoritatively given. This makes it very likely that the development of a capitalist economy will undermine the old status order.

The other main possibility, nationalism, appears to have more potency. Individual goals, or at least their pursuit, may be subsumed or incorporated within national aims. Arguably, a cultural heritage that stresses collectivist rather than individualist values might help foster a situation whereby sectional interests are restrained in the furtherance of the national economy. This might be particularly likely if the mode of industrialisation involved substantive state orchestration rather than being left to *laissez-faire* mechanisms. Japan and Germany might provide examples of this. However, the subjugation of sectional interests to this higher authority, nationalism, is almost certainly contingent on sustained economic success that provides long-term practical pay-offs for short-term restraint, thereby reconciling sectional and national interests. Furthermore, national economic success, as measured by position in the international economic growth table or by the feeling of a sustained rise in prosperity, itself relegitimates the authority of nationalism thereby perpetuating the cycle.

The other type of normative system that might restrain the pursuit of economistic ends pertains to what might be called the 'rules of the game', the culturally approved means of achieving the prescribed materialistic ends. Of particular importance here will be any institutional mechanisms that cut across the free play of market forces. Prices and incomes policies, arbitration procedures, concordats between government and industry or government and unions fall into this category. These can all be viewed as attempts to bring order into an essentially anomic situation. As such they run against the basic tenets of a capitalist economy. Accordingly, a number of writers have suggested that their chances of success, that is, of achieving widespread acceptance, may be compromised by the fact that the wider socio-economic system within which these restraints are meant to operate itself remains unprincipled, that is to say, the result of past market forces. The new rules of the game are to apply to changes in wages and prices, often defined in terms of flat rates or constant percentage increases unless a special case can be made out in terms of higher productivity or labour shortages. Thus if the acceptance of these institutions depends on how fair and just they appear to be, and such judgements rest on both the formality of the procedures and the substantive outcomes they produce, the failure to reorder the broader system of privilege and advantage may be crucial (Crouch, 1977; Fox, 1974, Ch. 8; Goldthorpe, 1974; Willman, 1982).

Further difficulties may be briefly discussed. For these institutional arrangements to be morally binding they must appear to be all-inclusive. The visible exclusion of some occupational groups or productive concerns, or their ability to breach the rules, unless it can be justified by some set of principles built into the framework, threatens the legitimacy of the whole order. Thus the ability of senior professional and administrative personnel to gain high pay rewards and fringe benefits or the ease with which multinationals can earn high profits (for example, in oil or pharmaceuticals) can undermine what would otherwise be a generally accepted institutional framework. This general acceptance is important. It is not enough for the leaders of industry, be they the heads of large unions or large companies, to accept the regulative power of these institutions. Consent has to be widespread as small groups of workers may have the power to disrupt the pattern of income increases contrary to the desires of their union leaders: union chiefs may be incorporated but not their members (Crouch, 1977). Yet visible breaches of the system threaten the legitimacy of that system. Similarly, in so far as price controls rest on some voluntary agreement between business federations and government, their efficacy may be threatened by the behaviour of 'rogue' companies, possibly multinationals directed from elsewhere, who do not feel bound by the rules, or by the exclusion of small businesses if they are able to raise further their prices and thereby undermine the system through their effect on real wages and thus substantive outcomes.

The earlier discussion of work by Crouch, Paloheimo and Lindberg suggests that some institutional and political contexts may make it easier to secure a system of normative restraints. Of particular importance is the degree of centralisation of bargaining arrangements. This is of significance for two reasons. First, a centralised bargaining system limits the number of separate agreements that are made and the scope for comparisons with other groups, thereby lessening the chance of a series of leap-frogging settlements. From this point of view company and industrial unions are preferable to craft and general unions because the latter facilitate multi-union company and industry bargaining. Furthermore, broadly-based labour federations that engage in real bargaining with employers' federations are preferable to loosely-knit, atomistic groupings that have no bargaining role, not only for this reason, but also because they force into the open the overall question of what the consequences of bargaining are likely to be. They are likely to facilitate the widening of concern from narrow sectional interests that are not concerned with the outcomes of their distributional conflict to an awareness that bargaining does have implications at the macro level for inflation, output and productivity.

In a similar manner greater participation and more shared information are likely to lead to a broadening of the frame of reference. Participation in decision-making bodies and information exchange or disclosure can take place within the enterprise and in national fora. They have the likely consequence of reducing the sectional nature of bargaining. This is partially because they promote greater awareness of macro consequences but also because they lessen the possibility of there being a 'free-rider': the group or individual who avoids the costs of restraint while benefiting from the restraint of others. Participants in decision-making cannot opt for the 'free ride' in advance and once they accept decisions they are to some extent bound by their prior participation. Under such circumstances non-compliance or failure to cooperate is very visible and will threaten the system thereby jeopardising the putative 'free ride'. Much the same result is likely if central-ised employee and employer federations do not bargain directly with one another but none the less participate in national fora which at least define parameters within which bargaining subsequently takes places.

The major drawback of these institutional arrangements is that they tend to draw union and business leaders into central-ised bodies and thereby widen the gap between leaders and members. The political context may aid union leaders at least in gaining the support of their members for their policies and bargaining agreements. The continued participation of left-wing parties in government may lead to policies of enhanced social welfare provision and demand management aimed at full employment that demonstrate the advantages of cooper-ation. Union leaders may bargain restraint in exchange for these policy commitments in centralised negotiations with government: bargained corporatism (Crouch, 1980, 1985). However, as the benefits from these policies accrue to rank-and-file members their support for wage restraint may also follow. Lange (1984) has pointed out that as these 'side payments' (i.e. greater social welfare and enhanced employ-ment prospects) are available to everybody, this overlooks the 'free-rider' problem. However, this ignores the point that if there are too many 'free-riders' the system of restraint will collapse and with it, in all probability, the electoral popularity of the left-wing party. In addition, as Lange indicates, the 'side payments' may have a symbolic function, being a sign of the cooperation between government and organised labour and a way of maintaining credibility that the benefits of cooperation will continue into the future.

It should not be inferred that the success or regulatory power of systems of restraint depends solely on voluntary normative compliance. On the contrary, deviant cases may have to be dealt with by legal sanctions such as fines. However, legal force will only support these institutional arrangements if they are widely accepted: if they are morally binding. In those circumstances, legal sanctions may bolster the system by dealing with a limited number of exceptions. More generally, a legally enforceable prices and incomes policy will have some impact because of the authority of the law, but without the underlying normative commitment its efficacy will be undermined by breaches, whilst resultant government unpopularity will tend to mean that the legislation is short-lived. Legal factors may restrict the power of organised labour to raise wages or of business to raise prices, but discussion of this will be confined to the next section. However, before doing so the argument concerning both sets of normative elements will be summarised.

Different societies may exhibit cultural variations in either or both sets of normative factors. Economism may be more or less widespread, normative restraints may be more or less weak. In so far as cultural variations exist, and this is a matter for empirical investigation, these may be explicable in terms of countries being at different stages of development or because they have followed a different historical path. It may be that as the development of capitalist society tears asunder the old social order 'economic man' emerges and multiplies. However, it is less obvious that if the old regulative restraints – the status order, deference – collapse, that they cannot be replaced by newer authoritative systems. Though the efficacy of these mechanisms may depend both on the existence of particular institutional and political contexts and also on whether as a consequence the economic system is successful in meeting individual aspirations.

(c) Power

Even if economism is high and normative regulation weak, the position may be stabilised if power is so concentrated that only a few groups can push through their claims. The point is paradoxical. First, if power is so concentrated that only one or a very small number of groups can exercise it, then that group or groups can dominate. The distribution of privilege and advantage will reflect that power. Distributional conflict will be resolved by the superior power of some groups. This will be true both in terms of relationships within the industrial sphere (micro-allocative mechanisms) and in terms of pressures on the government (macro-allocative mechanisms). Arguably, this is the situation that prevails in those stages of capitalist development when organised labour is weak and capitalist interests can entrench themselves in the political system. It is more likely to survive if financial rather than industrial interests predominate both because financial power is more flexible and because it is less likely to be fragmented in competitive processes than industrial power. Conversely, a situation of widely fragmented power will produce similar but not identical consequences. If producer groups have very little power they will be unable successfully to pursue large demands. This will be true of organised labour and business if they find themselves in a 'buyer's market'. Again, governments subjected to a variety of weak pressures are more likely to resist them successfully.

Claims may be pushed through with inflationary consequences in the industrial sphere when a number of different income-receivers have sufficient power. Similar consequences occur if governments can be pressured by a variety of powerful interest groups. Power both has to be concentrated in order to be effective and dispersed, so that a variety of claims can be pursued, for distributional conflict to result in anomic consequences. Groups of workers with sufficient power to push through wage claims and employers with power to raise prices is just such a situation. Oligopoly or monopoly in both labour and product markets provides the power for economistic claims to succeed. Similary, as Gordon (1975) notes, the exposure of government to interest groups whose electoral or financial support is needed, such as the beneficiaries of expenditure programmes, tax-payers who provide government finance and those who benefit from rising national income, has inflationary consequences.

Developments in capitalist economies tend to give rise to this sort of situation. The increased division of labour both within and between enterprises tends to raise the functional significance of any groups of workers who can monopolise the performance of a particular task. The increased scale of production, with its associated standardisation and bureaucratisation, provides fertile ground for worker organisation, whilst the same concentration of production gives rise to oligopoly in product markets. However, there may be counter-tendencies. The deskilling of work tasks or the use of migrant workers as an 'industrial reserve army' may weaken the market position of work groups. The ability of multinationals to switch production elsewhere may stiffen further the managerial bargaining position. In addition, particular trade union and industrial relations laws on 'closed shops' and strikes may weaken the effective power of work groups. Furthermore, the deliberate exploitation of some groups with a weak bargaining position such as the low-skilled migrant workers may damp down distributional conflict in favour of those with a monopoly of particular skills.

In like manner, not all business enterprises will operate in oligopolistic markets. Some sectors of the economy are still characterised by relatively small-scale concerns, whilst in other cases large-scale enterprises may be exposed to considerable international competition with resultant pressure to stabilise prices (and costs). In addition, governments may support these competitive processes by removing barriers to international trade and legislating against monopolies and restrictive practices. Thus the distribution of power within the industrial sphere may differ according to particular institutional arrangements and patterns of economic development.

Governmental exposure to interest group pressure is likely to rise with the extension of the franchise. Furthermore, attempts by governments to enter into agreements or contracts with the leaders of organised labour or business or to allow them to participate in national economic fora or decision-making bodies are likely to be associated with rises in expenditure without compensatory increases in income. As the discussion in the previous section has indicated, union leaders may bargain moderation for increased social welfare expenditure and the commitment to full employment policies, which in turn strengthens the position of organised labour. Similarly, governmental concern to encourage business to invest and expand production may lead to investment grants and tax concessions that enhance profitability and attract multinational companies.

However, governments are not passive agents. Within the

A Sociological Model of Inflation 43

constraints of a capitalist economy, particular governments can choose to resist some claims more than others, particularly those stemming from non-business interests. Governments can act to lower the power of particular groups, reduce their dependence on them and exclude them from effective participation in national economic decision-making. Clearly, left-wing parties in government that depend on financial and electoral support from organised labour have somewhat limited options.[7] Other governments may try to weaken organised labour as illustrated above by legislation on employment and trade union law, by encouraging labour mobility, or increasing unemployment. In addition, governments may try to influence public values as to what is feasible and thereby limit expectations as to what can be reasonably expected of a government in terms of factors such as the level of unemployment or welfare benefits and expenditure. By doing so they may be able to engineer electoral success even in the face of Brittan's excessive democracy. This is not to deny that such developments might have different consequences. Attempts to politicise industrial relations may heighten rather than reduce conflict if they are believed to be infringements of traditional practices. Governmental attempts to rewrite the 'rules of the game' unilaterally or to do so in a way which supports one side of industry may lead to non-cooperation or more active hostility. Again, the parameters of action are affected by particular historical and cultural circumstances especially those pertaining to the legitimate right normally accorded to the state to exercise power.

(d) Productive Capacity
The second structural element concerns the productive capacity of the economic system. In essence, the higher the level of output attained in the economy then the more likely it is that the inflationary consequences of distributional conflict can be averted. Economistic claims can be pursued relatively unrestrainedly and forcefully without resultant inflation if the economic system is highly productive. However, this in turn depends not simply on factors such as natural resources, the level of technology and the skills of the labour force, but also on the way in which productive potential can be enhanced and

utilised. The term 'animal spirits' has been used to characterise the general dynamism of industrial leadership in an economy. Again, cultural variations are possible in this area. These may be augmented by the nature of workplace relationships. The degree of cooperativeness of organised labour, the extent to which it facilitates or hinders the introduction of new work processes and procedures, and the extent of industrial conflict that limits production can have important consequences for production. They affect the extent to which productive potential is translated into actual performance in the short term or enhanced in the long term.

Dynamic Aspects of the Model
Until now the four elements of the analytical model have been discussed as if they were independent of one another. In practice, it is doubtful if this is likely to be the case. Already there have been hints that the presence or relative strength of one element will have implications for other parts of the model. It seems more likely, as will be discussed shortly, that actual societies will have one of two particular configurations of the four variables. One configuration corresponds to a 'virtuous cycle' that is highly conducive to avoiding or restraining inflationary pressures. The other corresponds to a 'vicious cycle' that exacerbates inflationary pressures. The former is better able to cope with inflationary shocks, such as higher import prices of commodities and raw materials like oil, whereas the latter is not only unable to cope with such external disturbances but very likely to generate its own inflation.

Consider first the implications of a productive system with a high and increasing productive capacity. In the short term this can fuel rising material aspirations, although according to Inglehart, in the longer term values are likely to be directed towards non-materialistic ends. However, if productive capacity exceeds or equals the current level of material demands this will tend to enhance the legitimacy of the socio-political system and, in particular, to underwrite the authority of any normative system which restrains the pursuit of economistic ends. A structural basis for normative restraint is provided because the favourable substantive outcomes, such as growth, employment and enhanced social welfare provision have implications for the formal procedures that produced them, that is, the restraint and moderation that restricts inflation and maintains international competitiveness.[8] Conversely, societies with low or declining productive capacities may find that they experience some national sense of relative deprivation *vis-à-vis* other societies that figure more prominently in the international economic growth table. In turn, this may heighten awareness of a gap between desired material goals and actual achievement and simultaneously undermine any existing system of normative restraint. This conclusion differs from that of Lange (1984), who suggests that pessimism rather than optimism about the economy is more conducive to restraint. He suggests that if economic conditions are favourable then this gives opportunities for gain through, for example, wage-drift and productivity bargaining whilst boom conditions generate investment without this having to be bargained for in corporatist arrangements. Conversely, economic pessimism may lead to restraint if it is thought that this will help lead to improvement. However, Lange discounts two factors: the extent to which economistic values may be sated for he assumes that people are economic 'maximisers' rather than 'satisficers'; and the extent to which economic prosperity might be thought to be contingent on past and continued moderation in pushing demands.

Consider further the implications of a relatively low level of material demands, or at least a level that is satisfied by the ongoing economic system, and a legitimated normative system prescribing how such ends may be pursued. First, these are likely to lead to an underutilisation of whatever power resources are available to income-receivers because they have no need to look for such mechanisms. Second, because conflict is abated, they are more likely to be associated with harmonious and orderly workplace relationships and thereby facilitate productive investment and expansion. This is likely to be further reinforced, if, as is probable under these circumstances, the government's fiscal problems are relatively slight, thereby providing a favourable atmosphere and appropriate interest rates for stimulating business activity.

In some cases, where restraint has been bargained in return for policy concessions, there will in any case be a government commitment to expansionary policies. Again, the converse situation may arise. Dissatisfied, unrestrained income-receivers will tend to seek out and create power resources. Disharmonious workplace relationships are likely to occur as claims are prosecuted vigorously. Under such circumstances the introduction of new production methods and procedures are likely to be resisted. In capitalist economies, particularly ones increasingly affected by multinational companies, this is hardly conducive to further investment and growth in productivity and output.

In short, as indicated above, it is possible to map out two feasible models with different, but opposite, configurations of the four variables and suggest that particular societies will tend to approximate to one or other type. Thus, if it were possible to measure the relative strength or weakness of each of the four variables: degree of economism; strength of regulating norms; power dispersal and concentration; and capacity of the productive system, societies should correspond to one of two models: the former constituting a 'virtuous cycle' and the latter a 'vicious cycle'.

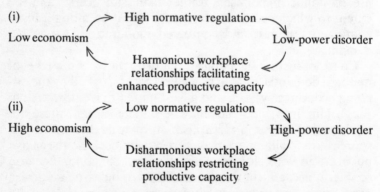

Figure 2.1: The virtuous and vicious cycles

Following Fox (1974), the two cycles are described respectively as having a 'high trust' and a 'low trust' dynamic. Unfortunately, it is more likely that the latter cycle will be stable over time than the former. It is difficult to break out of a 'vicious cycle' whilst a 'virtuous cycle', although having a certain durability, may come under threat. In particular, when the 'virtuous cycle' depends on cooperation, bargained or otherwise, between government and union leaders, then business leaders may challenge the system. One reason for this is that the expansionary policies which follow may be disliked because they may involve labour shortages. However, a further reason is that these expansionary policies are likely to involve higher, though more stable, rates of inflation than if very restrictionary policies were pursued.[9] These two factors taken together may provoke opposition by both industrial and financial interests who see power being shifted towards organised labour. In short, business interests may use short-term problems as an excuse for challenging a 'high trust' dynamic based on partnership between the industrial and political wings of organised labour. More generally, external shocks can threaten the survival of a 'virtuous cycle'. To be sure, one of the main advantages of the cycle is that it makes it more likely that restraint will be shown in order to adjust to a temporary set-back. However, long-term problems caused, for example, by world-wide recession or structural unemployment induced by a new labour-saving technology may undermine key elements of the cycle, in particular the material prosperity that is taken for granted by the population. Once one factor loses its strength other elements of the cycle are likely to become weaker.

Testing the Model
Many of the items that will be examined in detail during the case studies have already been indicated. Thus the ideological heritage of a society in terms of the significance of individual-istic or collectivist values and the success or failure of incomes policies or voluntary agreements between governments and union or business leaders, are obviously important factors in considering normative regulatory mechanisms. The centralisation of employer and labour federations, the centralisation of bargaining arrangements and the involvement of the leaders of peak organisations of employers and employees in governmental decision-making fora are important for discussing both the likelihood of normative restraint and the

structure of power. The latter also involves consideration of issues such as union density, the strength of left-wing political parties and the degree of competition in labour and product markets. The extent and intensity of industrial conflict is significant both for the structure of power and the state of workplace relationships, whilst the latter may also be affected by local participatory mechanisms.

One element, that of economism, is more elusive. Marshall (1983) has pointed out there has been a tendency to assume that economistic values of materialism and acquisitiveness flourish in capitalist societies. This arises mainly because the major factor linking workers to their employers is the cash nexus, hence they are likely to respond to investigations of their values by reference to economic factors because they frequently have an immediate salience. In this study use will be made of data on materialist and post-materialist values analysed by Inglehart and his followers. This will be supplemented by data pertaining to the strength of environmental and ecological movements and to worker interest in factors intrinsic to their work as further evidence of the strength of post-materialist values. In addition, use will be made of relevant surveys of worker attitudes that examine workers' interests and economic goals and, in particular, their sense of economic deprivation compared to other groups.

The choice of countries reflects the theoretical considerations that have already been outlined. On the surface the UK provides an example *par excellence* of the 'vicious cycle' whereas Germany and Sweden are frequently cited in terms of their economic success, possibly pointing to some 'virtuous cycle'. Yet the latter pair of countries differ in terms of a number of salient factors. In particular, union density and the political success of left-wing parties has been much greater in Sweden than Germany. Both, however, have a cultural tradition stressing collectivist values in contrast to the British heritage of individualism and *laissez-faire*. The USA shares many elements of this tradition but does not seem prone to the British sickness. Well-known differences in union density and the absence of a left-wing political party suggest that the USA too could provide a fruitful case study.

Other countries could have been discussed. France and

Italy provide examples of countries where both the political and industrial wings of the labour movement are split by ideological and religious factors, but lack of time and space precluded consideration of another country. Japan is frequently cited as another 'success story', yet perhaps too much of this is due to its very distinctive cultural traditions for a useful comparison to be made with western countries. However, one concession has been made in the interests of broadening the range of comparisons. In Chapter 7, East European societies, in particular Poland, will be discussed to see if the theoretical model has more general significance and in order to highlight the most crucial factors in western societies.

3   The British Disease: Cured?

For much of the post-war period Britain has been character-ised as the sick man of Europe. Precise definitions of the British disease are hard to come by but its main features, be they symptoms or causes, correspond well with the 'vicious cycle' of inflationary tendencies outlined in Chapter 2. Thus, frequent reference is made to the low rates of growth of output and productivity and to the relatively high rates of unemployment compared to most of the advanced industrial countries of the western world. A highly adversary system of industrial relations forms part of the account as this allegedly facilitates 'unrealistic' wage claims that are not warranted by the 'economic facts of life'. In turn, it is argued that the pursuit of these claims through strikes and other forms of industrial action has a variety of effects. If they are successful then prices are pushed up and workers 'price themselves out of jobs' as British goods and services lose their competitive-ness in international markets. Industrial conflict itself directly disrupts production and makes it likely that the introduction of new techniques and systems of production will be resisted. In addition, the unrealism of demands for economic wages spreads to the sphere of the social wage, the welfare benefits and services provided by the state. As governments try to meet these demands without financing increased expenditure through higher revenue they fuel the inflationary pressures by 'printing money'. The new result of these processes is a socio-economic system whose productive development is retarded whilst it produces a set of demands in excess of available resources.

This account can be expressed readily in terms of the low

trust dynamic of the 'vicious cycle'. On the surface it seems that economism is high and is not restrained by any set of normative values. Hence the failure of successive incomes policies to show any durability. In addition, it seems that organised labour has the power to force through its claims at the micro level of the workplace or firm, even though these gains are then offset by the price increases they induce. Most accounts of the British disease are silent about the role of oligopoly in transmitting inflationary pressures, but presumably they assume implicitly that wages pressures are so strong that price inflation is inevitable or that oligopolistic competition facilitates wage-induced price increases, as costs can simply be passed on to customers. Further, these accounts also suggest that the structure of power at the macro level is such that governments, fearful of electoral consequences, are vulnerable to pressures from organised labour and other interest groups. Lastly the disharmonious nature of workplace relationships is assured by the conflictful nature of self-interested sectional bargaining and this in turn lowers the capacity of the socio-economic system to meet the demands that are being generated.

Of course, this is a somewhat simplified account and it assumes or asserts the presence or absence of particular values, patterns of behaviour and distributions of power. In addition, it gives no indication of how or why such factors might have developed. In the following sections an attempt will be made to examine more rigorously the British situation as regards the four variables of the sociological model of inflation. The discussion will be set in the specific British context of a society which was the first to industrialise and did so against the backcloth of a highly individualist and *laissez-faire* culture. The analysis will be brought together to see if there really is, or was, a British 'vicious cycle'. The concluding section of this chapter will examine the Thatcher experiment, to see if this radical right-wing government's approach heralds a new age of realism: an end to the British disease.

ECONOMISM IN BRITAIN

The discussion in Chapter 2 has indicated already the difficulties in trying to measure the extent and pervasiveness of economistic values in any country. However, it was suggested that one possible guide was the use made by Inglehart and his followers of the distinction between materialistic and post-materialistic values and the corresponding attempt to identify the proportions of 'materialists' and 'post-materialists' in any given country. Unfortunately, there are some severe problems in utilising Inglehart's work for our purposes.

In the first place, Inglehart's identification of 'materialists' and 'post-materialists' does not rest simply on concern with material factors. His usual procedure has been to ask respondents which two out of a set of four factors seem most desirable to them. The four elements are 'Maintaining order in the nation'; 'Giving the people more say in important political decisions'; 'Fighting rising prices'; and 'Protecting freedom of speech'. Those respondents who choose the first and third factors are identified as 'materialists', whilst those choosing the second and fourth factors are described as 'post-materialists'. This procedure reflects Inglehart's interest in using Maslow's earlier work on a hierarchy of needs for it distinguishes between those who give priority to the basic needs of material well-being and physical safety and those who place greater value on the higher order needs of 'belonging' and 'self-actualisation'. However, this procedure has two disadvantages for our purposes. It produces a significant 'mixed' group of respondents who choose an element from both of the 'materialist' and 'post-materialist' pair of value priorities. More importantly, it also means that being identified as a 'materialist' depends not only on a preference for a material factor, 'Fighting rising prices', but on an element that cannot have the same implications for our discussion of economism, 'Maintaining order in the nation'. In the light of this difficulty, use will also be made of more specific questions used in some of Inglehart's surveys that relate more directly to economism.[1]

The other difficulties are less important. Much of Inglehart's data come from public opinion surveys sponsored by the European Community (Eurobarometers). As membership of the EEC changed during the 1970s so the data base altered. Inglehart is able to cover consistently six European countries (Belgium, Britain, France, Germany, Italy and the Netherlands) as well as the USA, which he surveyed independently. In addition, some of Inglehart's work covers Denmark, Ireland, Luxembourg and Switzerland. Lastly, as Inglehart (1985) himself indicates, the sample sizes of each survey are relatively small and this suggests that they should be used as broad indicators particularly when sample sub-groups are being discussed.

Table 3.1:   Post-materialists and materialists in six European countries and the USA

		1970	1973	% 1976	1979	1984
Britain	Materialists	36	32	36	27	23
	Post-materialists	8	8	8	11	16
Germany	Materialists	43	42	41	37	19
	Post-materialists	10	8	11	11	17
France	Materialists	38	35	41	36	35
	Post-materialists	11	12	12	15	12
Italy	Materialists	35	40	41	47	43
	Post-materialists	13	9	11	10	9
Belgium	Materialists	32	25	30	33	34
	Post-materialists	14	14	14	14	10
Netherlands	Materialists	30	31	32	28	21
	Post-materialists	17	13	14	19	21
		1972	1976	1980		
USA	Materialists	35	31	35		
	Post-materialists	10	10	10		

Sources: Inglehart (1981) Table 2, p. 888; Inglehart (1985) Table 6, p. 526.

In most of his work Inglehart (1971, 1977, 1981, 1985) finds that Britain has a relatively small proportion of post-materialists compared to other western societies. Marsh (1975) has a similar finding. The only exception to this is the 1984 data. It is difficult to know whether this marks a significant development or is an artefact of the small sample size. However, as can also be seen from Table 3.1, Britain does not have a noticeably higher proportion of materialists than the other countries. Inglehart (1977, pp. 36–7) reports the results of separate surveys conducted in 1972–73 that include not only the seven countries of Table 3.1, but also Denmark, Ireland, Luxembourg and Switzerland. Again Britain ranks low for post-materialists, with only Denmark and Ireland having a smaller proportion. In addition, both these countries as well as Germany, Italy and France have a higher proportion of materialists, with only Belgium having a smaller proportion.

This does not augur well for the view that economistic values are particularly pronounced in the UK. However, more detailed analysis does alter the position. First, if the ratio of post-materialists to materialists is considered, Britain ranked seventh amongst the eleven countries of the 1972–73 survey with only Italy, Germany, Ireland and Denmark having a lower ratio (Inglehart, 1977, p. 38). This measure may be a better indicator, because it discounts the mixed category. In addition, Inglehart's analysis shows quite clearly that Britain has the smallest inter-generational shift towards post-materialism of any of the eleven countries. This is important for two reasons. First, it suggests that economistic values may be becoming relatively stronger in Britain. Second, it suggests a fairly strong relationship between values and the overall level of prosperity.

The UK has been slipping down the economic league tables during the post-war period. As Table A.1, below, indicates, in 1960 only the USA, Luxembourg and Switzerland of the other ten countries had higher per capita output than Britain. By 1970 only Italy and Ireland were still occupying a lower position. Noticeably, these were two of the four countries with a lower ratio of post-materialists to materialists. A third of these countries, Denmark, seems to have shifted significantly towards post-materialism by 1976 (Inglehart, 1977, p. 33). Accordingly, the 1972–73 data show a very clear correspondence between the British ratio of post-materialists to materialists and her position in the international economic league table. Only Germany appeared to be more 'materialistic' given its level of economic prosperity, though by 1984 that too had changed (Table 3.1).[2]

Again, the very small inter-generational shift towards post-materialism in Britain correlates well with Britain's fall in relative economic prosperity. According to Inglehart's theory, values should reflect both current exigencies but also the level of prosperity and economic security during the socialisation period. Thus, one would expect the younger British respondents to be relatively less materialistic than the older cohorts but not to the same extent as their foreign counterparts. This is what the small inter-generational shift signifies. In addition, the 1972–73 data shows that amongst the youngest age groups, post-materialist values are less common in Britain than any of the other ten countries and materialist values at least as common as any other country except Denmark (Inglehart, 1977, pp. 36–7).[3]

It has already been pointed out that Inglehart's use of materialism and post-materialism does not depend simply on a preference for economic ends and, accordingly, may not be the most salient indicator for assessing economism. In his discussion of the 1973 data, Inglehart provides details that enable the economic factors to be analysed separately. In this survey respondents were asked to indicate two preferences from a list of twelve factors that included three economic goals: 'fight rising prices', 'economic growth' and a 'stable economy'. Britain had a greater proportion of respondents choosing the first two economic goals than any of the other nine countries (Switzerland was excluded from this survey) and had only a slightly smaller proportion than Germany when all three economic factors were considered together (Inglehart, 1977, p. 49).[4]

Lastly, Inglehart (1977, p. 155) discusses the degree of satisfaction with income. The data pertain to his 1973 survey except for Switzerland, for whom it comes from 1972. Only France and Italy have a higher proportion of respondents than Britain who answered that they were 'not very satisfied' or 'not at all satisfied' with their income. Again it is worth emphasising that Italy was one of the two countries that had a lower per capita income than the UK by this period.

When one considers these more specific indicators of preferences for economic goals and dissatisfaction with income it does seem that Inglehart's work provides quite strong evidence of the pervasiveness of economistic values in Britain compared with the other western countries. Even his own analysis of 'materialism' and 'post-materialism' provides some support for this conclusion, particularly as regards the younger age groups.

Further support for this conclusion can be reached by considering two related factors: support for ecological and environmental movements and concern with non-pay aspects of work. In the former case fairly strong support should suggest that material or economistic concerns are relatively modest as attention is being paid to the 'quality of life'. In the UK the political support for the ecological movement has been very modest. In the 1983 general election there were over 90 Ecology Party candidates. They averaged a paltry 1.1 per cent of the vote with 2.9 per cent being the highest share (Taylor, 1985, p. 161). This compares very unfavourably with the parliamentary success of 'green' candidates in countries such as Germany and Sweden. A more direct comparison can be made from the 1984 European Parliament elections. In the UK, ecology candidates got 0.5 per cent of the vote compared to over 8 per cent in Germany and Belgium. Indeed, nowhere in Europe did 'green' candidates stand with less success than in the UK (Jowett, 1985, p. 111). Admittedly, British voting figures are influenced by the first-past-the-post system of deciding elections as this tends to lower support for minor parties because of the fear of wasting votes. None the less, the data do suggest that 'bread and butter' issues dominate electoral politics in Britain to an even greater extent than Europe.

In a similar vein, widespread concern by employees with non-pay aspects of work such as intrinsic job satisfaction or control over workplace activities would modify any conclusions about the extent and pervasiveness of economism. However, there is little evidence to indicate that is the case. Certainly, the vast majority of industrial disputes are about wage-related matters, whilst numerous empirical studies of workers' attitudes have failed to find much evidence of concern with intrinsic job satisfaction.[5] Also there has been very little grass-roots pressure for greater participation in management or industrial democracy. The increase in participatory schemes in recent years in Britain reflects employers' initiatives aimed at legitimating managerial authority (Elliott, 1978, p. 160). There has been greater interest shown by some union leaders in industrial democracy, particularly in terms of representation on the Board of Directors, but this has mainly been for pragmatic reasons. It reflects concern that important decisions that affect employment opportunities are being centralised, for example, mergers that might lead to post-rationalisation redundancies, and as a consequence the desire to influence such decisions. Even so, other union leaders sharing these concerns have argued that their members' interests can best be served through collective bargaining and that they should not involve themselves directly in managerial functions.

More evidence of economism in Britain can be derived from surveys of people's attitudes towards economic inequality. In a much cited study, Runciman suggested that although actual inequalities of income and wealth were extensive, these did not appear to be very salient to many people. In particular, he found in his national survey of 1962 that over a quarter of his respondents said that there were 'no other sorts of people doing noticeably better than themselves or their families' (Runciman, 1966, p. 192). Furthermore, although lower-paid workers were more likely to think of people doing better than themselves, less than two-thirds of them did so. A further feature of Runciman's work was that even those who did feel that there were 'other sorts of people doing noticeably better' were remarkably reluctant to identify other occupational groups as doing so. This was particularly marked amongst the manual workers, who surprisingly were more likely to identify other manual workers than non-manual workers as 'doing noticeably better' by a margin of 25 to 19 per cent (Runciman, 1966, p. 196). Very few of Runciman's sample were prepared to mention explicitly as 'doing noticeably better' those groups who did receive the highest incomes and had the greatest wealth, that is those in senior managerial, professional and administrative roles.

Runciman has interpreted his results as showing both that awareness of inequalities is low and as indicating that people tend to compare themselves with similar people, hence limiting their scope for expressing concern about other people who are better-off than themselves. Daniel, in another national survey carried out in 1975, reached similar conclusions. He too found 'that a surprisingly large proportion of the general population feels that no-one is doing better than it is, and that proportion is now as great as it was ten years ago' (Daniel, 1975, p. 20). In addition, people were still remarkably reluctant to make cross-class comparisons when identifying those who are 'doing noticeably better':

the people most likely to compare themselves unfavourably with executives, bosses, managers, professional people, lawyers, solicitors, barristers, accountants, medical consultants, senior civil servants, television personalities and so on, are not those whose own income and wealth are farthest from them, but those who are closest to them. (Daniel, 1975, p. 22)

Lastly, two comparative studies have yielded similar conclusions. Scase (1977) found that Swedish manual workers were significantly more likely than their English counterparts to show awareness and resentment of inequalities, despite the fact that the objective structures of wealth and income equalities in the two countries were roughly similar. In addition, the Swedish workers were far more likely to identify non-manual workers and managerial or professional people as being better-off than themselves. Gallie compared British and French manual workers. He found that a large majority of both groups of workers thought that 'there was either a great deal or a lot of inequality'. However, the French workers were much more likely than the British ones to be concerned with inter-class inequalities and to focus on groups such as employers and managers in industry. Only a minority of the British workers thought these sorts of inequality were the most salient and almost as many made intra-class references, that is to other manual groups. In a further question Gallie specifically focused on attitudes to differences in 'the standard of living of a businessmen or lawyer on the one hand and of a worker on the other'. Although over 90 per cent of both samples of workers were aware of differences, the two groups differed radically in their perception of the legitimacy of these financial differentials. Whereas only 10 per cent of the French workers thought that these differences were completely just, 46 per cent of the British workers did so! (Gallie, 1983, Chs. 2, 3.)

The four studies seem to suggest that economism or concern with material values is surprisingly low in Britain. However, the data are essentially concerned with perceptions of class inequalities rather than absolute concerns with economistic ends. What it points to is a narrowness of horizons, or comparative reference groups, as it suggests that manual workers limit their aspirations by tending to compare themselves only with other manual workers, hence their relative unwillingness to identify the more obvious groups as being better-off or to show resentment of inequalities. This hardly suggests that British workers have the materialistic, acquisitive values suggested by the 'vicious cycle' syndrome. On the contrary, it would appear to indicate that their economic ambitions are relatively limited and correspondingly their desires for higher pay to reduce perceived inequalities should be modest, particularly as they do not seem to be as resentful of such inequalities as comparable workers in Sweden and France.

Appearances can be deceptive. It is worth noting that both national studies by Runciman and Daniel do find that a clear majority of their samples are able to identify groups better-off than themselves. In addition, Gallie's study suggests that when respondents are asked specifically about groups at the upper end of the income and wealth scales, in this case businessmen and lawyers, they acknowledge overwhelmingly the existence of significant economic inequalities. A further point is that Runciman claims that his own sequence of questioning 'was chosen in order to tie the answers to people's own immediate situations' (Runciman, 1966, p. 192). Thus, his results, and those of Daniel who used the same questions, concerning the limitations on people's reference groups, may be artefacts of the particular questionnaire. In short, awareness of inequalities may be more widespread than Runciman or Daniel suggest.

This view is reinforced by a consideration of other details of their surveys. Both Runciman and Daniel asked their respondents: 'What income do you think is necessary for you (your husband) in order to maintain a proper standard of living for people like yourself?' Again, the wording of the question – people like yourself – lent itself to a lowering of aspirations. However, contrary to Runciman's own interpretation of his data, his respondents did aspire generally to significantly higher incomes than they currently had. When their 'ideal income' was compared with their stated actual income most respondents had a large 'aspirations gap'. As can be seen from Table 3.2 over 60 per cent of the respondents thought that a proper income ought to be at least a quarter greater than their actual income. Daniel does not present his findings in the same detail as Runciman, so precise comparisons are impossible. However, he indicates that the relationship between proper and stated income 'was much the same as thirteen years ago' (Daniel, 1975, p. 27), though he goes on to suggest that people's aspirations might have become slightly more modest. Daniel points out that although there may have been no widening of reference groups or increase of aspirations since Runciman's study, none the less there is considerable desire for higher living standards and a concern with differentials between broad occupational groups.

*Table 3.2:	Gap between proper and actual incomes, 1962*

% age gap	Frequency	% age of respondents
Negative	86	8.1
0	150	14.1
1–10	67	6.3
11–25	111	10.4
26–50	228	21.4
51–99	271	25.5
100+	151	14.2
Total	1064	100.0

Source: Calculated from Runciman (1966), Appendix 5, p. 321. The totals exclude 351 respondents for whom the comparison could not be made.

This last factor is particularly important for it stresses the sectionalism of British workers, their concern with their pay compared with that of other occupational groups performing roughly similar sorts of work. Yet this is also the import of the studies by Scase and Gallie. Both writers found that British manual workers as opposed to their European counterparts are more likely to compare themselves with other manual workers, to confine themselves to intra-class deprivations. This suggests that what characterises British workers is an acute awareness of the wages and earnings of other workers with whom they have fairly direct or immediate contact. This then forms the basis of their own potential feelings of deprivation. The studies that have been reviewed do not point to any failure to be aware of significant inequalities nor to aspire to significantly higher incomes and their related living standards. They do indicate that the grosser inequalities are not particularly resented but that concern is highest with the income of those about whom knowledge is greatest. In the British case materialistic concerns are high but they manifest themselves not through broad class-related conflicts of interest but through calculations of comparison with other sections of the working class.[6]

The roots of this sectionalism lie in the form of British industrialisation and the implications of its *laissez-faire* pattern of economic development for industrial relations. The sectional nature of nineteenth-century labour organisation has been well documented by writers such as Hobsbawm (1964, Ch. 15) and Bauman (1972). Early craft unions were often formed on the basis of the old guilds. They were intended to preserve or enhance the economic advantages of their members over the labouring masses. Central to the mechanisms that they employed was manipulation of the labour market to restrict the supply of labour. Social cohesion was maintained by the forming of communities of occupational interest.

These processes were reinforced sometimes by the divisive tactics of employers. Foster (1974, Ch. 7) has argued that in some industries such as cotton, working-class organisation was deliberately fragmented by the device of establishing particular groups of workers as controllers and organisers of other sections of the workforce. Not surprisingly, such groups received high pay. Thus economic, technical and authority divisions were superimposed on one another.

The sectional nature of working-class organisation continued with the developments of the New Model Unions. They operated primarily to protect group interests. They posed little challenge to the economic system but instead accommodated their behaviour to its functioning. They practised a form of economic competition against other groups, albeit competition that was far from perfect but one characterised by market control, job regulation and demarcation of areas of work. As Bauman (1972, p. 154) points out one of the main charges made against skilled workers by the relatively unorganised unskilled masses was that of 'occupational egoism': self-interest exercised at the level of the occupational group regardless of how it affected the interests of other groups.

It is hardly surprising that contemporary studies record such strong emphasis on intra-class comparisons when the history of British unionism has been so affected by sectionalist factors. However, it also needs to be stressed that sectionalism was economistic by nature. As noted above, the unions accommodated their behaviour to the functioning of the prevalent economic system. Amongst others, Thompson (1967) has argued that the working class very quickly learnt the rules of economic life. Union organisers soon learnt to bargain cannily over time-rates and then piece-rates: bargaining aimed at maximising economic returns without necessarily increasing work or effort. In addition, employers were quite content to divert workers' attention from questions of control to issues of pay as this enhanced managerial control and limited potential challenge to the system (Bauman, 1982). Thus, bargaining was increasingly confined to economic matters, that is pay and conditions of work. Under the 'historic compromise' organised labour accepted in essence management's right to manage, tolerated a situation where workers' rights at the workplace were minimal, in return for the ability to contend over economic matters (Crouch, 1977, Part I). Adaptation to the conditions of a capitalist free-market economy had involved an economistic acceptance of that system.

This economism was highly consonant with the values of a *laissez-faire* economy and that, perhaps, is the key point. British industrialisation had depended relatively little on government action. This extended to the sphere of industrial relations that developed on a 'voluntaristic' basis. Management and employees were left to bargain over contracts that they had 'freely' entered into without, as in other countries, the government seeking to regulate extensively the terms of those contracts. This point will be developed in the next section, here it will suffice to stress that under these circumstances it was hardly surprising that organised labour adopted the 'dominant values' of self-interested economic behaviour, and sought to maximise its returns from the sale of labour in the employment contract. This was consistent both with the cultural tradition and with the interests of the business class. They benefited both from the divisions within the working class and the lack of challenge to their managerial authority. Not that economism failed to bring rewards to the skilled working class. Part of the fruits of early industrialisation and imperialism accrued to the 'labour aristocracy'. However, the significant point for our purposes is that this process sowed the seeds of twentieth-century economism and sectionalism. Once Britain's economic position declined relatively as other countries industrialised and the fruits of empire were lost, then it became problematic whether the socio-economic system could meet the essentially economistic aspirations of the working class. In this context it is worth repeating that amongst younger Britons post-materialist values are less common than amongst their European and American counterparts (Inglehart, 1977, pp. 36–7), suggesting that it has recently become more difficult to satisfy the traditional economistic aspirations.

Our discussion suggests that economism is relatively high in Britain. Historically, aspirations have been channelled towards economic ends. A careful review of Inglehart's studies of the strength of materialism and post-materialism and of recent surveys on workers' attitudes suggests that aspirations for significantly higher incomes and living standards are widespread. However, unlike some other European societies, these aspirations are not reflected in a class-consciousness directed at a capitalist or business class but in divisions or rivalries within the employee class. Groups of workers engage in sectional conflict with one another, carefully guarding their differentials over lower-paid groups or seeking to catch up with those who are just above. This provides the background for the anomic system of pay bargaining that has characterised British wage-determination in the post-war period.

NORMATIVE RESTRAINTS ON INCOME DETERMINATION

The sectionalism and economism of the British working class is not the only relevant product of British culture and industrialisation. A number of writers have stressed the role of the British tradition of 'individualism' in the development of industrial relations as another aspect of the *laissez-faire* heritage (Currie, 1979; Fox, 1983). This refers to values that stress only the role of individual rights and liberties rather than collectivist obligations and responsibilities to some higher authority. Fox (1983, p. 11) refers to 'demands that market relations between contracting individuals must be freed from all non-economic bonds, ties, obligations, traditional encumbrances, or claims based on some allegedly transcendental "higher goal"'. He also points out that managers who limited their own obligations to their workforce provoked an equivalent response.

The trade unionism ... was forced to adopt the same stance that had long been imposed by many employers, by governments, and by established ideologies, a stance which treated the worker as a contracting agent in a purely economic relationship which involved no obligations beyond the 'cash nexus'. The result was the 'us and them' syndrome; a posture of wary mutual inspection by two parties who ... pursued a zero-sum game within an essentially adversary relationship. (Fox, 1983, pp. 22–3)

The point is that workers did not feel any obligation to hold back on demands or aspirations that they might have. 'Nothing in the culture surrounding them convinced them that there was some "higher good" to which they should abrogate themselves; this was not part of the English individualist tradition' (Fox, 1983, p. 24).

Individual self-interest rather than a sense of collective interest with the firm or the nation forms part of a distinctive cultural legacy. Currie contrasts the 'individualism' of the British worker with the 'collectivism' of the German and

Japanese worker. In those countries both employees and employers do have a cultural tradition of obligations and duties that extend beyond narrow self-interest; to some extent individual rights are subjugated to collective obligations and, accordingly, business activity is not just a private matter but subject to public regulation or at least a sense of public duty. The British trade union collectivism should not be confused with this for it is essentially individual self-interest elevated to group self-interest, where the group is better able to achieve the goals and aspirations shared by its individual members. It is an instrumental collectivism aimed at furthering these shared individual goals (Fox, 1983, pp. 32–5). Thus the sectionalism of the British workforce is rooted not simply in the pattern of industrialisation but also in the cultural tradition of individualism in such a way as to make the exercise of normative restraints highly problematic.

The institutional mechanisms of industrial relations and wage determination both reflect this sectionalism and further inhibit the possibility of normative restraint. In brief, both union structures and bargaining systems tend towards fragmentation and decentralisation. The British union structure is a cumbersome combination of craft, industrial and general unions. The craft unions are mainly descendants of the old guilds and organise people with specific skills often with a view to monopolising the supply of such labouring skills in whatever situations they are required. This both reflects the sectionalism discussed above and provides ample scope for instrumental collectivism. In addition, as the industrial unions are distinguished by the fact that they recruit workers in a particular industry rather than by monopolising organisation in that industry, most industries and firms are characterised by a combination of craft workers, industrial workers and others belonging to the amorphous general unions. This provides ample opportunity for leap-frogging wage settlements as different groups may bargain at different times and use previous settlements as justifications for particular claims aimed at widening, preserving or narrowing differentials.

Further opportunities for this sort of competitive instrumental collectivism derive from the bargaining system itself. Until recently most wage determination was carried out at two levels. Industrial or multi-employer bargaining established minimum wage levels, but actual earnings were contingent on local bargaining conducted often at the level of the plant rather than the enterprise. This fragmentation of the bargaining system enhanced its anomic nature (Fox and Flanders, 1969). It gave ample opportunity for wage-drift as unions exploited local conditions such as the tightness of the local market or used productivity agreements. It facilitated a system whereby earning depended not so much on what one did or how one did it, but on how much one could get given one's bargaining power and often quite fortuitous particular circumstances.

To be sure, affairs have changed somewhat in very recent years as industry and multi-employer wage agreements have declined in significance and been replaced by single-employer bargaining (Brown and Terry, 1978). However, although this probably diminishes the scope for wage-drift deriving from local circumstances, it marks a further move towards decentralisation. As Marshall *et al.* (1985, p. 270) note: 'During the last ten years, for example, centralised industry bargaining between national trades union leaders and nationally organised employers has been almost completely replaced by sectional, decentralised single-employer bargaining on the basis of the market position of individual companies.' This smacks strongly of the sectionalist, free-for-all tradition of pay bargaining. Indeed, it is not simply that companies have broken free from higher-level bargaining fora, but unions too have been so decentralised that the critical level of organisation is often the factory or the workplace. This augurs poorly for any system of normative restraint for it suggests that bargaining is conducted increasingly in terms of the most narrowly drawn sectional interests. Not only does this maximise the possibility of leap-frogging settlements, if market conditions will so allow, but it makes it even less likely that an overall incomes policy can be agreed or imposed. As Metcalf (1982, p. 504) notes: 'Central control of pay has been made far more difficult by the collapse of industry-wide bargaining and by changes in the composition of union officials and shop stewards.' It is not just that unions may be competing with one another, although the recent significant reduction and amalgamation of unions has reduced this particular factor, but that often groups within the same union are trying to enhance their respective positions independently of one another.

The theoretical discussion of Chapter 2 suggested that centralised bargaining frameworks where both employers and employees had broad federations were most conducive to modifying inflationary wage claims. This was because in such circumstances the macro consequences of bargaining outcomes were most likely to be considered, whilst more decentralised systems facilitated the taking of a narrow sectional view. In addition, it was argued that participation in decision-making fora encouraged the broader view, particularly as this might lead to the sharing of information that could then provide the macro parameters of prices, output and investment within which wage determination could take place. In Britain the peak employer and employee associations, the Confederation of British Industry (CBI) and Trades Union Congress (TUC), are loose federations who do not play a significant role in wage bargaining. Even the industrial employers' associations are loose-knit federations and, as we have seen, they play a declining role in bargaining processes. Similarly, many trade unions either combine together quite disparate groups, as in the case of the general unions, or decentralise their bargaining functions to the regional, enterprise or plant level.

To be sure, both the CBI and the TUC have participated in numerous tripartite agencies established by the government. Particularly in the case of the National Economic Development Council (NEDC) these have sometimes served as important fora for discussion of general economic strategy and the articulation of putative relationships between variables such as output, wages, prices, profits and investment. However, tripartite bodies, with the exception of the NEDC, come and go with successive governments and, in any case, are little more than talking-shops. The cultural heritage is such that both the CBI and TUC, fearing a loss of autonomy, are reluctant to be drawn into too close a discourse with one another or the government of the day. In addition, they cannot commit their constituent members, the individual enterprises or unions, to any agreements into which they might enter. Accordingly, prices and incomes policies either have to be voluntary in a dual sense of both the peak associations and the individual constituents agreeing to accept them, or be imposed by legal compulsion. In either case they are likely to come under threat from individual enterprises or unions who seek to operate within the traditional ambit of self-interest. Even when, for example, the national leaders of the TUC and major individual unions may feel some sympathy towards a policy of incomes restraint because it serves some 'higher good' and can be bargained in exchange for other desirable objectives such as lower taxes or higher welfare expenditure, this may not suffice. The obvious case in point was the 'Social Contract' between the Labour government and unions during 1974–79. This came under increasing strain from rank-and-file union members who were influenced by the traditional culture of *laissez-faire* and (sectional) individualism.[7]

In the British case, the conditions for restraint are virtually absent. Thus, even when incomes policies have been introduced and have had some short-term impact, the tendency has been for market forces to reassert themselves quickly and for the initial impact to be off-set by a period in which real wage losses are restored (Henry and Ormerod, 1978; Henry, 1981). Indeed, the long-term tendency has been for increased unionisation amongst non-manual workers (white-collar, managerial, administrative and professional employees) precisely so that they can emulate the bargaining strategies of manual groups, restore eroded differentials, and overcome the restraints of incomes policies (Price and Bain, 1976; Jenkins and Sherman, 1979). All in all, British culture and institutions do not augur well for restraining the pursuit of economistic values.

POWER DISTRIBUTION

The considerations discussed above might matter less if the distribution of power in Britain was less conducive to the successful pursuit of economistic claims. The determination by sectional groups to use collective means to gain their goals would matter little if they lacked the power resources to force home their claims or if such claims could be strongly resisted by employers. However, the reverse has been the case.

In the first place, British workers are relatively well organised in trade unions. Unionisation has averaged well over 40 per cent in the post-war period (Table 2.1, p. 28 above) and rose in the late 1970s to about 55 per cent. Even though the effects of recession have reduced total union membership from its 1979 peak of about 13¼ million to a 1983 total of 11¼ million, union density still hovers near the 50 per cent mark (Department of Employment, July 1985, p. 28). In manufacturing industry and much of the public sector, unions are particularly strong. Union densities in excess of 70 or 80 per cent are frequently found. In large-scale enterprises, particularly amongst manual groups, densities in excess of 90 per cent are not uncommon. Closed-shop agreements, whereby only existing members of a particular union can work in a given plant or section of a plant (the pre-entry shop) or, more often, new recruits have to join the union (the post-entry or agency shop) bolster unionisation. By 1980 about a quarter of trade unionists were organised in closed shops (Gennard, Dunn and Wright, 1980). Elsewhere, particularly in small-scale concerns such as those frequently found in distribution or personal services, unionisation is much lower and closed shops relatively rare.

There is little doubt that trade unions are able to use their bargaining position to gain higher wages than non-unionists. Layard, Metcalf and Nickell (1978) suggest on the basis of 1973 data that where collective bargaining takes place, which implies unionisation, a mark-up in wages of about 25 per cent is obtained even when allowance is made for variations in skill. The actual mechanisms by which these gains are achieved differ. In some cases they reflect the existence of a closed shop or at least a very high level of unionisation. The union uses its monopoly position as a seller or supplier of a particular sort of labour to attain a monopoly profit for its members. In other cases the decisive mechanism is strike activity or at least its threatened use.

The point here is not just that Britain has a relatively high incidence of strikes compared to many other western countries

(Table A.5, p. 224) but that the strikes have tended to be particularly disruptive. Until recently they have been mainly short, fairly frequent and often unpredictable, rather than occurring at fixed points for which management could prepare in advance. In addition, the concentrated structure of British industry together with a division of labour that is extensive both within and between enterprises makes it peculiarly vulnerable to disputes. Even quite small groups of workers, provided that they have control of an indispensable task within the division of labour, can have a disproportionately large effect on the total productive system. Indeed, it has been pointed out that firms in highly concentrated industries have fewer strikes. This is because, in the absence of binding agreements with their fellow oligopolists, they are so vulnerable to strike action. Hence they have an incentive to buy off threatened disruption with higher wages (Geroski, Hamlin and Knight, 1982). Signs that workers may be prepared to strike, possibly manifested through other forms of industrial action such as overtime bans or go-slows, may be sufficient to induce higher wage offers.[8]

This in turn raises the issue of the bargaining position of employers. Tylecote (1981) suggests that typically British managers will have a soft bargaining stance. He points out that their low financial stake in their companies means that profit-maximisation is unlikely to have a high priority. Instead they satisfice with steady profits that are at an acceptable level for shareholders. The risks of disruption through strike action are to be avoided and the quiet life is preferred. This short-term perspective is reinforced by aspects of external financing. Institutional investors, who have come to predominate in large-scale industry in recent years, often need a steady, predictable flow of dividends that can meet their own financial obligations, whilst banks have tended to supply short-term loans and hence again do not supply an incentive for taking the longer time-horizon. In addition, Tylecote refers to factors that have already been stressed: the weakness of employers' associations and the fear that one's competitors may gain an advantage if they are not affected similarly by strike action. In combination, these factors suggest that British managers will perceive the costs of strikes as being relatively high in the short term whilst the rewards for resisting wage demands are postponed into the less salient long term.

Of course, Tylecote's analysis assumes that production is relatively oligopolistic, for it is this factor that enables higher costs to be passed on as higher prices. There is little doubt that British industrial production is highly concentrated. Certainly, there is no shortage of giant firms. In 1978, the UK occupied third place in the list of countries with the most industrial enterprises having a turnover in excess of $2.25 billion (Dunning and Pearce, 1981, Part II). This figure reflects the post-war increase in aggregate concentration of the British economy that has been well documented by Hannah (1983, Appendix 2) and Hughes and Kumar (1984). Whereas in 1948 the share of the largest 100 firms in manufacturing net output was only 22 per cent, it had risen to 40 per cent by 1970 and stabilised at 41 per cent in 1978. However, concentration as measured by the market value of all UK quoted companies has continued to rise in the 1970s. The largest 100 companies accounted for 53.9 per cent in 1972 but 63.8 per cent in 1982.

Data on aggregate concentration do not in themselves tell us anything directly about the more relevant item of market concentration, though it would be surprising if the two measures were unconnected. Such, indeed, is the case. Hannah (1983, p. 144) indicates that by 1969 in twelve out of thirteen major industrial groups the share of the five largest firms in net output was over 50 per cent and that in eleven of these twelve cases concentration had risen, often significantly, since 1957. A more detailed examination showed that for 157 products the unweighted average of their five-firm sales concentration ratio (that is, the proportion of sales accounted for by the largest five firms) was about 65 per cent in 1968, though this did not show any further rise by 1975 (George and Joll, 1981, p. 128). The same authors also refer to an earlier international comparison of market concentration that indicated that the UK was easily more concentrated than West Germany, France or Italy. Although all data in this area must be handled with care, particularly as usually they are based on domestic output figures and ignore imports that must have some effect on market competition, it appears that by the 1960s and 1970s British industry tended to be highly concentrated. The market structure did provide the appropriate context for a soft managerial bargaining position because it facilitated increased wage costs being passed on as higher prices.

The post-war commitment to full employment was a further element in this process. In so far as it could be met, it generated tight labour market conditions that were conducive to the bargaining outcomes outlined above. In practice, full employment became increasingly difficult to maintain (Table A.4, p. 222 below). Yet even when unemployment rose there were often labour shortages specific to particular areas or skills. In addition, strongly unionised groups were sometimes able to exert considerable leverage even when overall conditions were not particularly favourable: their ability to regulate the supply of labour through closed shops or apprenticeship schemes was often of importance in this context. Hence the tendency for the union/non-union wage differential to widen during slumps and narrow during booms (Oswald, 1982).

The commitment to full employment reflected the twin beliefs that in the aftermath of the Keynesian revolution governments could control the level of unemployment and that they would suffer the electoral consequences if they failed in this task of economic management. In addition, the associated aim of sustained economic growth was one of the few areas of agreement between the leaders of organised business and organised labour. The benefits to the latter are obvious, whilst the former hope to gain through increasing sales and profits. This suggests that at the macro level there would be consistent pressures for expansionary policies. In some cases these pressures could be augmented by specific attempts to involve organised labour in policies of income restraint, where the government might offer a bargain whereby commitment to growth, employment and social welfare expenditure were exchanged for the promise of wage restraint. These formed explicit parts of the two most recent attempts at engineering consensus, the offer by the Heath administration in 1972 being rejected by the TUC, whilst they were central to the Labour government's side of the 'Social Contract' that ran from 1974.

In the short term these policies augment inflationary pressures, but had sustained growth ensued then it is possible that parts of the 'vicious cycle' might have been broken. Economistic demands might have been more readily met and therefore moderated, whilst restraints might have become more acceptable because they were associated with long-term benefits. However, another element has affected the apparent consensus over expansionary policies. Financial interests, the 'City' as opposed to industry, have not favoured expansionary policies nor have they liked the detailed interventionary policies, such as prices and incomes regulation, that have sometimes accompanied them. The City fears the inflationary consequences of expansionary policies because this might threaten its capacity to engage in its core trading activities, such as commerce and insurance, that it feels are dependent on a stable, convertible currency. In addition, its own use of free-market exchange makes it unreceptive to state intervention. In a sense, it is the last bastion of *laissez-faire* ideology, though on occasions it finds willing accomplices from the ranks of organised business and labour.

The account that follows draws heavily on Ingham (1984). The City has the capacity to oppose effectively those developments in the post-war managed economy that it dislikes. The links between the City, Bank of England and Treasury that derive from common, interlocking interests and a social solidarity based on shared kinship and educational backgrounds (Lupton and Wilson, 1959; Whitley, 1973) give the City a degree of access to the political system that is far in excess of any other interest group. In addition, financial resources have a flexibility that is not possessed by either industrial capital or organised labour and financial interests are unified to a greater extent than industrial interests that are inevitably fragmented by elements of the competitive process. Thus the City has a greater cohesion than either organised business or organised labour, whose peak associations, as we have already seen, are weak federations lacking in key functions. It is only on rare occasions that either 'business' or 'labour' can unite to influence policy. Normally this has been to oppose and if possible defeat a particularly threatening legislative item. Thus the CBI mobilised business support successfully against the inclusion of compulsory 'planning agreements' in the Industry Act 1975 and effectively vetoed impending legislation on worker directors in the aftermath of the 1977 Bullock Report on Industrial Democracy, whilst the TUC fought against the Industrial Relations Act 1971 and saw its most disliked provisions repealed by the 1974 Labour government (Grant and Marsh, 1977, Ch. 8; Marsh and Locksley, 1983).

The City, on the other hand, has a clear sense of its own priorities. Ingham argues that these comprise an open economy, a stable high currency and high interest rates for holders of sterling. These are not conducive to strengthening the productive parts of the domestic economy. Indeed, because of its long-standing international activities the City is not very dependent on the growth of the domestic economy. To a considerable extent the Bank of England and Treasury share these policy concerns thereby reinforcing the political advantages of access and cohesion. In addition, the City can voice its dissatisfaction with government policy by its own activities. It is now clear that flights from sterling in the last 25 years have their source at least as much in Britain as in overseas collapses of confidence.

The effect of the City's pre-eminence is to limit the possibility of sustained growth but it has not been able to impose consistently its own priorities on successive governments. What it can do is prevent expansionary policies from being carried on for too long, and halt them with deflationary retrenchments. The result has been the stop–go cycles of post-war British economic history as governments oscillate between the Keynesian policies desired by industry and organised labour and the stable currency policies required by the financial élite (Ingham, 1984, Ch. 9). The paradoxical result has been that although inflationary pressures can be abated in the short term at the cost of rising unemployment and declining sales, both of which result in a switch of market power to the buyers from the sellers of labour and goods, in the long term the productive capacity of the economy has been reduced. This makes it even more difficult to meet the sectional claims of income-receivers for higher incomes and social welfare expenditure.

It is possible that the City has been able to increase its influence in recent years. Each time it is able to wring a policy concession out of government, for example, the greater convertibility of sterling, it increases its leverage to gain future advantage. Thus the price of short-term cooperation to resolve an immediate problem such as a 'run on sterling' may have a ratchet effect making it easier for the City to voice its disapproval in the future.[9] This may partially explain the apparent ease with which the Thatcher government introduced its policies to curb inflation and maintain the value of the currency. However, as we shall see later, maintenance of these policies may prove to be very difficult because the City does not have a monopoly of power.

A further consequence of any increase in the City's power is that it becomes increasingly difficult for any left-wing government to sustain itself in office by building a long-term policy of cooperation and restraint with organised labour. Each time a Labour government is forced to reverse policies and deflate rather than expand the economy, it lessens the prospect of coming to an arrangement with the leaders of organised labour. The continuance of bargained corporatism depends on both sides 'delivering the goods'. We have already seen that the leaders of organised labour have relatively little interest in policies of restraint, particularly as its own members are reluctant to be committed to such policies. The import of this discussion is that governments, even of labour sympathies, find it equally difficult to deliver their side of the bargain. In Britain the power of the City prevents organised labour exercising sufficient leverage even when it has the advantage of its party being in office.

THE 'VICIOUS CYCLE' COMPLETED

Earlier, reference was made to the adversary nature of industrial relations. This is hardly conducive to harmonious, cooperative workplace relationships. On the contrary there is considerable evidence that it is positively harmful. Apart from the obvious disruptions caused by a relatively high strike rate there is a general resistance to the introduction of new technologies and processes of work. In the prevailing climate of 'low trust', these are often viewed as potential threats to job security and pay. Changes in productivity may lead, on the basis of past experience, to maintained levels of output with fewer employees. There is no sustained commitment to long-term employment in a situation where each partner to a labour contract is, in theory, only concerned with narrow self-interest. In addition, recent 'rationalisation' in the aftermath of mergers such as that of GEC–AEI in the late 1960s or changes in management as at British Leyland in the early 1980s suggest that this may be a synonym for shedding labour. Even when employment is not threatened immediately, changes in work practices may reduce the opportunity for high earnings if overtime is reduced or the skill content of work tasks lessened.

More generally, work groups may use the introduction of new work processes and practices as a chance to pursue their sectional ends. After all, they may feel that they are entitled to share in the higher profitability that is the goal of these changes, even if they do not have to work longer, more arduously or exercise more skill. In addition, they may view this as another occasion for canny bargaining, perhaps exploiting a monopoly position or the possession of a scarce skill that is necessary for some key task. Changes in procedures can be used as an excuse for negotiating a more favourable contract.

In the light of these factors it is not surprising that Britain's labour productivity is so low. Taylor (1982, p. 84) quotes the former General Secretary of the TUC, Len (now Lord) Murray in his 1980 Granada Lecture:

It is less difficult for unions to win from their members acceptance of temporary wage restraint than it is for them to win agreement to changes in manpower practices. Indeed, Britain's poor economic record since the war is due much more to the ineffective use of our resources than to excessive wage claims.

To some extent Murray's observations are supported by the data shown in Table A.3 (p. 222). Until 1981 Britain was consistently at or near the bottom of the productivity growth-rate table, but in some periods, such as 1960–73, was also relatively low down the table depicting changes in money-wage rates. Of course, it is difficult to be sure of the pattern of causality as low productivity increases can lead to low wage rises, but this point does not invalidate Murray's comments.

Table 3.3: *Sectoral productivity levels*

		1970	1973	1975	1980
	manufacturing	48.9	52.0	53.8	76.9
Japan	private services	50.7	57.2	58.2	65.1
	manufacturing	81.3	77.2	81.6	89.3
Germany	private services	99.9	101.5	107.4	126.0
	manufacturing	83.7	80.7	85.4	98.1
France	private services	—	—	102.6	111.8
	manufacturing	41.7	40.8	40.2	38.4
UK	private services	55.0	55.8	56.4	55.7
	manufacturing	66.0	62.1	60.1	73.3
Italy	private services	61.9	63.5	64.5	67.9

Base USA=100

Source: OECD (1984), Table 18, p. 45.

As Table 3.3 indicates, the evidence of Britain's poor productivity performance is clear-cut. To be sure, not all of this is attributable to working practices. To some extent it reflects differences in the quality and quantity of capital equipment and poor management. However, even when allowance is made for these factors it is clear that productivity levels are low and, in any case, the lower capital endowment itself to some extent reflects the resistance to the introduction of new technology that has already been discussed. This is not to argue that all sections of the British workforce have been resistant to change, rather it is to demonstrate that the low trust dynamic does limit the growth of the productive capacity of the economic system.

The cycle is now complete. Low productivity and low rates of growth of productivity mean that the British growth rate is low. A low growth rate has pushed the UK down the economic league table (Table A.1, p. 219). It has become increasingly difficult to satisfy the economistic aspirations of the population. This is not so much because these aspirations are necessarily large by international standards but because the British growth rate has been low. It was noticeable from the earlier discussion of Inglehart's work that post-materialist values were least common in Britain. In particular, younger age cohorts were less likely than their counterparts elsewhere to have such values. Although these findings must be treated with caution, because Inglehart's distinction between material-ism and post-materialism does not simply depend on prefer-ences for material ends, it does suggest that Britain's long-term relative decline has had an effect. Material factors have a greater salience precisely because economic prosperity and advance has been less assured.

In addition, the mechanisms that in the past were used to divide the workforce and limit its aspirations to economic ends rather than issues of authority and control are now counter-productive. A sectionalised workforce has pressed for rewards that cannot be met given the ending of Britain's relatively advantageous position. Its sectionalism means that different groups are more likely to pursue their ends regard-less of the overall consequences for the economy. This has contributed to the fragmentation of wage-determination pro-cedures and made it more unlikely that broadly-based labour federations will emerge. The *laissez-faire* mode of industrial development has also contributed to this process. It has facilitated the growth of values of individualism among the workforce and employers, which make it less likely that they will subjugate their interests to some higher authority. Thus the possibility of authoritative centralised employee or em-ployer associations has been reduced.

Government has found it difficult to bring about restraint. This is partially because of the weakness of the peak associa-tions, the CBI and the TUC, but also because the *laissez-faire* tradition makes it unlikely that either organisation will want to be drawn into binding participatory systems or that their constituent members – individual enterprises and unions as well as individual managers and workers – will willingly accept any higher level agreements.[10] Also, the chance of bargained corporatism being successful has been lessened by the difficulties that both labour and moderate conservative governments encounter in engineering continued economic success. These difficulties have been exacerbated by the power and interests of the City which has been concerned about the effects of sustained expansion on the value of the currency and has acted to produce repeated deflations of the economy. Each successive deflation inhibits investment and therefore limits the prospects for future growth. This in turn makes it more difficult for any government to 'buy' the cooperation of the workforce.

The post-war period has not only seen a decline in Britain's economic position and increased difficulty in sustaining even a modest rate of growth (Table A.2, p. 220), it has also seen a rise in the power of organised labour. This is linked to increased unionisation and the growth of closed shops. However, increased industrial concentration and the growing interdependence of economic activity as the division of labour has intensified both within and between enterprises have also contributed to this development. They have enhanced the functional significance of key groups of workers thereby giving them greater leverage for effective bargaining. Management, operating in markets that have become more oligopolistic, is more prepared to accede to wage demands and pass them on to customers as higher prices. As some groups have gained by these processes, others have adopted them to retain or regain differentials. Distributional conflict has increased in intensity although in the long term the structure of relative earnings may remain fairly stable as attempts to gain higher relative earnings are off set by other groups' behaviour (Noble, 1985).

Apart from attempts to increase real wages or affect the structure of differentials, resistance to deflationary policies has also grown. Government deflations induced by tax rises or increases in the price of public goods and services reduce effective spending power. Similarly, rises in the prices of imported goods, whether occasioned by a devaluation or by commodity price rises, deflate the real value of earnings. Workers and employers have been likely to try to recoup their losses because of their short-term focus. They have no great expectation or confidence that short-term restraint will help matters to improve in the long term. Again, the concentration and dispersion of power facilitate their attempts to do so, even though they are likely to be self-defeating in the long term as a price–wage–price spiral ensues. This factor is particularly important in explaining why Britain's inflation rate rose so drastically after the 1973–74 oil price rise and took so long to come down (Table 1.1, p. 3 above).[11] Social forces tend to magnify rather than reduce the effects of exogenous price rises.

THATCHERISM: THE END OF THE VICIOUS CYCLE?

The Thatcher government has given priority to winning the fight against inflation. Its preferred strategy is based on a monetarist analysis of inflation which is to be squeezed out of the economy by lowering the rate of increase of the money supply. In order to do this the government's financial strategy places great emphasis on reducing the Public Sector Borrowing Requirement (PSBR), the difference between what the government spends and receives in revenue, even though there is no precise relationship between PSBR and the money supply. As increasing taxation is thought not to be popular the government has tried to reduce public spending, though there have also been increases in the prices of many public goods and services. Thus the corner-stone of the government's macro-economic policy is the reduction of public spending in order to reduce PBSR. This in turn should enable the government to limit the rate of monetary growth which it believes fuels inflation. In effect, it is trying to prevent the 'too much money chasing too few goods' syndrome. Aggregate demand is to be restrained by deflationary tactics.[12]

In order to pursue this policy, the Thatcher administration has set aside corporatist attempts to run prices and incomes policies. It is not prepared to bargain with organised business and labour to gain moderation in price and wage increases.

Instead it relies on a 'market' approach whereby firm control of the money supply sets the parameters within which price and wage determination takes place. In particular, wages are to result from the supply and demand for labour. If various groups of workers demand and attain wages that are unrealistic (that is, too high) then under the tight money regime they price themselves out of jobs. In the public sector this objective is to be achieved by setting firm 'cash limits' on expenditure which often do not allow for wage increases at the prevailing rate of inflation. 'Excessive' wage claims mean that fewer employees can be afforded. In the private sector discipline is to be asserted by a combination of high interest rates, that make it costly to finance 'inflationary' wage claims, and, on occasions, a high value for sterling, thereby making domestic producers more vulnerable to international competition. The consistency of these policy tools with the earlier discussion of City priorities need hardly be emphasised.

Although the Thatcher government has not had a formal incomes policy, this does not mean that it has no view on wages or wage determination processes. As indicated above, in the public sector an assumed or desired rate of wage increase is included in the calculation of the appropriate cash-limit. In the private sector it has taken increasingly to exhorting workers to accept lower wage increases. It argues that they must adjust to the realities of a tight money policy and the alternative (to lower wage increases) is that they will price themselves out of jobs. However, it has also sought to affect wage determination in other ways. In particular, it has tried to weaken the power of organised labour to force through wage increases. The main mechanism for this has been a series of euphemistically termed Employment Acts. Several of the measures contained in these Acts are designed to make strike action more difficult and costly: legal immunities are removed from certain activities such as secondary picketing, various sorts of 'political' or 'sympathetic' strikes and strikes called without a secret ballot. These changes make unions liable to extensive civil damages if they are sued by employers or other damaged parties for unlawful action. In addition, 'closed shops' are made vulnerable by making unions liable to heavy fines for unfair dismissals that have occurred as a result of closed shops that have not been endorsed in secret ballots by a very large majority of the workforce.

Apart from these measures which are designed to alter the balance of power between employers and employees, the government has tried to weaken organised labour through influencing general labour market conditions. There is little doubt that the high level of unemployment, in excess of 10 per cent since 1981 (Table A.4, p. 222), is being used in part as a way of disciplining the labour force which generally becomes easier to replace.[13] Further, it acts as a sanction against strike action because other legal changes allow employers not to re-employ particular strikers if they so wish. In addition, the government has reduced or eliminated various statutory provisions that protect workers' employment rights. Small businesses have been exempt from several regulations thereby making it easier for them to fire workers. Part-time and female employees are particularly vulnerable. The protection afforded to minimum wage levels by Wage Councils is to be weakened, particularly as regards young workers. Last, and by no means least, the real value of unemployment benefit has been cut on several occasions.

In sum, these measures can be seen as a very conscious strategy of 'dualism'. The primary workforce, possessing important skills or being trained for careers within their organisational hierarchies, retains relatively secure employment, pay and conditions of work. A sizeable secondary workforce is being established. The members of it lack skills and are easily replaceable from the 'industrial reserve army' of unemployed workers. Their vulnerability is enhanced by the measures discussed above. As they are subject to the full weight of market pressures their security of employment, pay and conditions of work suffer accordingly. In some cases, business enterprises supplement the government's strategy. The de-skilling of work tasks decreases their dependence on particular groups of skilled workers and widens the potential labour supply. The growing use of alternative sources of supply weakens the bargaining position of workers in either supplier. However, perhaps the most significant development has been the growth of sub-contracting particular activities to smaller enterprises. This reduces the number of core workers in the larger concerns and increases employment amongst workers who are vulnerable both because their employers have a weak and dependent market position and because they are less likely to be unionised given the difficulties of organisation in small firms.

In terms of our sociological model, the centrepiece of the Thatcherite experiment is an attempt to change the structure of power. At the micro level a combination of higher unemployment, legislative changes and employer strategies is designed to weaken the strength and bargaining position of organised labour as well as to increase the vulnerability of the poorly organised section of the labour force. At the macro level the government has cut itself off from some of the pressures for higher expenditure. In particular, it has avoided any semblance of bargained corporatism with the leaders of organised labour. In turn, this lack of obligation facilitates its use of higher unemployment as part of the strategy of weakening labour.

However, the Thatcher government's policies have implications for two of the other elements of our model. First, productive potential should be enhanced. This is because the changed legal framework should make strikes less frequent or, at least, more predictable. Also, the weakness of organised labour is intended to facilitate greater managerial control at the workplace and assist the introduction of new technologies and methods of work.[14] Second, the policies are intended to introduce a new realism. Workers are to be made aware of the relationship between higher wages and increased unemployment and thus induced to moderate their economic demands. This is not in any sense a form of normative restraint, rather it is aimed at changing workers' awareness of their self-interest. The individual or group has to be made to realise that it is not worth pressing for higher wages that their employer cannot afford. Accordingly, it redefines economism rather than subjugating it to some higher moral authority.

At first sight the Thatcherite experiment seems to have been remarkably successful in its primary aim of curbing inflation. As can be seen from Table 1.1, p. 3 above, the UK inflation rate fell from 13.4 per cent in 1979 to 5.0 per cent in

1984. However, Beckerman (1985) attributes much of this fall to a decline in world commodity prices between 1980 and 1982. He suggests that on average this factor ought to have lowered the rate of inflation by about 5 per cent in the advanced OECD countries. It is not clear from Beckerman's presentation whether this fall should have occurred from 1980–82 or, allowing for a small lag, from 1981–83. However, as can be seen from Table 1.1, the expected fall did take place for the average of all OECD countries over both periods. Beckerman goes on to argue that in any individual country there is no direct relationship between the level of unemployment and the level of wage increases. The crucial mechanism is the role of prices of imports and, in particular, commodity prices. If they rise, then domestic prices rise with attendant money wage rises. Those who believe that inflation is caused by attempting to lower unemployment below the 'natural rate' will deflate the economy. This lowers productivity and profits as demand falls. This suggests that real wages ought to fall in line with the trend in productivity and that workers who do not accept this are 'pricing themselves out of jobs'. As unemployment rises as another consequence of the deflationary policies, we have a classic example of the self-fulfilling prophecy! Conversely, the key mechanism in reducing inflation is the fall in import prices that directly lowers production costs and has a further impact through the lower money wage rises that ensue: in effect a downward price–wage–price spiral.[15]

The British experience was better than the OECD average – significantly so if the comparison is between 1980 and 1982. Then the inflation rate fell by 9.4 per cent compared to the OECD average of 5.1 per cent. There are some reasons for supposing that the 1980 UK rate was boosted artificially by the once and for all rise in Value Added Tax during 1979. This increase would have given some impetus to wage claims, and thus prices, in the following year. From 1981 to 1983 the UK inflation rate fell by 7.3 per cent compared to the OECD average of 5.5 per cent. This suggests that Beckerman's conclusions ought to be qualified. Certainly, the fall in world commodity prices must have played a major role in reducing British inflation, but for once the UK performance was better rather than worse than average. A comparison of 1978, the year before the second oil price explosion, with 1984, may give a clearer picture. Of the twelve countries in Table 1.1, Britain moved from having the sixth highest to the seventh highest rate over that period. Amongst all 24 OECD countries Britain moved from 12th to 17th (OECD, 1985, Table R10, p. 165). Possibly, therefore, the Thatcher government's restrictive monetary policies have had some effect. However, the price has been heavy in other regards. Table A.4 (p. 222), shows that over the same period the UK unemployment rate has risen by 6.9 per cent. This compares with an OECD average of 16 countries of 3.1 per cent! (OECD, 1985, Table R12, p. 167.)

If Thatcherism has scored a modest success in curbing inflation, its associated aim of lowering government expenditure has not succeeded so far. Its current expenditure has risen from 39.7 per cent of total output in 1979 to 44.3 per cent in 1983 (OECD, 1985, Table R7, p. 162). This failure to reduce public expenditure is not for want of trying. However, the Thatcher government is hemmed in by its prior commitments to increase expenditure on defence and 'law and order' as well as by the costs of the rising unemployment that it has caused. In addition, it cannot make significant cuts in state welfare expenditure because of the wide degree of public support for state provision in the areas of health, education, pensions and some personal services. By the mid-1980s numerous public opinion surveys had pointed to a general desire to maintain real levels of expenditure in these areas even if this meant that direct taxes could not be lowered. In some cases there was even majority support for maintaining or increasing expenditure even if it meant raising taxation. This suggests that there may be heavy costs in electoral unpopularity or, possibly, social unrest if the government attempts to make significant cuts in these areas. Commitment to the core elements of the welfare state, to the maintenance of citizenship rights within which the 'social wage' acts as a guaranteed minimum to which all are entitled places limits on even a radical right-wing government's freedom of manoeuvre (Taylor-Gooby, 1983; Marshall *et al.*, 1985).

The government's difficulties in pursuing its macroeconomic strategy by cutting state expenditure are mirrored in the micro sphere of wage determination. In the public sector, successive real wage cuts particularly in the area of services, is producing a new mood of militancy as embodied in the 1985 teachers' strike. In the private sector, the reliance on market forces is producing apparently perverse results. It is clear that pay settlements in manufacturing industry are now rising well above the rate of inflation and that the trend of money wage settlements is upwards despite the high level of unemployment. The underlying rate of increase in manufacturing earning was approaching 9 per cent by May 1985 (Department of Employment, July 1985, p. 54). OECD forecasts indicated that hourly earnings in manufacturing were expected to rise in 1985 and 1986 by at least as fast a rate in the UK as any other European country except for Greece, and that unit labour costs would rise more quickly than any other major country except for Italy where an equivalent increase was expected (OECD, 1985, Table 19, p. 39, Table 20, p. 40). These data support Beckerman's conclusion that there is no relationship between the level of unemployment and the rate of wage increases.

This finding is given further support by Layard and Nickell (1985). They suggest that only the number of short-term unemployed (that is, those out of work for less than six months) affect labour market conditions. The long-term unemployed spend less time and effort seeking jobs and therefore have only a modest effect on the supply of labour. Hence their limited impact on the market forces that affect the level of wages. Layard and Nickell, like Beckerman, are arguing that there is no natural rate of unemployment at which inflationary pressures are dissipated.

The recent rise in earnings reflects the modest economic recovery. As output and profits have increased in many sectors of the economy, workers have sought their share in this advance. Primary labour market employees have done better and it is clear that they have attained significant increases in real earnings. Low-paid workers have probably sustained a reduction in real earnings (Huhne, 1985). This widening inequality reflects the processes outlined above. Dualism does have some effect, but it is focused on workers in secondary labour markets. Elsewhere, skilled workers possess considerable industrial muscle which is scarcely affected by the government's legal changes. Even in the public sector, employees in key areas such as the provision of power supply and in water services have secured consistently above average wage increases. In the private sector many workers still retain considerable leverage. In addition, as the government lacks an effective competition policy for the large-scale oligopolistic sector of the economy, the discipline of market forces does not really prevail. A return to a high exchange rate would apply pressure on profits and costs and thus stiffen the managerial bargaining stance. However, this would also put a brake on the possibility of export-led growth and cause unemployment to rise still further.

Nor is there much prospect of relief on the 'supply side'. There has been no productivity miracle. The significant rises in labour productivity obtained in 1981 and 1982 were statistical illusions (Table A.3, p. 222). They reflected two factors. First, they were an adjustment to the fall of productivity in 1980 as output fell more rapidly than employment. Second, the collapse of many firms in 1981 and 1982 generally affected the less efficient firms and thus, by definition, meant that the survivors had a higher average level of productivity than had existed before.

Certainly, the incidence of strikes has decreased and the number of days lost in manufacturing industries has probably more than halved compared to the 1970s. However, it is difficult to believe that the climate of recession and unemployment is generally conducive to a new spirit of workplace cooperation and a lowering of resistance to the introduction of new technologies and methods of work. Rather, it is more likely that informal methods of work protest are operative and that workers utilise their position to resist change or at least demand a high price for accepting change. The poor prospects for Britain's competitive position indicated by the forecasts for unit labour costs mentioned above do not suggest that productive potential is rising sharply, a conclusion that is reinforced by the OECD's forecast that the UK productivity rate will fall from $2\frac{3}{4}$ per cent in the first half of 1985 to $\frac{3}{4}$ per cent in the second half of 1986 (OECD, 1985, Table 12, p. 27).

In the context of the sociological model of inflation this is not surprising. The government's emphasis on reducing the power of organised labour leaves it vulnerable to the industrial muscle of those whose power cannot be legislated away. The underlying sectional economism is still there. Indeed, Thatcherism has positively enhanced it.

First, the 1979 election success was predicated on a fairly conventional economistic appeal. The Conservative programme held out the prospect of cuts in income tax and a release from the constraints of incomes policies. It was aimed specifically at skilled manual workers whose differentials had been eroded during the period of the Social Contract and who had suffered real income losses through the combination of pay restraint, rising prices and a rising incidence of direct taxes. The Conservative's electoral success was greatest in the West Midlands, an area with a high proportion of such workers.

Second, the market solutions favoured by Thatcherism encourage people to get what the market will bear. They are directly conducive to an instrumental, calculative outlook. Next, some of the legal measures encourage a narrowly-based sectional view, for political and sympathy strikes lose their legal immunity. Workers may only lawfully strike in furtherance of their own industrial dispute, that is, their own self-interest. Last, the lack of concern with social and economic inequality that is a hallmark of Thatcherism, encourages the anomic free-for-all where people attend to their own interests rather than being concerned with any 'higher good'.

In addition, there is no reason for those who have an advantageous position to eschew using it. After all there is no reason to suppose that other groups will refrain from pushing their claims. Also, particularly in the private sector, there are no norms, as under an incomes policy, that might indicate what one might reasonably expect to get. Further, the expected benefits of Thatcherism have not always accrued. The promised tax cuts have only benefited those who were very well-off anyway. Davis and Dilnot (1985) have estimated that the combined effects of the government's tax and welfare benefit changes since 1978–79 have only made 6 per cent of the population better-off. Some 87 per cent are clearly worse-off, with the greatest cuts occurring among those with the lowest incomes. Clearly, the fiscal system has little effect on meeting the materialistic aspirations that are inherent in Thatcherism. Some income-receivers just have to put up with a decline in their living standards as they suffer both from their position in the labour market and the fiscal squeeze on their income. However, others can at least try to use their market power to off set their losses in net income caused by changes in the tax and benefit systems.

As one commentator has suggested, Thatcherism constantly appeals to the virtues of Victorian England, to 'the ethics of 19th century entrepreneurial individualism'. If taken seriously this implies that 'individual selfishness and organized greed are the only effective motivations for human behaviour'. It tends to 'promote a materialistic market-orientated individualism as the key to human social progress' (Jenkins, 1985). This approach worked when Britain was the first industrial nation and had the advantages of empire. When those advantages have been lost, international competition is strong and the UK has slipped well down the international league tables of output, growth and productivity, it hardly sounds like a cure for the British disease.

4 The American Equilibrium

In Chapter 3 we saw that the contemporary configuration of factors affecting inflation in the UK to a great extent bore the hallmark of British cultural traditions and its pattern of industrialisation. To a considerable degree the USA shares both of these legacies but to them must be added other historical elements that are peculiar to her. In particular, attention must be paid to the sheer scale of the domestic USA market, the successive waves of immigration and internal migration, and a unique set of political institutions.

In essence, the USA is a market society: the values of the market-place pervade not just economic life but other institutional areas as well. Central to these values are not simply beliefs in market exchange, but also in a rugged self-interested individualism coupled with a *laissez-faire* emphasis on limiting the extent of government intervention in economic activity. The roots of this belief system lie partially in the shared Anglo-American cultural tradition:

> principles of autonomy and self-government have formed the basis of institutional life; an adversary procedure of contest has dominated the law, parliament and industry; and the conception of good citizenship has incorporated a spirit of stubborn independence and a willingness to resist 'arbitrary authority'. (Dyson, 1983, p. 37)

This cultural tradition, imported by the Founding Fathers and buttressed by the nature of the break with British rule, gained further support from the relatively early industrialisation process. As with the British case, this was a mainly *laissez-faire* matter with the government playing a modest role compared to the later transitions to industrial production in Western Europe and Japan (Shonfield, 1965). This 'spontaneous' industrialisation process itself fostered entrepreneurial ideologies that stressed the beneficial consequences of the forces of economic competition. Possibly because of the limited presence of a feudal tradition, the philosophy of Social Darwinism, with its emphasis on the benign power of natural selection in economic life, was significantly more influential in the USA than the UK in the latter part of the nineteenth century (Bendix, 1956).

The implications of this view were clear-cut. Entrepreneurs, or their managerial agents, ought to be free to manage without government interference, that could only disrupt the beneficial workings of the forces of competition. Hence business was essentially a private matter, autonomous and distinct from state activity. However, this perspective also recognised more conspicuously than in the British case the vital role of the state in preserving the institutional framework within which competition could take place.

As a consequence anti-trust legislation intended, at least in theory, to limit the rise of monopolies, was formulated with some vigour. Certainly, American legislation with its emphasis on preventing mergers that might produce a large market share, and on granting powers to break up existing monopolies seems stronger than its British counterpart (Howe, 1971). A further consequence of this tradition is that where monopolies might be inevitable, as with the provision of energy sources or communications systems, the Americans have preferred the development of public utility companies that are privately-owned but subject to state regulation, rather than the British solution of nationalisation.[1]

The pattern of industrialisation both reflected and supported the cultural tradition. However, an important additional factor was that the scale of the American economy was so much greater than its European counterparts. The implications of this for the efficacy of the competitive process in the USA will be discussed in a later section. Here, the consequences for the organisational structure of American companies will be discussed briefly.

The large size of the domestic American market was directly related to the early development of the multi-divisional form of organisation (Chandler, 1976, 1977). The larger American firms are typically multi-plant if not multi-product enterprises. Production is scattered in a variety of different sites and states whereas control over financial and strategic decision-making is located in a central headquarters. The multi-divisional firm developed in the 1920s in the USA as opposed to the post-war period for its European counterparts. Accordingly its implications have also materialised earlier.

First, it gives management considerably more leverage in its relationships both with organised labour and local government through the threat of withdrawal of production to other states or even other countries. Thus it has important implications for power relationships that will be explored more fully later. However, it also has important implications for the style of management–worker relations.

As noted above, financial and strategic decision-making is conducted at a central headquarters. This means that the form of the payment system will be centrally determined. Central management is likely not only to negotiate company-wide pay agreements in terms of basic rates of pay, but also the form of any piece-rate or bonus-rate schemes (Tylecote, 1981, Ch. 2). The reason for this is clear. If too much discretion is allowed to plant management to determine these elements then it opens up the possibility of escalating wage costs through unpredictable local wage-drift. It is part of the control strategy of central management that defines the parameters within which local management has to operate. However, it also means that the evolution of the large-scale multi-divisional firm itself tends to facilitate the development of centrally determined rules and procedures for governing management–worker relations rather than a reliance on face-to-face interaction, for the payment system lies at the centre of these relationships. It corresponds to the shift from a personal to a bureaucratic mode of control (Edwards, 1979).

Unions have adapted to the cultural underpinnings and structure of the American economy. Perhaps more than anywhere else in the western world, American trade unions are 'business unions'. They are primarily concerned with the 'bread and butter' issues of pay, fringe benefits and conditions of work. They are organisers and sellers of labour power seeking initially recognition from employers for the right to bargain collectively, and then, having obtained that right, the best possible deal for their members. They reflect the predominant market orientation of their society and pursue sectional group interests rather than the interests of the working class as a whole or seeking to challenge or transform capitalist society (Rosen, 1975; Estey, 1981).

The initial development of American unionism reflects this sectionalism. The first successful union movement, the American Federation of Labour (AFL), was organised on craft lines. The formation of unions based on a particular group of workers with common skills, rather than on the basis of working in the same industry, lent itself more readily to business unionism. Unions were more easily able to attain their goal of maximising the economic returns to their members if they were 'selling' the same skills, rather than a diversity of attributes.

In addition, conflict between unions could be limited, if, as was the case, individual unions were granted a monopolistic right to represent particular categories of worker by the AFL, and if the central organisation also gave its constituent unions autonomy over collective bargaining and did not seek to impose centralised controls. Thus the structure and policies of the AFL fitted into the prevailing socio-economic system in terms of its emphasis on economic goals and its representation of discrete groups of workers selling the same skill. The former factor both was consonant with the market values of 'possessive individualism' and left management autonomy over the running of enterprises unimpaired. The latter factor was consistent with the rise of bureaucratic modes of control as it facilitated the standardisation of rules and procedures covering particular categories of worker.

In the twentieth century the emergent pattern of industrial relations where large-scale industry predominated was one of company-wide bargaining between the central headquarters of the company and the relevant craft unions. Where small-scale production was more important, then industry-wide bargaining tended to be more pronounced. Bargaining was increasingly constitutionalised in terms of the formalisation of contracts to cover a particular period of time and of the development of grievance machinery for use during the period of the contract. The contracts made explicit the specification of the details of economic exchange in the collective bargaining between the two autonomous agents. The union selling labour power, the company purchasing it. The grievance machinery was intended to smooth management–labour relationships by providing machinery for resolving or adjudicating on disputes over matter including the precise working out of the contractual arrangements. Both, therefore, were aspects of the bureaucratisation of workplace relationships.[2]

If American unions are 'business unions' *par excellence* and thereby reflect the prevailing market values, the political process as a whole also mirrors these values. Not for nothing has so much analysis of American democracy been couched in terms of economic parameters such as the market for votes (Downs, 1957; Buchanan and Tullock, 1969). American politics lacks the sharp ideological cleavages that predominate in most other western countries. Instead, it is built round the conception of parties trading for support amongst blocs of voters.

For example, the old city political machines won power in effect by promising to use that power for the direct benefit of those who elected them. Thus the support of particular ethnic groups might be gained in exchange for promises of direct payments in the form of public works or welfare payments, not to mention the spoils of office for their leaders and representatives. More recently political parties and individuals have competed for votes by 'positioning' themselves on the issues. When in office they construct a voting record, or when out of office a programme of action, that is designed to appeal to sufficient groups of voters to gain election or re-election. Interest groups, be they ethnic, economic or related to specific issues such as civil rights or the environment, construct performance indicators for candidates based on their voting records, and thereby measure their suitability for support by that group's adherents. In essence candidates for office sell themselves for support. They compete in the marketplace for votes using the most sophisticated of media and advertising techniques to present themselves to the electorate.

The evolution of this process reflects the prevailing market ideology. It has also provided a mechanism for integrating successive waves of new immigrants into the political system, though as will be seen later, their main impact has been on labour market conditions. Indeed, some commentators have pointed to the success of immigrant groups being secured when their representatives can attain their share of political office. However, this process also reflects the fragmentation of the American political system.

This point is too well known to need much comment here. Yet it should be emphasised that a system that contains a separation of powers both between the federal nation state and the constituent states and, at both levels between two elected legislative chambers and an executive elected partially or in whole, in addition to separate municipal administrative structures, is hardly conducive to clear-cut lines of political cleavage. Rather it lends itself to a situation where each electoral contest is conducted in terms of particular and often local or short-term contingencies. Thus candidates will 'sell' themselves in terms of those factors, whilst conversely, organised groups will offer support to those candidates whose position on the salient issue, for that group, is most benign. As a consequence, candidates nominally of the same party may have views and legislative records that differ radically, whilst interest groups may support candidates from different parties.

ECONOMISM IN THE USA

The preceding discussion has outlined the pervasiveness of market values in the USA. It suggests that economistic values ought to be widespread. However, our earlier discussion of Inglehart's work on 'materialist' and 'post-materialist' values suggests a caveat. Most groups in America have attained such high living standards because the USA, until the 1970s, was the most affluent society in the world (Table A.1, p. 219), that economic well-being can, up to a point, be taken for granted. If this is so, then Inglehart's theory suggests that narrow economic concerns should have less salience and post-materialist values should have greater prominence.

Inglehart's data are somewhat ambivalent on this point. Table 3.1, p. 53, suggests that the USA has consistently a lower proportion of materialists than Britain, Germany, France and Italy but a higher proportion than Belgium or the Netherlands. However, the proportion of post-materialists is smaller than in all these countries except for Britain and Germany.

His more detailed survey data of 1972–73 slightly clarify the position. The older Americans are more likely to have post-materialist values than their European counterparts in the other ten countries surveyed. However, this is not true of the younger Americans who occupy a roughly median position. Indeed, Inglehart (1977, pp. 36–7) points out that apart from Britain, the USA has the lowest inter-generational shift towards post-materialism. When an overall comparison is made, the USA ranks third out of the eleven countries, behind only Belgium and the Netherlands, in the ratio of post-materialists to materialists (Inglehart, 1977, p. 38).

As was discussed in Chapter 3, Inglehart's use of materialism and post-materialism is not just contingent on preferences for economic values but also depends on the goal of 'maintaining order in the nation'. However, it was also pointed out that he provides sufficient details of the 1973 survey for preferences for economic ends to be analysed separately. His American respondents were the least likely of the ten countries surveyed to give as first or second preference, out of a list of twelve factors, the three economic objectives of 'fight rising prices', 'economic growth' and 'stable economy'. These accounted for 31 per cent of the American first and second choices as opposed to an EEC average of 42 per cent. In addition, the Americans were more likely to express preferences for those items that Inglehart relates to 'belonging' or 'self-actualisation' than the other countries, except for Belgium, Netherlands and France (Inglehart, 1977, p. 49).

This more specific analysis suggests that the Americans are less concerned with materialistic or economistic ends than most of their European counterparts. Belgium and the Netherlands are the principal exceptions. Presumably, this reflects the high levels of affluence enjoyed by the American population. At the time of the 1972–73 surveys American per capita income was well in excess of most EEC countries, being exceeded only by Switzerland and matched by Denmark. However, the American growth rate was considerably lower than that of most of her European counterparts during the 1960s and 1970s and, accordingly, she began to slip down the economic league table, being below most of the EEC countries by 1980 (Table A.1, p. 219; Table A.2, p. 220). This may explain the relatively low shift towards post-materialist values amongst the younger American respondents. They were socialised at a time when American economic dominance was coming under challenge, whereas their elders were socialised when American standards of living were generally clearly higher than their European counterparts. Hence older Americans would be likely to be relatively indifferent to economic goals, compared with their European counterparts, whilst younger Americans, having grown up during a period of relative decline, would not be likely to show this differential to the same extent.

Although this might explain the low inter-generational shift in American values it still seems that there is no precise relationship between the relative incidence of materialist and post-materialist values in the USA, and the general level of prosperity. In particular, Belgium and the Netherlands consistently show lower proportions of materialists and higher proportions of post-materialists despite not surpassing the American per capita income until the late 1970s, a period well after most of Inglehart's survey data and even further after the period of socialisation for the survey respondents. This suggests that two conclusions about economism can be drawn from Inglehart's data. First, economic factors are more important than material success alone would indicate, thereby suggesting that the cultural emphasis on market values does have an independent effect. Second, it suggests that American prosperity has led to some attentuation of these values but not to the extent indicated alone by America's absolute levels of affluence.[3]

Data from other empirical studies tend to support these conclusions. In a 1959 survey Americans were asked about their personal hopes and fears. Economic concerns were most frequently voiced (Cantril, 1965, pp. 34–6). Respondents from eleven other countries were also surveyed in the late 1950s or early 1960s. The Americans were only slightly less likely to mention economic aspirations and worries than on average were other nationals. This was despite the fact that most of the other societies were Third World countries whose GDPs were well below the level of western industrial economies in general, let alone the USA in particular (Cantril, 1965, Table VIII:7, p. 163).

Mackenzie's 1966 survey of affluent manual craftsmen in Providence, Rhode Island, also points to the centrality of material concerns in American society. Mackenzie asked his respondents, who also included very small sub-samples of clerical workers and managers, what sorts of people were in the middle and working classes. Middle-class people were described in income-related terms by over 70 per cent of each of the three groups; whilst the working class was described in a similar manner by majorities of both the craftsmen and the clerical workers. Only the managers preferred to use occupational rather than material factors when identifying the working class (Mackenzie, 1973, Table 42, p. 127).

The typical factors mentioned were income, education or a combination of education and income, and style of life. However, Mackenzie makes clear that these factors should not be viewed separately from one another. Education was very rarely mentioned by itself. Normally, it was seen as something that led to the ability to attain a higher income. In a similar manner, although style of life was relatively frequently mentioned separately, it was generally seen as deriving from and reflecting income levels. Thus education, income and style of life formed a causal chain of inter-related elements. The identification and description of social classes depended primarily on material factors rather than on occupational role or social prestige (Mackenzie, 1973, pp. 125–38).

Perhaps not too much should be read into these findings, particularly given the relatively small sample used by Mackenzie. However, they do emphasise the material concerns of American workers even when, as with these craftsmen, they were receiving incomes that were significantly above average. In addition, Mackenzie also provides evidence in support of our earlier argument about the nature of American trades unions. A clear majority of each of his three sub-samples saw the purpose of trade unions in purely instrumental terms (Mackenzie, 1973, Table 49, p. 144). Unions are there to get the best possible deal for their members, that is, the individual workers.

This gives credence to the notion that American trades unions are primarily business unions, who justify their existence to their members by the returns they can accrue in terms of pay, fringe benefits and conditions of work. In this context, political activity is looked upon as a particular form of investment, aimed at electing candidates who will be relatively favourable to labour interests – favourable, that is, in the sense of passing legislation that facilitates union activities or enhances workers' rights, or supporting expansionary economic programmes. Thus union goals are narrowly conceived focusing on pragmatic rather than ideological aspirations (Brody, 1980, Ch. 6).

In connection with this it should be mentioned that the trade unions have rarely posed a serious direct threat to managerial prerogatives. Management has long been ceded the right to manage: unions are concerned with the best returns for their members. As in the British case, their collective mode of action is a form of instrumental collectivism: individual interests are aggregated so that they might more readily be attained.

Management has often resisted unionisation because it threatens managerial power in the area of wage determination. However, unionisation is quite compatible with formalised, bureaucratic managerial methods of control because it allows for precise calculation of labour costs and still leaves management relatively free to extract as much work as possible from their labour force (Edwards, 1979). Hence, American management too has accepted a form of compromise which tolerates unionism whilst leaving managerial prerogatives unchallenged.

Mroczkowski (1984) has suggested that recent developments may herald an end to this formal independence of unions and management. He points to a variety of trends: the rise of profit-sharing schemes covering some 17 million employees by 1983; the increased use of joint labour–management committees to anticipate and deal with workplace problems; the renewed interest in the quality of working life; the introduction of quality control circles by management as a way of engendering greater commitment; and the growth of co-ownership schemes. However, the evidence that he presents does not amount to a major shift in worker orientation. Rather, as he acknowledges, the changes are an attempt by management to gain greater control of their workforce. In particular, they are likely to be used by paternalistic management in non-unionised spheres as a form of pseudo-participation – the illusion of participatory management being engendered in order to elicit greater worker compliance, actual participation in management being far removed from decision-making areas.

None the less, the renewed interest in the quality of working life – that is, the intrinsic aspects of work performance as opposed to the extrinsic economic rewards – is of some note. It does question the underlying economistic ethos and suggests some broadening of interest that is in line with our interpretation of Inglehart's work. Further support for this view can be based on the rise of essentially midde-class protest movements in the last twenty years that have not been connected with 'bread and butter' issues.

One of the main examples of this was the anti-war movement of the late 1960s and early 1970s. This in turn greatly influenced the success of McGovern in obtaining the Democratic presidential nomination in 1972. Other political campaigns that placed a relatively greater stress on 'quality of life' issues were the third party candidacies of McCarthy in 1976 and Anderson in 1980. Inglehart (1981) himself points to another case: the campaign in the early 1980s that effectively halted the nuclear energy programme.

All these movements were strongly supported by those groups who had the most sustained experience of economic well-being – the well-educated, secure middle classes. All of them tended to have modest support from organised labour with its traditional concern with economic issues. Indeed, Rosen (1975, p. 344) points out that their concern with economic worries sometimes heightened making manual workers less liberal in the late 1960s and early 1970s than they had been.

Overall, it seems that economism is higher in the USA than would be warranted by consideration alone of the absolute level of living standards. Concern with the quality of life, environmental and other post-materialist values is relatively concentrated amongst middle-class people and their off-spring. Organised labour still focuses on narrowly-defined economistic goals, pursuing them both by bargaining with employers, and by pressures on governments for expansionary full employment policies.

NORMATIVE RESTRAINTS

As with the UK, the heritage of individualism does not augur well for the development of normative restraints in the USA. We have already seen that the AFL unions were structured on craft lines. In addition, the AFL itself served as no more than a loose umbrella organisation, leaving collective bargaining to its constituent members. The development of industrial unions and their federation the Congress of Industrial Organizations (CIO) in the 1930s did little to alter matters.

Since 1955 the two federations have been merged into one organisation, the AFL–CIO. However, the autonomy of the individual unions has been maintained. They are still responsible for collective bargaining whilst the AFL–CIO takes on broader political functions, in particular pressing for favourable governmental programmes and legislation.[4] The weakness of the peak employees' organisation is signified by the fact that by the early 1980s only about 70 per cent of unionists belonged to trade unions who were members of AFL–CIO; and two major unions, the Teamsters and the Autoworkers, were disaffiliated from it (Estey, 1981, Ch. 3).

The situation on the employer's side is not dissimilar. The major employers' associations are fragmented both at the national and the state level. Again, membership is very incomplete (Wilson, 1982). In addition, as with the union side, the employers' organisations have their main effect in lobbying and pressuring government rather than in the sphere of wage determination. We have already seen that wage bargaining is decentralised to the level of the enterprise and, in some cases, the plant.

The absence of strong peak associations of employees and employers reflects the tradition of individualism. It allows the basic units, unions and companies to bargain in a relatively autonomous manner. The decentralisation of bargaining makes it more rather than less likely that the short-term self-interest of the participants will have primacy for there is little reason for them to take a broader view. Again, the similarity with the British case is marked, even to the extent that as with the TUC the AFL–CIO has never had much sympathy for egalitarian tendencies, thus removing one more possible restraint on the pursuit of narrow sectional goals.

Superficially, the USA does appear to differ from the UK in terms of the role of legal regulation of industrial relations. A succession of major, mid-century legislative items, the Wagner Act 1935, the Taft–Hartley Act 1947, and the Landrum–Griffin Act 1959, appear to give legal factors a far greater significance in the USA than the UK. However, these Acts have their main influence on the framework within which bargaining takes place rather than on the pattern of bargaining itself. The Acts are concerned primarily with issues such as the right of workers to form or join unions, the ability of unions to organise closed shops, the way in which strikes can be called, and the constitution of individual unions. These are important matters that have implications for the power relationships between unions and management rather than on normatively prescribing restraints on the use of power. Their British equivalent would be the Industrial Relations Act 1971 and the succession of Employment Acts of the early 1980s which were modelled, at least in part, on American law and were also aimed at altering power relationships.

The actual content of industrial relations processes has remained relatively untouched by legal restraints. Basically, legal provision has facilitated collective bargaining, particularly through the Wagner Act, but has left the bargaining to the (self-) interested parties. Even when the law has provided for external regulation, as with the National Labor Relations

Board (NLRB) established by the Wagner Act, this has not affected the substance of bargaining processes. The NLRB is concerned with the legality of particular industrial relations practices not with the content of the bargaining process itself.

This pattern of decentralised bargaining, weak peak associations and a voluntarist legal framework that facilitates and structures collective bargaining rather than regulating its content, does not suggest that income-receivers will be restrained from pursuing their narrow sectional goals. On the contrary, it suggests that short-term interests will be paramount with each group trying to maximise its own position regardless of the long-term implications for macro factors such as inflation and unemployment, let alone social inequality (Aberg, 1984).

Other elements that might facilitate restraint are also lacking. The USA has never developed an enduring set of tripartite agencies in which representatives of organised business and labour could meet with government officials and members. This both reflects and reinforces the weakness of the peak associations. It means that not only are long-term binding agreements between broadly-based federations impossible but there is also an absence of 'talking-shops' that might at least facilitate the sharing of information that would define the parameters within which subsequent wage and price determination might take place. Similarly, the absence of any significant political party clearly allied to organised labour precludes the possibility of bargained corporatism: the trade-off between organised labour and a broadly sympathetic government.

The combination of cultural traditions, decentralised bargaining and institutional arrangements does not suggest that prices and incomes policies are likely to be particularly effective. Indeed, circumstances seem even less propitious than in the UK. In practice, there have been fewer attempts than in the UK to introduce such policies. In addition, the attempts under Truman (1950–53), Kennedy and Johnson (1962–66), Nixon (1971–74) and Carter (1978–80) have all been short-lived. They have mainly depended on the voluntary cooperation of business and unions and this has not been forthcoming for long. For example, the Kennedy–Johnson administration's use of price and wage guidelines foundered as in particular the Secretaries of State for Commerce and Labor, Connor and Goldberg, came increasingly to reflect the view of their constituents, organised business and labour, rather than seeking to impose some broader perspective (McQuaid, 1982, Chs. 6, 7). The Nixon administration's introduction in 1971 of three regulatory bodies: a tripartite Pay Board with business, union and government representatives; and independent Prices and Dividend and Interest Rates Commissions, also failed. The former body soon collapsed in internal disagreement whilst the latter bodies were withdrawn in 1973 (McQuaid, 1982, Ch. 8). In both cases the weakness of the peak associations and their reluctance to be drawn into systems of restraint were crucial.

Pencavel points to an additional difficulty in implementing prices and income policies. He shows that in comparison to the UK, a far smaller proportion of American employees are covered by collective bargaining agreements. In the 1970s comparable figures were about 45 per cent of production workers and 30 per cent of all private sector employees in the USA, and 81 and 72 per cent respectively in the UK (Pencavel, 1981, p. 156). This means that it is far more difficult for American regulatory policies to have wide coverage. They are very likely to omit the unorganised sectors of the economy. Pencavel goes on to point out that even 'the Korean War price freeze of January 1951 covered only 65 per cent of the items weighted in the consumer price index' and 'the comprehensiveness of Nixon's wage–price controls lasted only a few months' (Pencavel, 1981, pp. 166–7). Not surprisingly, he concludes by suggesting that price and wage restraints have had a moderate short-term effect but when the policies have concluded, market forces have reasserted themselves and the losses have been made good (Pencavel, 1981, p. 177).

Finally, in this section, mention should be made of one factor that is not present in the British situation. We have already referred to the fragmentation of the American political system. This tends to reproduce at the macro political level some of the factors that have been described in the micro sphere of wage and price determination. The unrestrained pursuit of economic ends by groups of income-receivers is mirrored by the activities of elected politicians seeking advantages for their constituents.

Senators and Representatives will try to secure re-election by using their elected office to gain favours for their state or district. They are likely to pay prime attention to directing federal money in the form of grants or procurements to their geographical constituency. A favoured mechanism is to gain membership of a relevant Congressional Committee such as Agriculture, Defence or Aerospace and use this position to direct projects or finance in the 'right' direction. Chairmanship of a Committee or Sub-Committee is even more advantageous. In addition, there is a built-in ratchet effect as renewed federal expenditure is desirable election by election to engender industrial growth, employment and prosperity in the legislator's home area.

These mechanisms exist independently of more general pressures for federal expenditure such as welfare payments that might bring benefit to all regions and areas. The marketplace for votes echoes the sectional bargaining processes of the micro-economic sphere, in the sense that it too is sectional and unlikely to be subjugated by appeal to some 'higher good'. Individual Senators and Representatives are unlikely to hold back on their demands unless they can be sure that others will also show restraint, and, even then, they may be under strong pressure to push their own case in order to maintain electoral support. Thus this aspect of the political system positively exacerbates the pursuit of heavy expenditures which might be inflationary.[5]

POWER RELATIONSHIPS

(1) Within the Company

The discussion of the American situation has paralleled so far the earlier consideration of the UK. In the USA, economistic values are extensive, though not as much as in the UK, but normative restraints are even more limited. However, power relationships are in many ways radically different.

First, the degree of unionisation is markedly lower in the

USA. In the post-war period on average only about 25 per cent of the workforce has been unionised (Table 2.1, p. 28). In recent years the figure has fallen to about 20 per cent. To be sure, the overall figures conceal significant variations. Manual workers are more unionised than non-manual ones; manufacturing industry more than most other sectors; and men more than women. Even geographical variations are significant, 39.2 per cent of New York's non-agricultural labour force being unionised compared to only 6.5 per cent in North Carolina (Estey, 1981, Ch. 1). Overall though, organised labour is clearly weaker in the USA than the UK.

Not only is this the case, but in addition American management is generally more likely to be resistant to wage claims. Some of the reasons for this have already been mentioned. In particular, attention has been drawn to the early development of the multi-divisional organisation form and the greater leverage it grants to management. It gives management the possibility of switching production to other parts of the USA or overseas. In some cases management may threaten to relocate production where wage costs are lower. The potency of this threat is clear even in the light of the sharp regional variations in unionisation indicated above, let alone if one considers the even lower levels of unionisation in many Third World countries.

Mention has been made also of the high rates of immigration and internal migration in the USA. These have important implications for the tightness of labour market conditions. Again it means that American management has more flexibility as regards not only where it locates its productive capacity but also whom it employs. It also means that American management can adopt a tougher bargaining stance than its British counterpart.

An additional factor that has not been discussed so far is the structure of competition in the USA. It is a truism of economic discussion that the giant multi-nationals of the modern era are mainly American in origin. Dunning and Pearce (1981, Part II) point out that by 1978 there were 831 companies with an annual turnover of over $2.25 million. Of these companies 370 (44 per cent) were American, leaving Japan with 125 and the UK with 75 trailing far behind. However, absolute size is not always a good indicator of competitive forces. In the case of the USA the large size of the domestic market suggests that market competition might be more vigorous than the presence of these giants might presuppose.

Consideration of available data indicates that competition in product markets is considerably more pronounced in the USA than either the UK or Sweden of the other case studies, and only slightly less than in West Germany. Domberger (1983) has compared the USA with the UK. He looked at the market share of the five largest UK companies in 153 manufacturing industries and the corresponding share of the four largest USA companies in 450 sectors.

Table 4.1: Distribution of concentration range of largest UK and USA companies, 1972

% share of industry	UK %	USA %
0–19	12.4	19.3
20–39	20.3	37.3
40–59	30.0	26.2
60–79	19.0	12.2
80–100	18.3	4.9

Source: Domberger (1983), Table 1.1, p. 10.

Even allowing for the slight difference in yardstick (the four as opposed to the five firm concentration ratio), the position is clear. British industry has a more oligopolistic market structure. It is more likely to be dominated by a relatively small number of firms. In a similar vein Kristensen (1981, p. 3) indicates that in 1972, the four largest American companies accounted for 50 per cent or more of sales in 127 out of 429 industries, whilst in 1970 that figure was reached in 17 out of 21 Swedish industries. Finally, Pryor (1973) has compared a variety of western countries in terms of the average share of the four largest firms in each industry. Most of his data pertain to the early or mid–1960s but British concentration is underestimated as his data come from 1951 and, as was seen in

Chapter 3, concentration has increased sharply since then. Pryor provides a variety of measures, but using the USA concentration as an index of 1.0, the average Swedish concentration had a value of about 1.5, the UK of between 1.1 and 1.2, and West Germany of about 0.9.

The stronger competitive pressures in the USA strengthen the likelihood of American management being more willing to resist wage claims than their British counterparts, for they are less likely to be able to pass on higher costs as higher prices. One should not over-generalise this point. In some sectors of the economy unionisation is strong and competition is weak. In such areas it is more likely that high wage claims can be successfully prosecuted with a resultant wage–price spiral. Certainly, numerous studies indicate that trade unions are able to earn higher money wages for their members. Ashenfelter (1978) estimates this premium at 12 per cent in 1967, rising to 15 per cent in 1973 and 17 per cent in 1975, though he also indicates that it varies considerably from industry to industry. In addition, trade unions appear to be able to insulate their members from the effects of short-run market forces that might otherwise lower their money wages (Ashenfelter, Johnson and Pencavel, 1972).

This suggests a high degree of dualism in the American economy. Those sectors that belong to the 'planning system' (Galbraith, 1974) contribute to the cost–push inflationary process. However, the 'market system' has a power balance that is far more conducive to the restraint of inflationary pressures. The combination of competition, low unionisation, relatively plentiful labour and, in some cases, centralised management control, is quite potent. Even in the more oligopolistic sectors the balance of power is more conducive to the restraint of wage claims than in Britain because unionisation is less widespread and there are significant possibilities for easy relocation of industry.

The bargaining system is itself constrained by a broader framework. Here two factors are of significance, the legal framework and the general level of unemployment. It has already been mentioned that a series of major statutes have significant implications for the rights of workers to join unions and the legality of various union practices. In brief, the

Wagner Act 1935 encouraged collective bargaining by enabling workers to join unions without fear of dismissal. The Taft–Hartley Act 1947 limited union powers. Pre-entry closed shops were made illegal, although the post-entry union shop was still allowed. However, these too are illegal in several states that have passed 'right to work' legislation. Various 'unfair' employee practices were outlawed. Lastly, the ability of union leaders to call strikes was limited by allowing for the calling of a cooling-off period followed by a union ballot in 'national emergency strikes'; though, as Estey (1981, Ch. 6) points out, these emergency powers have been little used and in those cases when a compulsory ballot has been called it has always resulted in a rejection of the last offer made by the employer. None the less, these powers may weaken a union's position for fear that they may be used. They shift the parameters within which calculations of the costs and advantages of strike action are made. In particular, a union may not be able to call a strike at the most opportune moment.

The Taft–Hartley Act thus places some restrictions on the exercise of union power. It tilts the framework within which bargaining takes place in a favourable direction for management. So, too, does the general level of unemployment. Until recently, unemployment levels have generally been higher in the USA than the other advanced western countries (Table A.4, p. 220). The reason for this is not unrelated to the inability of organised labour to wield the same political clout as organised business.

(2) With Government
It was no accident that the Taft–Hartley Act was passed during a brief period of Republican Party ascendancy in Congress. However, organised labour has not been able to repeal its most disliked provisions, those pertaining to the 'open' shop. Nor has it been able to strengthen the Wagner Act, some of whose provisions have been weakened by companies delaying union recognition and the cumbersome method of resorting to the NLRB and possibly to subsequent litigation (Brody, 1980, Ch. 6). This suggests that, unlike in the UK, organised labour cannot veto adverse legislation or

remove it when a more sympathetic party comes to power. The political weakness of organised labour is further indicated by the fact that: 'Among the industrial democracies of the world [the United States and Canada alone] have not instituted a policy that gave the first priority to continued full employment' (Moynihan, 1973, pp. 94–5, quoted in McQuaid, 1982, p. 131). The subsequent watering down of the 1977 Humphrey–Hawkins full employment Bill during the Carter administration and despite the Democratic congressional majority, reinforces this point (Brody, 1980, Ch. 6; Vogel, 1983).

Whereas in the discussion of the UK it was argued that the City had achieved a position of great influence, financial interests do not have the same significance in the USA. This is partially because they did not have a comparable international status during American industrialisation but also because of a deepfelt mistrust and anti-bank feeling that dates back to the nineteenth century (Dyson, 1983, pp. 44–5). Instead, industrial interests have attained great power in the political arena.

This reflects a number of factors. First, there are numerous studies pointing to the substantial presence of business personnel, including corporate lawyers, in the American legislature and executive, and to the frequent interchange of personnel between the business and political sectors (Mills, 1956; Mintz, 1975; Zweigenhaft, 1975; Useem, 1980; Salzman and Domhoff, 1980). This institutional access is reinforced by the presence of business representatives on key advisory and policy formulating bodies such as the Council of Foreign Relations and the Brookings Institution (Shoup, 1975).

In addition, there are signs that large-scale business interests have become increasingly well-integrated and organised in applying political pressure. The role of the Business Council and the Committee for Economic Development have been stressed (Domhoff, 1975; McQuaid, 1982). Last, the whole climate within which political decision-making takes place is dominated by business values as has already been emphasised, whilst the government depends on private investment as the main engine whereby economic and social advance is gained. Thus, threats of non-cooperation can prove extremely effective in constraining legislatures from adverse policies, a factor that can apply even more forcibly at the local than the national level (Crenson, 1971).

The argument is not that American government is the political wing of the big business system, but rather that organised business is better able than any other group to steer policy towards its objectives and to prevent what it considers to be adverse legislation. Of course, there may be periods when its influence is less pervasive and it suffers defeats on important issues. Vogel (1983) maps the rise of consumer and environmental public interest groups in the early 1970s and points to this as a period of decreased business power. However, he also outlines its recovery in the late 1970s as indicated by the defeat of labour law reform, the gutting of the afore-mentioned Humphrey–Hawkins Bill, and the success in getting capital gains tax reduced in 1978. In comparison, other interest groups tend to be successful only in very limited fields, often single issues, whilst organised labour is simply less organised, lacking in institutional access, and without comparable leverage to exert on government (Wilson, 1982).

This analysis leads to a complex set of conclusions. The relative dominance of business interests and, in particular, big business interests, in the political arena has important implications for labour and employment legislation. Since the Wagner Act 1935 organised labour has not been able to gain further significant changes that would shift workplace power relationships in its favour. On the contrary, legislative changes have tended to weaken their position. Other tech-nological and organisational changes, particularly those associated with the regional and international relocation of industrial activity, have also strengthened the employers' position. Thus, compared with Britain, managerial domi-nance at the workplace, and the ability to resist potentially inflationary wage claims, have been high.

At the macroeconomic level matters are more compli-cated. We have already noted that there is an inbuilt inflation-ary bias in the political process. This arises because Senators and Representatives seeking periodic re-election try to direct federal expenditures to their constituencies in order to sup-port employment or welfare. As there are no corresponding pressures for raising taxes or cutting general items of expenditure such as national welfare schemes, there is a bias towards federal overspending and budgetary deficits: the fiscal crisis of the state. This means that inflationary pressures of the excess demand variety are likely. However, there are also important counter-tendencies.

First, there is clear evidence that the public does 'blame' political leaders for high unemployment or inflation. Thus the chance of securing re-election depends not just on local 'pump-priming' but also on a more general assessment of economic performance (Nordhaus, 1975; Hibbs, 1979). Clearly, public priorities are likely to shift towards perception of inflation as a problem as it increases. Hence this should give incentive to politicians to curb inflationary pressures by some combination of expenditure reduction or tax increases.

Second, there is clear evidence that Republican administrations are more concerned about inflation and Democratic ones about unemployment (Mumper and Uslaner, 1982). This reflects the differential basis of their electoral support. The Republicans gain higher levels of support amongst the more affluent groups, who tend to be more concerned with inflation, and from the self-employed and small business people who are more committed to the virtues of a balanced budget because if reflects the contingencies of their personal lives.[6]

Last, big business although generally in favour of mildly Keynesian policies because they generate increased demand for their products is also concerned about the consequences of permanent deficit spending (McQuaid, 1982, Ch. 5). this reflects fears about inflation and concern about labour markets becoming too tight. In this regard, the success of business interests in watering down the Humphrey–Hawkins Bill has already been noted. The big business solution to deficit spending is, of course, to cut expenditure, particularly in the welfare field. In so far as inflation has become perceived widely as a problem, they are likely to find Republican administrations particularly susceptible to pursuing this policy. However, even Democratic administrations are susceptible to these pressures, as they too are concerned about re-election and also need business cooperation, although they are more likely to offset expenditure cuts with some tax increases (McQuaid, 1982, Ch. 7).

AN UNEASY EQUILIBRIUM

The discussion of the three variables – economism, normative restraint and power relationships – points to the evidence of neither a 'virtuous' nor a 'vicious' cycle. Instead, it indicates a cycle of offsetting tendencies.

Economism does not seem to be as high as in the UK but none the less is high given the standards of living already attained in the USA. Normative restraints on the pursuit of economistic values are very weak. However, the structure of power relationships is not conducive to the successful prosecution of high wage claims and the consequential perpetuation of a wage–price spiral. The political system does generate pressures for potentially excessive government expenditure, but even here the combination of electoral feedback and business pressures means that executive and legislative alike will attempt to curb these inflationary forces before long. Thus, in general, unlike the British case, the concentration and fragmentation of power in the USA serves to nullify rather than reinforce the inflationary impact of relatively high economism and low normative restraint.

This would suggest that the USA ought to occupy a roughly median position in the international inflation table. Indeed, this has been the case for some time. In recent years the USA has consistently had a lower than average rate of inflation, being above the OECD average only in 1968–70, and 1979–80. Among the seven major OECD countries (Canada, France, Germany, Italy, Japan, United Kingdom and United States) its modal position has been the third lowest rate since 1967 and it has never been worse than fifth. In comparison with the other three case-study countries it has never had the highest inflation rate and has generally vied with Sweden for second place, with Germany usually having the lowest and the UK the highest rate (Table 1.1, p. 3 above).

The configuration of factors should enable the USA to cope well with exogenously-produced inflations. Management should be better able to resist wage claims intended to compensate workers for higher prices of imported products thus limiting the price–wage–price spiral, whilst politicians will also be encouraged to rein in the inflationary increase before it goes too far. The relatively small share of international trade in American output and expenditure should also help this process. In fact, Table 1.1 shows that the American performance after the 1973–74 and 1979–80 oil price increases was only about average compared to the OECD average or the other major countries. However, it was noticeably better than that of the UK.[7]

This equilibrium of forces is coming under increasing strain. The discussion of economism suggested that younger Americans are becoming relatively more materialistic than their European counterparts. This development could reflect the relatively slow rate of increase of productivity in the USA and its consequences for both the American growth rate and the USA's decline in the international league table of per capita income (Tables A.1, A.2, and A.3, pp. 219–222). Should this decline continue, then a significant gap could develop between the material aspirations of the American population and the productive capacity of the socio-economic system.

The prospects do not appear to be good. Production relationships are not particularly harmonious. The American strike rate is high by international standards (Table A.5, p. 224). However, these strikes tend to be more predictable than British disputes and include a smaller proportion of unofficial stoppages, reflecting both the legal restraints and the grievance machinery that have already been discussed.

More generally an adversary system of workplace relationships predominates. As in the UK feelings of trust and a spirit of cooperation are marked by their absence. Management has normally used other methods of gaining compliance with their authority. Piece-rate schemes have been widespread in many parts of manufacturing industry. They appealed to the assumed economism of the workforce. However, their efficacy in motivating higher productivity can be thwarted by informal restrictive practices as many studies have shown (Roy, 1952; Burawoy, 1979).

Recently the use of piece-rate schemes has declined as

other methods of control have been developed. Edwards (1979) has stressed the use of technological control where, for example, the speed of the production line or the use of automated work processes generate their own productive levels. However, as these control devices are rooted in an assumption of conflicting and adversary interests between management and workers they are hardly conducive to developing a spirit of active cooperation. Rather, it seems likely that productive relationships will continue to be alienating and demoralising. In this context the attempt to introduce participatory programmes as a palliative is likely to be of little consequence. The recent fad of re-importing Japanese managerial techniques such as quality control circles is not likely to be effective when the whole ethos of company relationships is founded upon American cultural values of individualism and the associated sectionalism of group egoism, rather than Japanese collectivist values (Dore, 1983).

If this is the case, then there seems no reason why the American productivity performance will improve or the American growth rate show a sustained improvement. The likely outcome will be that the equilibrium outlined above will become more difficult to sustain. Economism will become stronger and, in the absence of any enduring system of normative restraints, income-receivers will apply stronger pressure for higher rewards. The cost of resisting this pressure may be higher levels of unemployment in order to further weaken organised labour. However, as British experience shows, this is of doubtful long-term efficacy. In addition, American unemployment is already high by international standards (Table A.4, p. 222) and a further deterioration in the trade-off between unemployment and inflation will pose severe problems for politicians trying to gain re-election. In short, distributional conflict is likely to become more intense unless the new control techniques and technologies are successful in raising the American productivity performance.[8]

5 The West German Miracle

West Germany is widely considered to be the paradigmatic example of a successful post-war economy. The indications of success are many. The growth rate has been consistently high resulting in a per capita income that is now amongst the highest of the advanced industrial countries. Although this growth rate has slackened during the 1970s and 1980s it is still high compared to those of most of its western rivals and certainly well in excess of those of the UK and the USA (Table A.2, p. 220). In addition this economic advance has been accompanied by levels of inflation and unemployment that are exceptionally low (Table 1.1, p. 3 above; Table A.4, p. 222).

How then has the German economy been able to achieve this 'miracle' and, in particular, how has a relatively low level of inflation been combined with a low level of unemployment? Conventional explanations stress the ideological and institutional framework. The functioning of a 'social market' economy together with the consensus implicit in the term 'social partnership' are thought to be crucial factors. However, although they form part of the answer they indicate only superficial factors and not the underlying mechanisms.

THE SOCIAL MARKET ECONOMY AND SOCIAL PARTNERSHIP

The 'social market' economy involves a combination of two elements. Economic activity is characterised by market exchange in an essentially privately-owned economy. The

116

government's role is basically to underpin the market aspect by maintaining and enhancing competitive conditions whilst ameliorating the adverse effects of the system by providing a substantial set of social welfare benefits.

Maintenance of the market system occurs not so much through rigorous enforcement of competitive practices in individual product markets but more through limitations on the scope of government intervention. The government tries to establish and support the conditions favourable for market-determined investment and growth.

Industrial concentration, although not as high as in the UK is still significant and has been rising in recent years. Dunning and Pearce (1981, Part II) indicate that Germany is fourth in the international league table of giant firms with annual sales turnover in excess of $2.25 billion with 58 of the 831 firms in this category. Webber (1983b) points out that on average the ten largest enterprises accounted for 38.5 per cent of production in their sector in 1968, and by 1977 this had risen to 43.7 per cent. A clue to the factors facilitating the dominance of large-scale companies is provided by the relatively relaxed merger policy of the later 1960s and 1970s. Storey (1981, pp. 67–8) indicates that in 1973–77 'only two of 773 mergers reported [to the Cartel Office] were prohibited'.

Thus the key to the 'market' element of the 'social market' economy does not lie in the rigorous enforcement of competitive market structures or limitations on the size of firms. Indeed, not only does German industry show considerable concentration but it is also significantly cartelised. Most German firms belong to at least one of the main employers' federations. Webber (1983b, p. 63) indicates that about 80 per cent belong to the Federation of German Employers' Associations (BDA) and 95 per cent belong to the Federation of German Industry (BDI). As Maurice and Sellier (1979) point out, the strength of these employer organisations reflects the prior early cartelisation of German industry. In a sense they are an institutional embodiment of pre-existing cartels. This is not to say that they exist as price-fixing or output limiting concerns, but rather that they reflect tendencies for industrial enterprises to harmonise productive activities and not to compete as entirely distinct entities. The

BDA is particularly important in this regard. It is organised on a sectoral basis and although intended formally to consider questions of industrial policy, it cannot help but act as a forum for exchange of information particularly as its decision-making bodies are dominated by representatives of the larger firms.

The process of harmonisation and orchestration of industrial activity is far removed from the textbook world of perfect competition in which firms make decisions entirely independently of one another. It is supported by a further distinctive feature of German industry: the active role of the major banks. They not only provide long-term finance but also they are involved in giving expert advice and disseminating information. Of particular importance is the representation of banks on the *Aufsichtsrat* (Supervisory Board) of German companies. It is not so much that the banks' representatives will consciously try to harmonise business decisions but rather that they will inevitably facilitate flows of information about other companies' activities that will have implications for major decisions. In this context it is worth emphasising that one of the main functions of the Supervisory Board is to approve major investment decisions. This integrative function is not contingent upon the same person representating a particular bank on a variety of Boards, although this does occur, for given the banks' role in long-term finance of investment, any representative is bound to make reference to the overall pattern of development in that industry.[1]

What then is the 'market' element? It is really the commitment to providing the conditions within which market activities can take place. This has two components. First, successive governments have tried to establish a stable financial framework within which 'private' economic decisions can be made. Second, they have tried to refrain from direct intervention in those micro-economic decisions. Thus the pattern of goods and services that are produced is said to reflect the functioning of freely-functioning markets.

The central element of the financial framework has been a monetarist policy that by careful regulation of the government's budgetary stance mitigates against the possibility of inflation. Successive German governments have been keen to act against inflation both by controlling the money supply and by deflationary fiscal policies. One reason for this policy of financial rectitude has been the relative autonomy of the German Bundesbank. It is far freer than most other state banks to pursue what it considers to be sound monetary policies, that is, to moderate the rate of monetary expansion if it feels this to be the prudent course.

However, the sound money policy also has considerable political support. It was developed by the Christian Democrats in their long post-war period of political ascendancy. But it was also accepted by the Social Democrats. To be sure they have been keener to make explicit usage of Keynesian demand management policies. Schiller, who became Chancellor in the Grand Coalition of 1966, introduced the Concerted Action programme. This built on the Stability and Growth Act 1967, which was aimed at reconciling price stability with low unemployment and steady growth. Concerted action brought together representatives of the unions and employers' associations to try to agree a macro-economic framework that would facilitate the attainment of these goals. They engaged in exchanges of information, or macro-orientation data about the future direction of the economy. The exercise corresponded to 'indicative planning' or 'global steering' rather than direct intervention in the functioning of the economy. The government hoped that wage claims might be limited by the establishment of wage norms that would emerge on a consensual understanding of what the economy could afford. Thus it was hoped that concerted action would facilitate price stabilisation without hindering growth. So, in essence, this development was no more than an adjunct to the underlying sound money policy and the 'social market' economy (Kuster, 1974; Clark, 1979; Dyson, 1981).

By then the Social Democrats had renounced the more socialist of their policies at the 1959 Bad Godesberg Congress. Their leaders clearly saw private enterprise as the main engine of economic and social prosperity. They accepted that government's role was to support that motor:

Referring to the need not to undermine the investment propensity of capital, Brandt cautioned that the 'cow' must not be milked to death.

Rather the coalition had to 'keep it in good condition and ensure that is stays in the pasture, or in the milking-shed and does not land up somewhere else' (that is abroad). (Webber, 1983b, pp. 65–6)

Thus Brandt in 1971; whilst his successor Schmidt was described by Webber (1983b, p. 69) as feeling that 'adequate profits were a pre-condition of the investments without which there could be no growth, job security, real wage increases, or social progress'. Clearly a consequence of this dependence on the private sector would be a commitment to price stability for the presence of banking interests on the Supervisory Boards would ensure that German business would be likely to value this to an even greater extent than their counterparts elsewhere.[2]

The concerted action programme did point to one of the main supporting structures of the 'social market' philosophy: the notion of 'Social Partnership'. This concept implies that employers and employees are partners whose activities are interdependent. Unlike the Anglo-American model that has already been discussed this suggests that as partners in a cooperative venture they have duties and obligations to one another. As such there may be occasions when individual or group interests have to be subjugated to a greater, collective purpose.

This concept owes much to German cultural traditions. Currie (1979, p. 18) suggests that the 'Germans held, and perhaps still hold, the notion of something other and higher than the individual, something which by definition had authority over the individual, and something by reference to which the individual's true interests and needs may be better judged than they could ever be judged by the individual himself alone.' Currie goes on to suggest that the higher authority was the nation and that this collectivist culture encouraged a reciprocal sense of rights and duties between individuals and the nation.

In a similar vein, Fox (1978) has pointed out that traditionally German employers have been responsible for the welfare of their workers and that the state has reinforced this sense of duty. Accordingly, the bonds between employers and employees have been broader than the cash nexus. Again, this encourages a sense of collective purpose, of cooperation towards some higher goal – in this case the success of the company rather than the zero-sum game of adversarial conflict as in the UK or USA. Clearly, this lends itself to the idea of a 'social partnership' between the sides of industry, who are responsible for the continuance and success of the company and, ultimately, the nation. There are also distinctive ideological functions, for the stress on cooperation rather than conflict has important implications for how differences ought to be resolved. These will be returned to in a later section.

At this point one practical import of 'social partnership' will be briefly discussed. 'Crisis cartels' have been developed as a way of rescuing companies facing commercial failure. The government tries to bring employers and unions together to agree a rescue package. The agreement is drawn up with national bodies, that is the relevant employers' association and industrial union. The key point is that survival of the firm as a going entity can and does take precedence over sectional interests including the claims of creditors. The government tries to build on the collectivist cultural values by offering a package of support which benefits both 'partners' so that each will gain some advantage whilst making the concessions necessary for the firm's survival.

The presence on supervisory boards of representatives of a variety of outside interests – in particular, banks, customers and other corporate concerns with commercial relationships of supply or purchase with the firm in crisis – greatly facilitates the government's endeavours to reach an agreement. The diversity of interests represented on the Board makes it more likely that a broad view will be taken of how failure would affect the economy as a whole or other commercial or business interests. Hence the costs of failure are not simply the private, internal costs of the company, as would normally be the case in the UK or USA, but include broader external and social costs. This increases the pressures on the 'partners' to reach agreement and makes it much more likely that a 'crisis cartel' will be successfully established (Esser, Fack and Dyson, 1983; Dyson, 1984).

'Crisis cartels' provide an example of social partnership at the macro level because the interests represented and the institutional devices used transcend the level of the firm. However, social partnership has been embodied in a series of institutional mechanisms at the level of the firm, in particular in the form of co-partnership and co-determination.

CO-PARTNERSHIP AND CO-DETERMINATION

As is well known, West Germany has established a complex set of institutions for co-partnership and co-determination. The arrangements have been defined by a series of laws of which the most important are the Co-Determination Act 1951; the Works Constitution Acts 1952 and 1972; and the Co-Determination Act 1976. These Acts entitle workers to some participation in the management process. In some cases this involves the right to representation on decision-making bodies; in other cases there is the right to be consulted or informed prior to decisions being made. By implication the various laws stress the need to provide institutional mechanisms whereby either consensus can be created, or at least potentially conflicting claims can be considered prior to or instead of overt conflict. Thus, they give formal recognition at the level of the firm to the interdependence of the social partners, and the rights of both groups to have account taken of their interests.

The post-war legislative programme builds on or replaces earlier legislation which had been destroyed by the Nazi regime, as well as on post-war innovations made by the British occupying authorities. Its introduction has to be understood not just as an attempt to replace and systemise earlier developments but also as part of an effort to build a 'new' Germany. In particular it should be seen as a conscious attempt to legitimate the new regime by restructuring the basis of managerial authority: an authority which was weak owing to the discrediting of German business leaders who had collaborated with Hitler.[3]

The Co-Determination Act 1951 applied only to the iron, steel and coal industries (the Act is sometimes known as the Montan Act after these industries). It gives workers' representatives parity of representation with shareholders' representatives on the Supervisory Board of companies employing over 1000 people. As the Board normally had eleven members, both workers and shareholders were entitled to five representatives. The eleventh member, the chairman, was an outsider elected by the other ten members. Whereas the shareholders' representatives were elected by the annual shareholders' meeting, the five workers' representatives were chosen by a complex process. Two, a manual and a salaried non-manual employee, were appointed from its own ranks by the Works Council, the elected representative body of the whole workforce. A further two were nominated by the national union, one being an employee of the company, the other an outsider. The last worker representative was chosen after consultation between the Works Council and the union and was neither an employee nor a member of the union. These complex arrangements underscored the principle that the company was not just a private concern but had broader obligations and responsibilities.

In addition to this parity of representation on Supervisory Boards, and hence the power to co-determine supervisory decisions, the workforce also had representation on the Management Board. This body is normally appointed by the Supervisory Board but as the workers' representatives had the power to veto the appointment of the Labour Director, effectively that appointment was indirectly an employee prerogative. The actual choice usually involved consultation between the Works Council and the national union.

Thus in the Montan sector, employee representation was and is extensive. The Supervisory Board, which has the powers to appoint the Management Board, approve major investment decisions and review managerial decisions, appears to be bi-partisan. The presence of the Labour Director on what is often a three-person Management Board gives further involvement in day-to-day management decisions. In addition, there is further potential influence as the Works Councils have the right to co-determine or be consulted on some decisions.

The Works Constitution Act 1952 applied to companies employing over 500 people. Worker representation on the Supervisory Board was limited to one-third. The representatives were to be elected directly by the workforce. There were restrictions on who could be elected so that union officials were only eligible in the larger companies. There was no representation on the Management Board.

The Act also re-established elected Works Councils for all companies employing over 100 people. These Councils had important rights of co-determination, particularly in social and welfare matters. For example, they had to decide with management the hours of work, principles of remuneration other than basic wages which were the subject of negotiation at the national level between the relevant union and employers' association, piece-rate schemes and welfare facilities. In case of disagreement between the Works Council and the management there was recourse to an independent arbitor. In addition, the Works Council had the right to be consulted over lay-offs and to be informed about economic matters such as the company's production and financial situation or impending mergers.

This formal system fell far short of union demands. The unions felt that the Works Constitution Act, and to a lesser extent the Co-Determination Act, both split worker representation and limited the effectiveness of that representation. As regards the former Act, they felt that the legislation cut off the Works Councils and the employee representatives on the Supervisory Board from the unions. In particular they disliked the fact that the unions had no formal role in the election of the Works Councils nor, save for the larger companies, in representation on the Supervisory Board.[4] In addition they noted that the one-third representation on the Boards hardly constituted a real 'social partnership', for they could easily be outvoted.

They were also dissatisfied with the powers of the Works Councils which were limited in a number of ways. They had no power to call strikes in support of demands or grievances. Company secrets, often widely defined, could not be divulged to outsiders, including union officials. Last, the Works Councils were expected to operate with the company's interest at heart, rather than as the representatives of one particular interest, that of the employees. This reinforces the notion that has already been described of the presumption that there is some corporate interest transcending sectional interests.

Union leaders were more satisfied with co-determination in the Montan sector, but even here they and outside commentators pointed to shortcomings that limited the scope of genuine 'social partnership' (Daubler 1975; Furstenberg, 1978; Adams and Rummel, 1977). The functioning of the Supervisory Board was criticised for it was argued that shareholders' representatives could meet with managers prior to meetings and manipulate information available to the full Board. In addition, important decisions could be made in sub-committees. The authoritative Biedenkopf Report (1976, pp. 48–50) points out that technical and planning matters were left to management, whilst investment decisions were not really discussed by the full Board. Although Biedenkopf points out that worker representation on the Supervisory Board ensured discussion of the social consequences of economic decisions.[5]

The role of the Labour Director also attracted criticism. It was argued that his activities were often confined to those of personnel management, with the somewhat paradoxical result that he might be responsible for communicating information about closures and redundancies to other worker representatives. The key economic and financial decisions were being taken by other members of the management team. In addition the Labour Director was cut off from the union. This reflected the fact that any prior union role had to be relinquished on joining the management, and the tendency for him to be increasingly incorporated into the management team with an acceptance of their orientations. Thus the issue of loyalty, potentially divided between the company and the workforce, was normally resolved in favour of the former.

This is not to say that the various institutions of co-partnership and co-determination have brought no benefit to the workforce or had no implications for decision-making. There is ample evidence to suggest that the presence of workers' representatives on either the Supervisory or Management Board, as well as the activities of the Works Councils, have had significant effects. Heidensohn (1971) points out that in the Montan industries, management was forced to consider the social implications of their closure programme: a point that is particularly salient in the light of the 1984–85 miners' strike in Great Britain.

In addition, several writers (Furstenberg, 1978; Adams and Rummel, 1977) refer to surveys showing that a high proportion of the German workforce both participated in elections for the Works Councils and placed considerable value on these institutions. None the less, it is also clear that influence was mainly confined to the spheres of social and personnel matters, with direction of economic affairs firmly in the hands of management and the shareholders' representatives. Indeed, management seemed quite content to allow the Works Councils in particular to spend considerable time discussing welfare facilities, social problems and similar issues as this distracted them from considering the more fundamental economic questions.

Both the Social Democrats and the main unions were divided about the advantages of 'social partnership' within the company. But by the early 1960s both were committed to a policy of reforming and extending the existing institutions to make 'social partnership' more of a reality. The alternative course of transforming society towards socialism by measures such as nationalisation and direct state controls had been rejected by the party at Bad Godesberg in 1959 and by the main unions at Dusseldorf in 1963. The political and industrial arms of the labour movement had chosen to work within the capitalist system and accept much of its social market philosophy, though with a more Keynesian slant than the Christian Democrat creators of that framework (Markovits and Allen, 1984).

It was not easy for the unions, even when their Social Democrat allies were in office, to bring about significant changes to the system. This was partly because the Social Democrats were never in office with an overall majority. After the Grand Coalition with the Christian Democrats ended in 1969, the Social Democrats depended on the support of the Free Democrats to remain in office. The latter were reluctant to extend the co-determination system mainly through fear of giving the workforce, and particularly the unions, too much power and weakening individual property rights (Markovits and Allen, 1984, p. 162). Also the em-

ployers' federations were opposed to any significant extension of worker influence lest managerial decision-making on
key economic and financial matters be impaired.

In the 1970s two further major Acts were passed – the
Works Constitution Act 1972 and the Co-Determination
Act 1976. The first Act extended the powers of the Works
Councils. Some additional items of personnel planning
such as recruitment and training became matters for co-
determination rather than consultation, whilst an increased
range of economic and financial issues became subject to
consultation or prior information disclosure.

The Co-Determination Act 1976 was far more controversial. The unions wanted to achieve parity of representation on
Supervisory Boards outside the Montan industries. Mainly
because of the Free Democrats, actual legislation fell far
short of union demands. In firms employing over 2000 people
– about 600 companies in all – there were to be six shareholder
and six worker representatives. However, one of the worker
representatives was to be elected by salaried middle management. Such a member was almost certain to vote with the
shareholders' representatives. In addition, the chairman,
who had a casting vote, was to be chosen by a two-thirds
majority of the shareholders' representatives. Effectively,
the new arrangements did not provide for parity of representation but normally had an inbuilt majority of eight to five for
the shareholders' representatives.

It is too early to report on the consequences of the 1972 and
1976 legislation. Both Acts strengthen the notion of 'social
partnership' by increasing the representation of the subordinate partner on decision-making bodies or adding to the
range of issues they can affect. Yet, the reforms fall well short
of parity of representation. They seem to correspond to
the minimum concessions that employers would grudgingly
concede.

None the less, the reforms do strengthen the underlying
concept of an accountable management, one that at the very
least has to consider the social as well as the economic
consequences of its decisions. In this sense they increased the
legitimation of managerial authority. They also do so in a
slightly different manner. The increased representation of

workers on the Supervisory Board strengthens the idea of the company being a corporate body with some public purpose transcending the interest of any single group. This idea has already been encountered in the earlier discussion of 'crisis cartels'. A key element in the formation of such cartels was the presence of representatives of a wide range of interests on the Supervisory Board. This made it more likely that the crisis would not be assessed solely in terms of its costs for those with a direct financial interest, creditors and shareholders, as would be the case in the UK or USA, and that the different interests might have a joint role to play in helping the company to survive. The recent changes would appear to bring the workers' representatives more centrally into that process.

Our discussion suggests that 'social partnership' works. It seems that the Germans have developed a complex set of institutions that legitimate managerial authority and contribute to an orderly resolution of crises and potential conflicts of interest. The arrangements may not be ideal from the point of view of the unions but they appear to bring practical short-term benefits to the workforce in terms of social and welfare factors; and if they contribute to higher production they also help bring long-term economic benefits. However, before concluding that at least in Germany, normative restraints do work, we should assess whether organised labour has an alternative to accepting a role as a subordinate partner. Has it the power to pursue a different strategy?

THE POWER OF ORGANISED LABOUR

We have already indicated that business interests are relatively strong and well-organised in West Germany. The well-established employers' federations represent the overwhelming majority of companies and tend to be dominated by the larger firms. The BDI concerns itself with broad questions of social and economic policy – it is in a sense the main business pressure group; whilst the BDA is mainly concerned with industrial issues. In addition, unlike the UK and USA, financial interests are strongly integrated with industrial ones, suggesting that their influence will be complementary (Webber, 1983b).

In comparison organised labour is both weaker and divided. First, only about 35 per cent of the German workforce is unionised (Table 2.1, p. 28 above); and over 80 per cent of this membership is in the 17 industrial unions that together comprise the German Confederation of Trade Unions (DGB). The separate white-collar union, the German Salaried Employees' Union (DAG), and the German Civil Service Union (DBB) have the remaining 20 per cent of union membership.

This relatively low level of unionisation greatly limits the potential strength of organised labour. This strength is diluted further by three factors – the legal limitations on strike activity; the post-war augmentation of the domestic labour supply by East German refugees and migrant labourers; and the formal exclusion of union organisation from the workplace in favour of the non-union-based Works Councils. These factors reduce the effectiveness of unions at the industry and company levels as will be discussed shortly. However, before doing so, the capacity of the unions, in particular the DGB, to influence national economic and social policy will be analysed briefly.

We have already seen that national economic policy has been based on the idea of the 'social market' economy augmented when the Social Democrats came to office by a moderately Keynesian system of indicative planning and use of wage orientation data. Both wings of the labour movement have accommodated themselves to an economic system dependent on private capitalist accumulation. The conversion of the Social Democrats to this reformist position reflected its exclusion from political power and its consequential need to broaden its electoral appeal by modifying its position. In addition the social market economy appeared to be working well, growth was high, and inflation and unemployment were low.

The introduction of the Concerted Action programme in 1967 did not involve a radical departure. Direct government intervention in the market economy did not increase. Instead, it was an attempt to harmonise economic policy. It stressed the role of information exchange, the provision of orientation data to enable more rational and consistent decision-making by the relevant economic actors. Although the Stability and Growth Act 1967 had given the government fresh fiscal and monetary powers with which to manage the macro-economy and deal with the economic recession of 1966–67, the crux of the new programme was concerted action. As Kuster (1974, p. 70) writes:

This key measure stipulated that in case one of the overall aims of the act was endangered, 'the Federal government should provide the orientation data for simultaneous and mutually agreed upon measures [concerted action] on the part of Federal, state and local authorities, labour unions and employers' associations' in order to remove the threat.

At the point of introduction both stability and growth were threatened by a combination of recession and strike activity. The new policy was used to initiate a period of wage restraint agreed between the government, union leaders and representatives of major employers' associations. The 'orientation data' became a way of indicating what would be an allowable rate of wage increase. The role of the government's earlier creation, the Council of Economic Experts, was crucial in formulating these wage guidelines and assessing the likely consequences of alternative outcomes. Although there were benefits to all groups as economic growth resumed, the policies came under increasing strain. In the late 1960s the rise in real wages lagged behind the rise in real growth. This triggered off a series of wildcat strikes. In response, the unions raised their wage demands which in turn were resisted by the employers' associations (Kuster, 1974; Clark, 1979; Webber, 1983b; Markovits and Allen, 1984).

Concerted action became increasingly one-sided, for although the implications for wage rates were fully discussed, profit rates were never included. In addition the composition of the participatory body tended to be biased towards the representatives of the employers' associations. Above all the framework within which discussion took place was one dominated by business values. We have already seen that Brandt and Schmidt, the Social Democrat leaders, were committed to making the social-market system work. They needed business success. However, they also needed to persuade union leaders to cooperate in (price) stabilisation policies. In so far as the older generation of union leaders shared the social consensus this was possible, but even this support was problematic for Clark (1979) indicates that survey data showed that workers were opposed to participation in concerted action if it meant binding wage guidelines. In addition they were concerned about the potential loss of union autonomy.

Union support was jeopardised further by the government's tendency to sacrifice expansionary policies on the altar of fiscal and monetary rectitude. For example, legislation in the mid-1970s allowed the government to tighten its fiscal stance by cutting back on social welfare expenditure particularly in the fields of unemployment pay, health and sickness, and pension benefits (Markovits and Allen, 1984, pp. 148–9; Esping-Anderson and Korpi, 1984, p. 198). Keynesianism was taking second place to monetarism or, put another way, growth was subordinated to (price) stability. The government's priorities reflected the German fear of inflation and the desire to stamp out what would elsewhere be regarded as a mild inflationary surge. This factor also probably accounts for the support of the older generation of union leaders. However, the government's policies also reflected its subservience to business interests who did not want too fast a rate of economic growth, lest labour shortages should occur with a consequential shift in power relationships at the level of industry or company bargaining.

The Social Democrats were having increasing difficulty generating the economic and welfare benefits with which they were 'buying' the quiescence of organised labour. This accounts in part for their concern to strengthen the co-determination and co-partnership system in the early 1970s. They were trying to maintain union support by acceding to union demands in the industrial rather than the economic sphere. In addition they hoped that by strengthening the notion of social partnership they might also support the social consensus, that is legitimate the on-going socio-economic system.

As we have already seen, business opposition was able to dilute the proposed changes, particularly in the Co-Determination Act 1976. At the same time, there were further indications of the extent of business power as the government was pressed successfully to drop its proposals for employee capital-formation funds, change its employer training programme, and reduce the burden of company taxation (Webber, 1983b, pp. 70–2).

In 1977 the unions withdrew from concerted action. This was not only because the Co-Determination Act had fallen so far short of their expectations but also in protest at the employers' challenging in the courts the constitutionality of the new Act. Although in 1979 this legal challenge was defeated, the action following the dilution of the legislation indicated all too clearly to the union leaders their subordinate status in the social partnership.

If this describes the situation at the national level, what of union power in industrial bargaining? The main union federation, the DGB, and the relevant employers' association, the BDA, are both organised on an industrial basis. Bargaining covering basic wage rates, the basic work tasks of different groups and general working conditions is highly centralised. It is conducted on an industry-wide basis between the DGB and the BDA. Contracts reached between the two parties are legally binding and enforced over the whole industry. Actual earnings also depend on company bargaining between the Works Councils and company management that covers areas such as piece-rate schemes and overtime bonuses. This can give rise to significant wage-drift over and above the nationally agreed wage rates (Muller-Jentsch and Sperling, 1978).

For a number of reasons the bargaining position of the national unions is usually relatively weak. First, the union density of about 35 per cent compares unfavourably with the 80 per cent of companies that belong to the BDA. In addition, BDA membership is relatively concentrated amongst the larger companies, so that they cover about 90 per cent of employees in private industries. The cohesiveness of the BDA means that the companies can normally muster a united front. This reflects their cartel-like origins and the role of the major banks, whose presence on the Supervisory Boards tends to bind together companies who otherwise might be in disarray because of their competitive position.

The cohesion of the employers' associations is strengthened further by the centralised bargaining agreements, for this affects all of them. Similarly, they will all be affected by any strike called by the union in support of its position. Tylecote (1981, Ch. 2) argues that this is likely to lead to a tough bargaining stance and resistance to wage claims. Indeed, there is clear evidence, particularly in the 1970s, that employers' associations have been prepared to sit out strikes or even to initiate lockouts to discipline the unions (Markovits and Allen, 1984).

There are, of course, legal restrictions on the use of both strikes and lockouts. Unions cannot call strikes whilst a contract is in force. This makes it difficult for a union to co-ordinate strike action as contracts may expire at different points of time. A strike is only lawful if procedures for dispute resolution have been followed and exhausted. There are limitations on how vigorously a strike may be prosecuted, for example as regards the compulsion to carry out maintenance work (Schmidt, 1974). Essentially, the legal framework sees society as interdependent and thus seeks to restrain one party from seeking to destroy its partner. Indeed this presupposition of social harmony leads Muller (1974, p. 163) to point out: 'conflict settlement must aim at the achievement of a stable order.'[6]

Thus the legal climate is not particularly conducive to strike activity. By implication union support for wildcat strikes is unlawful, whilst other strikes may expose the union to potential damages if the courts do not think that strike activity is 'socially justifiable', that is, occurs for a proper purpose and after exhaustion of appropriate procedures. The low German strike rate cannot be seen as a reflection of underlying social harmony, but reflects also these legal constraints. Indeed, many German unions recognising that their strike potential is limited have entered into legally binding arbitration procedures with their employers' association.

A further constraint on union strength arises from the fact that any agreement on wages or conditions of work won by the union has to apply to non-union as well as union members. This encourages the 'free-rider' and is hardly conducive to an increase in union membership. In addition the appeal of union membership to non-unionists is limited by the quite significant wage-drift attained by company bargaining. This can add at least 20 per cent to basic wage rates (Muller-Jentsch and Sperling, 1978, p. 283).

Two other factors can be identified as weakening the position of the unions in the post-war period. First, employers have had access to external sources of labour. The immediate post-war period saw a significant influx of refugees from East Germany, many of whom were skilled workers. Krejci (1976, p. 117) estimates that prior to the construction of the Berlin Wall in 1961 there were over 2.5 million refugees. They had an effect in stimulating the post-war economic recovery as they both augmented the supply of labour, particularly in areas where skills might otherwise have been scarce, and increased consumer demand. However, by the same token, they weakened the bargaining power of organised labour.

The other external source of labour was the migrant or guest-workers. By 1965 they accounted for over 1 million of the German workforce and at their peak in 1973 they numbered nearly 2.5 million or about 10 per cent of the workforce (Sturmthal, 1982, p. 757). Unlike the refugees, they have been relatively unskilled and have tended to be employed in the secondary labour market, that is, in those jobs that are poorly paid, lacking in career opportunities and mainly insecure. As a consequence their presence has not only boosted the labour supply in general terms but has also shielded the indigenous workforce from some of the worst effects of recession and economic down-turn.

Dohse (1984) points out that it was the guest-workers who were most likely to experience selective lay-offs and least likely to experience upward occupational mobility. In addition, as they lacked the legal status and rights of the domestic labour force they were likely to take the brunt of long-term unemployment. Sturmthal (1982, p. 758) estimates that between 1973 and 1977 something like 900,000 guest-workers must have returned home, a trend that is likely to continue with the Return Promotions Act 1983, which offers financial inducements to leave.

These developments have two main consequences for union power. First, they indicate that the unemployment figures for the post-war period have been deceptively tight.

To be sure, the immediate post-war labour surpluses have long since evaporated, but the possibility of importing labour during the 1960s meant that the effective labour supply was considerably greater than that signified by the unemployment statistics. The 'industrial reserve army' was located externally rather than internally. In any case, the presence of illegal immigrants who do not appear in official statistics suggests that the unemployment figures probably under-represent the real position.

Second, the guest-workers can be made the victims of recession. Unemployment is and has been exported quite consciously, thereby limiting the rise in official unemployment. As Dohse (1984) suggests, to some extent inducing guest-workers to leave is the cost of buying industrial peace. In any event the unions are more interested in representing the interests of home workers, who in turn blame unemployment on the foreigners. This suggests that whereas in times of boom the introduction of guest-workers has weakened the bargaining position of the unions, in times of recession it has undercut potential militancy. In both cases, of course, the domestic workforce has benefited.

The other factor that has weakened the position of the unions is the familiar one of the increased internationalisation of economic production. Large German firms, as with those in the UK and USA, tend to be multinational. Production is increasingly likely to take place abroad perhaps utilising cheaper sources of labour (Frobel, Heinrichs and Kreye, 1980; Sabel, 1982). As elsewhere this disciplines the domestic labour force. Industrial militancy and failure to accept new technologies and patterns of work may be costly in terms of future investment and jobs.

This takes us back full circle to the individual company where these critical decisions are made. Formally, workers' representatives are able to influence these decisions, as well as those in other economic, financial and strategic areas, through their membership of the Supervisory Boards. However, as we have seen, it is in just these areas that worker influence is most severally circumscribed. In addition, the Works Councils only have the right to information on these major matters and then are often bound to secrecy because of the confidential nature of such issues.

The Works Councils do have the right to bargain over local wage factors but, as we have also seen, they cannot support their position through strikes. However, the workforce does seem to possess some industrial muscle for when in the late 1960s management cut back on the wage-drift elements of earnings, this provoked a wave of unofficial strikes (Markovits and Allen, 1984, p. 135).

In addition, we have also seen that the Works Councils and the other institutions of co-partnership have been frequently criticised for splitting the potential power of organised labour, because of their formal independence from the unions. In practice, this is not so apparent as over 80 per cent of the work councillors are members of the DGB (Furstenberg, 1978), whilst the unions are also able to monopolise representation on the Supervisory Boards. In addition, recent years have seen attempts to integrate the shop stewards, the shop-floor union representatives, with the Works Councils so that they operate in harmony rather than as split channels of worker representation (Muller-Jentsch and Sperling, 1978). Thus, there is less scope than hitherto for management to adopt a strategy of divide and rule, although the underlying problems of the scope and strength of the power afforded by the participatory institutions still remain.

In summary, it appears that organised labour is relatively weak at the national, industry and company levels. Its capacity for effective action is severely limited *inter alia* by its numerical weakness, the strength and unity of the employers' associations and legal restraints on strike action. This makes it difficult to know to what extent the unions acceptance of social partnership is an acknowledgement of this lack of power or reflects a genuine commitment to the values of social consensus borne out of the collectivist German cultural tradition.

In general terms it does look as if the institutional restraints have been imposed on a not too reluctant union movement. Yet the shift in union aspirations and priorities in the early 1960s did reflect the underlying realities of power. However, the unions' accommodation to the prevailing socio-economic system also signified an awareness of the benefits of that system: the material advantages of the sustained post-war recovery. this suggests that restraint and moderation were being purchased by economic success. If so, social partnership is contingent on the system 'delivering the goods' in the form of high living standards and social welfare payments. A slow-down in the rate of economic growth may threaten the social consensus to the extent that economistic aspirations are not satisfied.

ECONOMISM IN GERMANY

On the surface there is little reason to feel that materialist concerns rank any lower in Germany than elsewhere in the western world. Certainly the aforementioned shift in the official position of the DGB as contained in the 1963 Dusseldorf Programme supports this view. This gave primacy to the pursuit of economic goals rather than the transformation of society.

As regards managerial goals, Lawrence (1980, Ch. 4) suggests that German managers are more concerned with 'technik', that is getting things done and the quality of production, than with the pursuit of profits. However, this may be because profitability is taken for granted. Indeed, this view is supported by Budde *et al.* (1982, p. 14), who conclude from a comparative study of British and German management that in both cases 'the satisfaction of capitalistic economic objectives remains paramount'; these objectives being related essentially to the growth in profits and level of profitability. Tylecote (1981, Ch. 2) goes even further by suggesting that the strong numerical representation of banks on the Supervisory Boards makes it more rather than less likely that managers will be constrained to follow shareholder goals, though this view is not supported by Budde's findings.

In a sense this is surprising. The rapid growth of the postwar German economy and the attainment of very high living standards might have been expected to sate these materialist aspirations. By 1980 Germany had the fourth highest per capita income of the 'non-oil' countries (Table A.1, p. 219) and the increase in foreign travel and international communication systems must have heightened awareness of this favourable situation. Some support for this view can be derived from the already discussed work by Inglehart, and also from Dalton.

In general, Inglehart finds that Germans are no more likely to exhibit 'post-materialist' values and if anything are more 'materialist' than the other nationals surveyed (Table 3.1, p. 53). Indeed, his 1972–73 data indicate that the Germans had the ninth lowest ratio of post-materialists to materialists out of eleven countries (Inglehart, 1977, p. 38). He also finds them recording the seventh highest level of dissatisfaction with their incomes out of ten countries (Inglehart, 1977, p. 155). His more specific analysis enables the purely economic factors to be separated from the indicators of 'safety' that together form the basis of his distinction between 'materialists' and 'post-materialists'. Here again the economism of the German respondents is remarkable as they were most likely out of ten nationals to mention the three economic factors as their first or second priority (Inglehart, 1977, p. 49).

However, Inglehart and Dalton provide other data which qualify these findings. First, they both note that younger Germans are very much less materialistic than their elders and that even by 1973 the younger Germans were more likely to exhibit post-materialist values than their British or American counterparts. Only in France and Belgium did the youngest age cohort exhibit a higher ratio of post-materialists to materialists. Indeed the inter-generational shift from materialist to post-materialist values was more pronounced in Germany than anywhere else (Inglehart, 1977, pp. 36–7, Dalton, 1977, p. 463).

These findings suggest that the high living standards of the 1960s and early 1970s have had some effect and those younger age groups who have been most recently socialised tend to some extent to take material prosperity for granted. Inglehart provides further specific evidence of a shift in values that applies to the older age cohorts. He reports the findings of a series of surveys that have been conducted regularly since 1949. What is of importance is that a growing proportion of respondents indicate that 'Freedom of Speech' is most important, whilst the proportion choosing 'Freedom from Want' declines. 'In 1949 "Freedom from Want" was the leading choice by a wide margin ... by 1958 "Freedom of Speech" had moved ahead. In 1970, "Freedom of Speech" was chosen by more people than all other choices combined' (Inglehart, 1977, p. 107).[7] Inglehart adds that the change is so great that it cannot represent simply generational shifts, that is younger cohorts being less concerned with the material value of 'Freedom from Want', but shifts within each cohort as they grow older and more attuned to rising German prosperity.

The most recent survey data tend to support this conclusion. The proportion of materialists has been falling and that of post-materialists rising (Table 3.1, p. 53). By 1984 the ratio of post-materialists to materialists was second only to that of the Netherlands of the six countries surveyed. These conclusions are further strengthened by two recent developments, the rise of the German 'green' party and the recent emphasis paid by union leaders to the 'quality of working life'.

The 'green' party has focused on the issues of environmental control and nuclear energy both of which are identified by Inglehart (1981) as relating to post-materialist values. Certainly, these concerns seem far removed from the conventional, economic 'bread and butter' issues. The 'green' party has achieved remarkable electoral success. It recorded 5.6 per cent of the vote in the German Federal elections and 27 of its members were elected to Parliament. It also has representation in six of the eleven *Lander*, gaining between 4 and 8 per cent of the vote (Rothacker, 1984). In the more recent European elections, it recorded 8.2 per cent of the vote, the highest share achieved by any ecological or environmental party (Jowett, 1985, p. 111).

The other recent development has been the switch by union leaders from the mid-1970s onwards to stressing issues relating to the 'quality of working life'. Markovits and Allen (1984) point out that they tried to develop a Humanisation of Work Programme. This was in reaction to the changes in work tasks occasioned by rationalisation and the introduction of new technology. Of particular concern were the alienating or dehumanising implications of the new structure of work tasks and the associated deskilling or dequalifying of the workforce. The unions tried to use the co-determination machinery or strike action to influence the ways in which new work processes were introduced in order to avoid these deleterious effects.

Of course, these issues together with a related concern, the introduction of a 35-hour week, had economic as well as qualitative implications, for deskilled work is normally lower-paid work, whilst a shorter working week not only reduces time spent in stressful activity but might also reduce unemployment. In addition, to some extent, the unions were forced to focus on these 'qualitative' issues because they had little chance of directly affecting the 'bread and butter' issues of real wages and unemployment during the late 1970s and early 1980s due to their lack of power. Indeed, by then unemployment, as elsewhere, was rising sharply (Table A.4, p. 222) and the share of wages in national production was falling (Markovits and Allen, 1984, p. 144). Even so, this development is mildly supportive of the thesis that with the long-term sustained rise in prosperity, narrowly-based economic and material issues were losing their potency.

However, it is not clear that this state of affairs will survive if there is a lengthy period either of substantial unemployment or of near static real wages. Krejci indicates that the structure of income distribution has been stable in post-war Germany. He suggests that this is due to the lack of resentment of economic inequality, even though in 1970 the top fifth of households had 45.6 per cent of income compared to the 5.9 per cent share of the bottom fifth. In turn this lack of resentment is related to the overall rise in living standards: 'As long as individuals were satisfied with the general increase of real income and were not disturbed at lagging behind others, there might have been greater satisfaction with the development [of income distribution by size]' (Krejci, 1976, p. 94). The clear implication is that disruption of this taken-for-granted state of affairs might bring questions of income distribution to the forefront.

Certainly there has been a marked relationship between changing wage levels and industrial strikes. The 1966–67 recession reduced the rate of increase of real wages and, as we have already seen, provoked a significant rise in strike activity in 1967. Again in 1971 a strike wave occurred that was related not to the absolute level of wage increases but to their shortfall compared to rises in production in 1969–70. The recession of the mid–1970s also triggered off a 'new wage consciousness' highlighted by the metal-work and printing strikes of 1978, though even so militancy was less pronounced than might have been expected and the German strike rate remains low by international standards (Muller-Jentsch and Sperling, 1978; Markovits and Allen, 1984; Table A.5, p. 224 below).

In part, this is because the costs of recession have not been borne entirely by the indigenous workforce. As already noted the guest-workers were more susceptible to being laid off and in many cases have returned home as their contracts of employment have ended. Even so, there does seem to be some restraint on how claims are pursued. As Dyson (1981, p. 51) notes: 'distributional struggles which involved the exercise of power in the economic system were constrained by the primacy that was attached by actors within industry itself to the attainment of the economic goals of stability and growth.' Perhaps, in this regard, it is worth making one final reference to Inglehart's survey data. We have already noted that the German respondents of the ten-nation 1973 survey most frequently gave priority to the three economic issues included in a list of twelve. These issues were 'economic growth', 'fight rising prices' and 'stable economy'. Most other nationals attached more significance to economic growth than did the Germans. However, the Germans were far more likely to make the other two factors their first or second choice than any other nationals (Inglehart, 1977, p. 49). Fear of inflation and economic instability, reflecting the inter-war German economic history, may be a significant cultural factor.

A VIRTUOUS CYCLE

It does appear that materialist values are held in check to some extent by a combination of cultural values and the benefits of post-war prosperity. However, we have not yet discussed whether this post-war prosperity is itself contingent on the structure of power and normative restraints that have already been outlined.

At one level this is clearly the case. The much vaunted low level of industrial disputes is related both to the mechanisms of 'social partnership' and to the relatively low power of unions. It is not just that the low strike rate is directly conducive to orderly production and thereby higher production. In addition, as Lawrence (1980, Ch. 6) points out, German managers can rely on supplies of components and materials from other firms who are also likely to be strike free. The net result is that productive activities can be planned more rationally and predictably and that lower stocks of components and materials can be held. Furthermore, it becomes more likely that the servicing of faulty goods or the replacement of bad parts will take place promptly. Both are important parts of successful marketing where the German experience and reputation stands in marked contrast to that, say, of the UK.

Apart from this, the use of participatory schemes at the workplace may itself directly improve productive performance. In a well-known study Blumberg (1968) has argued that this is the normal consequence of the use of participatory schemes. He contends that worker participation by increasing job satisfaction and morale led to higher output and productivity. We have noted already that surveys show that German workers place a high value on their participatory schemes and that turnout for Works Council elections is high. This is not to say that they do not feel some sense of alienation from their companies, but rather that commitment is higher than otherwise might be the case. If so, we should expect greater commitment to have the effects indicated by Blumberg.

Some light is thrown on this by a recent study by Cable and Fitzroy (1980). They looked at a small number of firms that had introduced participatory schemes over and above the miniumum requirements of German law. This participation took the form of access to information normally confined to management as well as involvement in strategic decision-making about investment, prices and products. These 'high participation' firms also had collective profit-sharing schemes. Cable and Fitzroy compared these firms with 'low participation' companies which only exceeded the statutory requirements by having a collective profit-sharing scheme. The 'high participation' firms had a better economic performance. Their growth rates and productivity increases were higher. They were more profitable and efficient. In addition, although during the period of the study unemployment was generally increasing, the 'high participation' firms had a smaller fall in employment than the 'low participation' ones.

Cable and Fitzroy suggest that the combination of collective profit-sharing and participatory schemes is conducive to a 'high-trust' relationship (Fox, 1974). Workers are more committed to their firms. They are prepared to be more cooperative because they share collectively in the consequences of cooperation in so far as this increases profitability and because their participation in decision-making makes decisions more legitimate and therefore more acceptable. This cooperativeness is a much more positive element than simply limiting industrial stoppages. It implies that there will be less resistance to the introduction of new technologies and systems of work and that workers will not just comply with instructions but work positively towards their successful fulfilment.[8]

Crouch (1980) and Streeck (1981, 1982) have pointed to further aspects of this phenomenon. Crouch focuses on the fact that labour is dependent on the controllers of capital to use profits for investment to provide future employment opportunities. He suggests that the high involvement of financial institutions in German industry is conducive to a high level of domestic investment for any given level of profitability because they are long-term rather than short-term providers of capital, as in the British case. This provides a key element whereby higher investment creates higher overall employment. In turn, this means that there is higher employment than otherwise would be the case in the individual sectors of the economy. This encourages greater cooperation by the industrial unions that, in turn, enhances profitability and, thereby, investment. As we indicated in Chapter 2, this is another variant of the 'high trust' cycle but at a higher level of abstraction: workers 'trust' that higher profitability will result in higher domestic investment. In so far as that trust is justified the cycle can be maintained.

The argument is taken a stage further by Streeck. He suggests that the German system of industrial relations has given rise to a 'virtuous circle':

The structure of industrial relations at the workplace has permitted high productivity, high productivity has allowed for high real wages and elaborate social insurance provisions, and the latter have contributed to union moderation in general and union acceptance of the industrial relations system in particular. (Streeck, 1981, p. 153)

Streeck sees this desirable state of affairs as stemming from three factors. First, the fact that the unions are organised on an industrial basis. This helps orderly relationships to develop because inter-union conflicts can be avoided and leap-frogging wage settlements become less likely. In addition, it means that unions have to take a broad view. Here, Streeck explicitly uses Olson's argument that they have to take account of the impact of their activities on the economy as a whole and that they have to find policies that can gain the support of a broad range of workers in the industry and not just a sectional group based on a particular skill or craft. Streeck, like Crouch (1985), likens this to the 'solidaristic wage policy' of the Swedish unions that will be discussed in Chapter 6. Streeck also suggests that the union structure is conducive to pursuit of the collective goal of growth because this brings benefit to all concerned (Olson, 1982).

Streeck also gives some weight to two other factors. He suggests that both the legal system and the increased involvement of union organisation with the workplace representative system has helped to develop this orderly system of industrial relations that stands at the centre of the virtuous cycle.

In a later paper, Streeck (1982) has suggested that union leaders were originally drawn into 'social partnership' because it satisfied their need to provide material benefits for their members as well as because of the aforementioned concern with the broader impact of their activities. However, he goes on to point out that they have increasingly tended to be incorporated into the industrial and state system. Their involvement with Works Councils, Supervisory Boards and Concerted Action led them to seek stronger, more centralised control over their members in order to be able to 'deliver' cooperation and restraint. This explains the ideological shift in the DGB's position. Its pragmatic post-Dusseldorf position is, of course, highly consonant with the economic rationality of a management strongly committed to shareholder goals of profitability and to the 'social market' economy in general.

Streeck's analysis of the German labour movement differs radically from that of Goldthorpe (1978) for Britain. For, whereas the latter sees the maturation of the British working class leading to heightened distributional conflict as wage claims are prosecuted with increasing vigour, the former sees a German labour force that is increasingly incorporated and cooperative. However, Crouch (1985) points out that the very factors that facilitate this development, the centralisation of the union movement and the control that the leadership exerts over its members, give it a capacity for strategic action in its relationship with government. It can choose to rein back wage demands when the economy enters recession thereby minimising the impact of deflationary pressures, whether caused by exogenous forces or by the government's monetary and fiscal policies, from severely affecting the level of unemployment. Thus compared with Britain, deflation is likely to have a sharper impact on prices than on employment levels.

Streeck's 'virtuous circle' is very similar to the 'virtuous cycle' of Chapter 2. However, in that model the role of economistic values and orderly power relationships is far more explicit. Indeed, this leads to an important corrective to the emphasis given by Streeck to the role of normative and institutional restraint, for he tends to underplay the power advantage enjoyed by the controllers of capital over organised labour in Germany. To be more explicit, the industrial relations system that does have many of the functions attributed to it by Streeck is itself constructed on and buttressed by the weakness of organised labour: the long period of rule by the Christian Democrats, the low density of unionisation, the cartel-like employers' federations, the legal restraints on strike activity and the exogenous labour supply. Indeed, many of the participatory institutions so valued by the workforce have been designed not so much by organised labour as for it, with the explicit intention of conceding as little as possible and of building in as many restraints as possible. If incorporation has taken place it has been into a capitalist system and on capital's terms. The leaders of the labour movement have accommodated themselves to market capitalism.

This is not to say that this accommodation has not brought considerable benefits that have already been described. In particular a policy of restraint and cooperation when the Social Democrats were in power did bring some changes to the participatory system and particular gains in the state social welfare system.

However, our focus is on the implications for the containment of inflation. In the German system, at the macroeconomic level growth is partially sacrificed to stability. This reflects the dominant role of financial institutions and the way in which the historical fear of inflation shifts the balance of political advantage towards curbing inflationary pressures. So strong are these forces that in the 1970s even a Social Democrat government did not hesitate to cut unemployment benefits in order to maintain fiscal rectitude. At the microeconomic level, the relative lack of bargaining power means that the rise in money wages can normally be restrained to accord more closely with rises in productivity than in most other western countries (Table A.3, p. 222). In both cases organised labour is in a subordinate position, unable to pursue effectively distributional conflict because of its lack of power and not simply or mainly because of the restraints of the institutions of 'social partnerships'.

This is not to say that the normative restraints of the industrial relations system do not have a role to play. Certainly, they help to maintain a cycle in which productivity is enhanced, materialist aspirations are satisfied and normative restraints are reinforced. In addition, they make it more likely that a union leadership which depends on the system for delivering benefits to its members will fail to develop an effective challenge to the socio-economic order and will thereby maintain its subordinate position. This suggests that if there is a German 'virtuous cycle', it corresponds more to Figure 5.1.

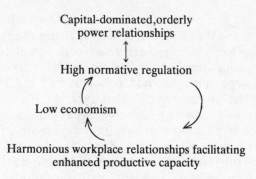

Figure 5.1: The German 'virtuous circle'

However, there is a further function provided by the normative restraints. They provide time for readjustment. When growth has slowed down and/or inflation been imported, as in the mid- and late 1970s, the restraints on sectional distributional conflict mean that problems are not immediately magnified. A price–wage–price spiral is not triggered off automatically as in Britain in 1974–75. In a sense the combination of past material advance, the restraining set of institutions and the weak power position of organised labour at both the national and industry levels acts as a buffer limiting the immediate response – a buffer that is reinforced if part of the adverse impact of economic recession can be displaced disproportionally on to the migrant workforce. Accordingly, Germany has been considerably more successful than most other western countries in restraining its inflation and recovering from externally induced inflations (Table 1.1, p. 3).

What is not clear is whether this favourable state of affairs can be sustained if the socio-economic system ceases to bring about the sustained rise in living standards that has been one of the hallmarks of the German miracle. In recent years the German growth rate has slowed, investment is increasingly going abroad and unemployment, despite the export of guest-workers (a process that in any case cannot go on for ever) is rising. The advent of a Christian Democrat coalition in 1982 has lessened the possibility of informal cooperation with the trade union leadership. In any case, writers such as Streeck (1984) suggest that business leaders may use the recession as an excuse for limiting the role of centralised bargaining, instead relying more openly on the use of market forces to restrain wage increases and on enterprise corporatism to maintain the 'virtuous cycle'. However, there are some signs that after a decade of relatively slow economic growth the workforce is growing more militant and more prepared to press its economistic claims that are now not so readily met. Certainly, the bitter strikes of the mid-1980s over the 35-hour week are an ominous indicator that the German 'virtuous cycle' is creaking to a halt.

6 The Swedish Virtuous Cycle

Sweden has aroused considerable interest amongst English-speaking writers in recent years. This attention has been stimulated by a number of reasons. For some writers the focus of attention has been the Swedish industrial relations system and in particular the sharp decline in overt forms of industrial conflict to very low levels (Table A.5, p. 224). This has led to concern with the structure of unions and employers' associations, the bargaining framework, and the institutional processes for resolving industrial conflicts.

For other writers the principal concern has not been industrial relations *per se* but the Swedish economic performance as a whole. The maintenance of high living standards through a continued good growth rate and significant productivity increases has been of note (Tables A.1, A.2 and A.3, pp. 219–222). However, even more interest has been paid to a level of unemployment that is particularly low by the standards of the western industrial economies, yet is unaccompanied by the high rates of inflation that conventional economic theories, both of the cost–push and excess demand varieties, would suggest (Table A.4, p. 222; Table 1.1, p. 3 above).

Another focus of attention has been the political supremacy of the Social Democratic Labour Party (SAP). Its long period in office together with its close relationship with the main union federation, the Swedish Confederation of Labour (LO), has caused considerable speculation about whether Sweden might provide the first example of a peaceful, reformist transition to socialism. Speculation that has been enhanced both by the high level of state social welfare provision and by recent moves to transfer share ownership from private ownership to collectively-owned wage-earner funds.

The political role of the SAP together with its partnership with the LO has been so important in shaping not only the contemporary industrial system but also the political culture of Sweden that this will be discussed first. It provides an essential framework for the more specific discussion of the analytical variables of the sociological model of inflation.

THE DOMINANCE OF LABOUR

The SAP first took office in 1932. Since then it has been almost continuously in government. Its period of ascendancy was only broken by the shaky rule of a coalition of bourgeois parties from 1976 to 1982. In no other western country has a left-wing party been in office for so long in the same period.

The significance of this long period of political control is twofold. First, it has given considerable stability to the pattern and direction of government policy. The SAP's continuity in office has been associated with the continued use of macro-economic Keynesian policies of a counter-cyclical nature aimed at maintaining economic growth and full employment. So pervasive have been the expectations generated by this programme, that its central tenets seem to have been accepted even by the bourgeois parties. Thus, in their short period of office, the bourgeois parties gave considerable priority to maintaining high levels of employment through fear of losing electoral support, even though this meant levels of public expenditure that would have been considered unacceptably high by most right-wing governments (Schmidt, 1984; Martin, 1984, pp. 295–7).

In a very real sense these widespread expectations about low unemployment, coupled with beliefs about the appropriate role of the government in managing the economy towards that end, constitute a 'dominant ideology' that is radically different from that normally associated with a capitalist market economy. This ideology not only has implications for non-socialist parties in office, but, as will be seen later, affects attitudes to a series of institutions and policies.

Second, the continuity in office of the SAP has given significant political leverage to the most prominent institution of the working class, the LO. The alliance between the political and industrial wings of the labour movement is one of cooperation and partnership rather than incorporation. Scase (1977, Ch. 6) points out that manual workers look to the LO on industrial matters and to the SAP on broader social matters. In addition, as Lash (1985, pp. 231–2) rightly indicates, the LO has frequently taken the lead in developing policies that have been subsequently turned into government action. This partnership has reinforced the development of the working-class hegemony hinted at above – a process that has been further strengthened by the numerous union-run cultural and educational organisations that promote support for working-class institutions and values (Scase, 1977, Ch. 6; Lash, 1985, p. 233).

The result has been to enhance support for the SAP as the political party of the manual working class and for the LO unions as their industrial organisation. The declining proportion of manual workers in the occupational structure ought to have increased the electoral problems of the SAP. However, Korpi (1978a; 1983, Chs. 4, 5) shows that the SAP has been able to offset this factor by maintaining a very high level of support amongst manual workers, increasing their electoral turnout and making sharp inroads into the white-collar vote; all three tendencies being in marked contrast to those of most other western countries, in particular the UK. As a result the SAP has been able to maintain the support of well over 40 per cent of the electorate in the post-war period (Table 2.2, p. 31 above) and gained an average of over 50 per cent of the votes cast (Korpi, 1983, Table 3.5, p. 38).

The ability of the LO to influence its political partner also enhances its legitimacy and authority as long as economic success maintains the credibility of the partnership. Again, despite the fact that it recruits virtually entirely from manual workers, LO membership has risen from 41.2 to 50.2 per cent of the labour force between 1950 and 1980, whilst union membership as a whole has risen from 51.3 to 80.6 per cent over that period (Martin, 1984, Table 3.3, p. 345). Union density has been far in excess of any OECD country (Table 2.1, p. 28) and union membership is now considered to be so normal that even the majority of white-collar and salaried employees are unionised. Korpi (1978a, p. 102) shows that in the secondary and tertiary sectors of the economy (manufacturing industry and services) by 1975, 95 per cent of male and female manual workers and 70 per cent of salaried employees were unionised.

The LO's Role in Collective Bargaining

The role of the LO is in marked contrast to those of equivalent peak labour organisations in most western countries. For example, in comparison with the TUC in the UK and the AFL–CIO in the USA, it has a far greater role in wage determination and significantly more control over its constituent unions. It shares these features with the German DGB but differs from it because of its high involvement in the formation of the SAP's economic and industrial policies.

The origins of the LO's role lie in a response to the earlier significance of the Swedish Employers' Confederation (SAF). Ingham (1974) has argued that the early formation and strength of the SAF itself reflected the small scale of the Swedish economy. This meant that large-scale non-competitive firms developed who, because of their oligopolies and cartels, found it easier to organise collectively than most of their European counterparts. Individual unions were in a relatively weak position particularly if individual firms used lockouts against them. A natural response was for the unions to organise collectively and to intensify this level of conflict. Hence the formation of the LO to represent manual unions and the corresponding white-collar federation, the Central Organisation of Salaried Employees (TCO). In addition there are two smaller confederations, the Central Organisation of Salaried Employees (SACO) and the State Employees' Organisation (SR). These have now merged as SACO–SR.

The intensification of conflict as manifested by a very high strike rate in the 1920s and early 1930s made both the SAF and LO aware of the costs of collective conflict. It led directly to the development of centralised agreements. Initially there is little doubt that the SAF was the dominant force in these arrangements. Their early ascendancy was reflected in the so-called December Compromise of 1906 and the labour laws of

1928 that underpinned the 1938 Basic Agreement. They consolidated managerial prerogatives by embodying managerial rights to hire and fire workers and to organise work activities. In addition, collective agreements were legally enforceable and ruled out strikes and lockouts whilst they were in progress.

This 'peace obligation' was maintained in the 1938 Basic Agreement. However, the improved bargaining position of organised labour caused by the presence of the SAP government was recognised by the introduction of some minor limitations on management's right to hire and fire. In effect, the roots of what have been termed the 'historic compromise' had been formed. Management ceded to unions the right to organise and bargain collectively. In return the unions ceded to management the right to manage at the workplace, granting them virtually undisputed control over the workforce and the direction of work activities. In addition the subsequent development of the centralised bargaining system, buttressed by labour courts and arbitration procedures, institutionalised conflict and was associated with the sharp fall in the strike rate. Last, both management and unions accepted the Keynesian policies of the SAP and the commitment to counter-cyclical policy adjustments designed to maintain economic growth and full employment (van Otter, 1975; Martin, 1977, 1984, Part 2).

The 1938 agreement enhanced the power of the LO over its constituent unions as it legitimated its authority. It also led to individual unions having to seek permission from the LO before engaging in strike action. The crucial mechanism here was the development by the LO's economists of a highly distinctive post-war policy: the solidaristic wages policy.

The essence of this policy is the attempt by the LO to reach agreement with the SAF on a general wage increase to apply across all industries and occupations. It is highly contingent on the representativeness of the two peak organisations. As we have already seen the LO grew to represent at least 90 per cent of manual workers through its 25 affiliated national unions. The SAF has some 25,000 member companies in its 38 member federations, and these firms employ about two thirds of the workforce (Ingham, 1974, p. 55; Ryden, 1977).[1]

The LO's concern with a general increase reflects its egalitarian ideology. Indeed, in some cases the policy results in higher wage increases for those in lower-paid jobs. The level of the wage increases reflects an interesting economic judgement. It takes into account the high degree of dependence of the Swedish economy on its exports, where, for example, the metal industries export nearly 50 per cent of their output (Lash, 1985, p. 221). The wage increase is set with a view to allowing the 'competitive' sector of the economy to maintain price competitiveness with the rest of the western world after allowing for technical progress but whilst allowing scope for sufficient investment. Thus, it builds in an inflationary rise, which is likely to be larger in the non-competitive domestic or 'sheltered' sector which is more service oriented and accordingly less likely to experience significant productivity increases.

Apart from its egalitarian nature and its concern to maintain Sweden's competitive position, the solidaristic wage policy has direct implications for the relative competitiveness of Sweden's domestic industries. As the wage increase applies irrespective of the industrial sector or the economic position of any individual firm it has long-term implications for the expansion and contraction of particular sectors and enterprises. In the case of individual firms, those with below average productivity rises compared to their rivals will suffer a cycle of declining profits, reduced investment, falling output and employment and eventual economic extinction. Conversely, those with above average productivity will be able to extend and increase production and employment. In order to increase the labour mobility inherent in this wage bargaining strategy, the LO has encouraged successive governments to pursue an active labour policy of easing the costs of job transfer by financing retraining schemes and information centres.

The development of this strategy in the post-war period suggests a refinement of the 'historic compromise'. Managerial prerogatives at the workplace are retained but given a new imperative by the centralised solidaristic wage bargaining. Union goals are economistic but also facilitate and demand technological and organisational change by management. In addition, the compromise now rests on the assumption that not only will governments utilise Keynesian macro-economic policies designed to maintain full employment but they will also pursue micro policies to facilitate the active labour policy of the LO. Hence it is highly contingent on the presence of a sympathetic government, one that is either linked to the labour movement or at least gives the maintenance of full employment a high priority.[2]

This brief account greatly simplifies both the development and working of the policy. In particular it overlooks the problem of whether government planners are able to calculate with sufficient accuracy the counter-cyclical policies necessary for full employment to be obtained. It also discounts the difficulties involved in calculating the appropriate wage increase that allows for price competitiveness in the competitive sector whilst still leaving sufficient funds for investment.[3] As this last issue takes us to the crux of our problem, it will be discussed now at some length. The next few paragraphs draw heavily on the excellent account by Martin (1984).

The historic compromise is contingent on the government's ability to maintain an expanding economy that can fuel rises in living standards and the social wage. There is clear evidence that the acceptance by successive governments of this responsibility has resulted until recently in a sustained high growth rate, low unemployment and high social welfare expenditure (Korpi, 1978c; Castles and McKinlay, 1979; Schmidt, 1984). Yet, as Sweden is essentially a private enterprise economy, this means that private business decisions, particularly in the sphere of investment, are crucial for this process.[4] Thus economic conditions must be suitable for private capital accumulation. The state has certainly played its part as the Keynesian macro-economic policies provide sufficient demand to stimulate new investment, assuming, as has not always been the case, that the government planners have been sufficiently accurate in their calculations. In addition, the state has used discriminatory fiscal measures such as tax exemptions to encourage investment.

However, private investment decisions depend more specifically on the availability of finance. Thus profitability is of prime significance as the direct source of investment funds as well as being the key to acquiring outside finance through new equity issues or bank loans. As has been indicated the egalitarian nature of the LO's solidaristic wage policy has microeconomic implications for the distribution of resources between firms. As wage rates are established regardless of a company's 'ability to pay', those firms that are unable to pay are forced out of business whilst the more successful ones are left with surplus funds that are available for investment.

Wage increases are determined by calculating a wage fund based on consideration of a tolerable level of price increase in the 'competitive' sector of the economy, an allowance for the effect of technological advance on productivity and output and a margin for profits that are essential for necessary investment. Too high a rate of wage increase squeezes profit margins and limits funds available for investment and/or forces prices up to an uncompetitive level. Too low a rate of wage increase leaves surplus funds that will almost certainly result in wage-drift above contractually determined wages as firms compete to retain and attract labour. However, large-scale wage-drift undermines the egalitarian nature of the LO's policy as higher-paid workers tend to benefit more. It thereby also threatens the basis of collectivist support for the LO and SAP. Conversely, if the level of wage increase is too high not only are investment funds in short supply but wage-drift is very low. This too can weaken support, in this case from those workers who do expect to do a bit better than the general wage increase.

The LO walks a dual tightrope with its solidaristic wage policy. It has to be mindful of the implications for private accumulation which, as in the German case, provides the motor for economic growth, full employment, rising living standards and enhanced social welfare: the bases for the electoral success of its political allies, the SAP. It also has to beware of losing its own broadly-based support by facilitating too little or too much wage-drift.

Both aspects of the LO's dilemma are distributional issues which are alleviated when economic growth is facilitated. Hence the LO has a long-term incentive to pursue cooperative policies with government and management that are designed to increase productivity and growth. This is the basis of the LO's support of managerial prerogatives to promote technological change and of governmental stimuli for labour mobility and retraining. However, it has become clear that the LO has been trying to shift the parameters of the 'historic compromise' in order to enable its goals to be attained and in the process these goals have themselves been transformed.

The wave of unofficial strikes of the late 1960s indicated a breakdown in the Swedish industrial peace. Industrial conflict, apparently, had not been fully institutionalised. Although the extent of the upsurge was exaggerated because the official strike statistics exclude minor stoppages and because both the LO and SAF have an interest in under-reporting stoppages in order to preserve the appearance of industrial peace, there was a definite increase (Martin 1977, p. 65; 1984, p. 248; Korpi, 1981). This alerted the LO to the dangers of centralisation, for the strikes were widely seen as a reaction to the centralised wage policy.[5]

Martin (1977) has persuasively argued that the LO's response was to pay increased attention to democratising workplace life, thereby impinging on hitherto untouched managerial prerogatives. The LO hoped that this would provide a new role for the local unions, who had lost most of their bargaining functions to the LO, and thus maintain the LO's cohesion and the support of its membership. However, as Martin indicates, the LO's shift in policy was not just a reaction to the unrest of the late 1960s. There was also considerable concern that the social costs of change were falling too heavily on the labour force, particularly as regards the human costs of retraining and the introduction of new technology. In addition, the unions felt that as management was already introducing pseudo-participatory schemes, like those at the automobile companies, Saab and Volvo, they too had to show their concern with the 'quality of working life'.

The result was that in the early and mid-1970s the LO pressed for and achieved a variety of changes in the laws controlling employment and labour practices. The most important of these were enhanced work safety provisions, greater security of employment, employment promotion schemes for disadvantaged people, representation on the Board of Directors, and participation in management prior to strategic decision-making. Collectively, these changes imposed major limitations on managerial authority, for they introduced substantial constraints on managerial powers to hire and fire employees, introduce new technology and change the organisation of work tasks. Of particular importance is that, in marked contrast to most other western countries, the Swedish unions do not have to wait until after changes have been introduced before challenging them. In Sweden, management has to provide advance notice of proposed changes, and if agreement with the local union cannot be reached, the status quo is maintained until management can justify its position with the appropriate arbitration body, such as the Labour Court. The onus of proof is normally on management (Martin, 1977).

The LO's influence with the SAP was instrumental in gaining these legal changes although they were also supported by the Centre Party. How successful they were in enhancing support for the LO and SAP is problematic, as the latter lost power after the 1976 elections that followed these legal reforms. However, the shift in emphasis by the LO was not confined simply to workplace democratisation.

The late 1960s had seen increased concern with some of the environmental problems of economic development. The SAP's poor performance in the 1966 local elections was attributed to issues such as urban and regional decline that had been taken up by the Centre Party and the New Left. The government's response had been to shift its attention from simple macro-economic handling of the economy to the micro aspects of economic performance. In 1967 it launched a 'new industrial policy' that aimed at greater state control by providing regional and sectoral planning as well as the allocation of state investment funds. The government was intervening much more directly in the allocative mechanisms of the market (Martin, 1984, pp. 230–5).

However, the basis of the LO's position was to force it into an even more interventionist posture. We have already seen that the LO's solidaristic wage policy required it to pay great attention to the relationship between wages, technical progress, prices, profits and investment. The bargaining process with the SAF became increasingly formalised and tripartite because the government, although not a party to the wage agreements, could not remain disinterested in their outcome.

The crucial area of concern was the relationship between profits and investment. In a private market economy profits are necessary for investment. The LO's economists frequently differed from those of the SAF as to what level of profits was necessary to finance directly or otherwise the required level of investment. As Martin (1984, pp. 265–8) clearly indicates, the issue was one of distributive conflict. The lower the level of profits, the higher, other things being equal, the level of wages that could be afforded and, in all probability, the smaller the ratio of wage-drift to contractual wage increases. The LO's economists were led to formulate proposals that on the one hand sought the maximum use of profits for investment and on the other hand focused on other sources of finance for investment. The former led to government fiscal incentives to retain and reinvest profits, the latter led to the famous Meidner proposals for wage-earner investment funds.

In order to facilitate the centralised bargaining process the LO had encouraged the creation of a national economic forum which tries to calculate the parameters of prices, technical progress etc. within which the next wage-round will take place. In order to stabilise – that is, make more predictable – the outcome, the LO has also tried to incorporate the other labour federations, the TCO and SACO–SR, into the process so that the LO solidaristic wage rise will be compatible with those negotiated for white-collar and public sector workers (Elvander, 1974). Not surprisingly they have resisted, whilst the SAF used the period of bourgeois government to try to disengage from the centralised collective agreements. The SAF claimed that the wage levels being set were too high to allow for the appropriate, private financing of investment. In addition, their solidaristic nature was too damaging for many firms. However, the strength of the LO was such that they were able to resist a return to market-based wage bargaining during 1976–82, and when the SAF returned to office in 1982 the scene was set for the establishment of the 'Meidner' funds.

The funds were originally conceived as a step on the road

towards economic democracy. Meidner envisaged that a proportion of profits would be held in a collective union fund. The funds would be reinvested in industry and would therefore accumulate quickly giving the unions significant blocs of shares, sufficient to control the companies in 20–30 years. Thus they complemented the solidaristic wage bargaining by attacking inequalities of wealth and power. Meidner (1980) saw them as having three aims: making sure that surplus profits did not go to capital owners; counteracting the concentration of private share-ownership; and increasing employee influence through the rights of ownership. However, as the proposals developed they were increasingly advocated as a solution to the problem of investment. For any given level of profits there would be a higher level of investment because an element of profits would not be distributed to shareholders but reinvested through the wage-earner funds. Therefore, other things being equal, it lowers the share of profits and raises the share of wages in any wage round. In addition, wage restraint can be justified because if profits are increased, the surplus is now more likely to be reinvested because of the wage-earner funds and not distributed as dividends to augment private wealth holdings. (Albrecht and Deutsch, 1983; Martin, 1984, pp. 268–78).[6]

The introduction of the wage-earner funds marks a further step in the transition of the Swedish model. However, although the historic compromise has been reshaped with the recent moves to democratise the workplace and economic life, certain core elements have remained constant. In particular, the peak organisations (the LO and the SAF) have consistently played an important role. Against the background of the Keynesian full employment policies practised by the LO's allies, the SAP, who have enjoyed a near monopoly of political power, they have engaged in centralised wage-determination negotiations. These negotiations have explicitly taken account of the potentially inflationary implications of decisions on wages and profit margins. In this regard they have sought to assess what inflation would be tolerable given the Swedish economy's exposure to international competition. This is not to say that the LO and SAF have always found it easy to agree on what the outcome of bargaining should be, but rather that they have shared an awareness of the macro implications of their decisions.

The centralised bargaining system has come under threat recently. The LO's solidaristic wage policy is disliked by some of its constituent unions and members because of its effect on differentials. The SAF have disliked the growing influence of the unions occasioned by the legislative gains of the LO through their SAP allies. These strains will be discussed later at greater length. However the centralised system and the associated solidaristic wage policy have been key elements of the post-war Swedish political economy. With them has gone a shared commitment by the LO and SAF to cooperative and harmonious workplace relationships and a general emphasis on increasing economic growth and production, this economic advance being necessary to meet the population's aspirations for enhanced living standards and social welfare provision.

ECONOMISM IN SWEDEN

The difficulties of assessing the extent and intensity of economistic values in Sweden are compounded by the exclusion of the country from the studies by Inglehart and his followers of the development of 'post-materialist' values. This exclusion reflects Sweden's non-membership of the EEC and hence the absence of Eurobarometer data on which Inglehart relies so heavily.[7] This means that Swedish economism will have to be tapped by other indirect measures, particularly those focusing on relative deprivation, orientations to work, the causes of strikes, and support for environmental and ecological movements.

In successive publications, Scase (1972, 1976, 1977) has argued that Swedish manual workers are more resentful of economic inequalities than their English counterparts. However, this does not itself imply that the Swedes are more economistic for Scase is careful to point out that what he is measuring are differences in the awareness and legitimacy of economic inequalities. Thus Scase (1977, Ch. 5) argues that Swedish manual workers were very much more likely than their English counterparts to identify white-collar or business, managerial and professional personnel rather than other manual workers as being the 'sort of people' who 'are better-off than yourself': 45 per cent of the Swedes as opposed to 20 per cent of the English workers mentioned such non-manual occupations (Scase, 1977, Table 5.2, p. 120). In addition, when specifically asked to compare their earnings with those of white-collar employees, 63 per cent of the Swedes thought they were worse-off, and only 4 per cent better-off, whereas the corresponding figures for the English sample were 23 and 44 per cent (Scase, 1977, p. 121). These differences occurred although the objective structures of income and wealth distribution are roughly similar in the two countries.[8]

As Scase (1977, p. 123) indicates: 'The evidence clearly suggests that the Swedish sample demonstrated a greater awareness of the inequalities which existed between themselves and white-collar workers than the English.' In addition, Scase goes on to show that the Swedes were more resentful than the English because they were more likely to disapprove of the perceived inequalities and to think that their own earnings ought to be higher. As was indicated in Chapter 3 Scase's findings support Runciman's and Daniel's conclusions that relative deprivation is low in Britain.

However, these data cannot be used to show that the Swedish manual workers were more economistic in the sense that pursuit of economic gain was more important than other factors. For this conclusion to be reached the two groups would have had to be compared in terms of the relative priorities they attached to the pursuit of materialist as opposed to non-materialist ends. What the data do suggest is that distributional conflict might take a more broadly-based form. The sectionalism that characterises British earnings comparisons is far more muted in Sweden. There comparisons are far more likely to be between manual and non-manual workers as a whole or, indeed, between wage-earners and profit-receivers. This reflects the egalitarian ideology of the LO and the role of its educational and cultural institutions in socialising its members into these values. In turn, the Swedish workers' perceptions and resentment of economic inequality will have important implications for the way in which economistic values, of whatever strength, are pursued and in particular for the possibilities of normative restraint.

In another well-known study, Korpi (1978c) has questioned whether instrumental values are widespread amongst Swedish manual workers. Again care has to be taken in using Korpi's data for his frame of reference was not economism *per se* but the issue of whether the possible embourgeoisement of affluent workers was reflected in their orientations to work.

Korpi suggests that the emphasis given by some sub-groups in his sample (e.g. immigrants, migrants and young married workers) to extrinsic economic rewards rather than the intrinsic aspects of the work itself suggests that they did have markedly instrumental orientations to work. However, there were no such tendencies in the sample as a whole. In addition, Korpi (1978c, p. 171) points out that union membership is as likely to occur because 'one should be solidaristic with the labour movement as because of personal benefit from being a member of the union'. This finding is used by Korpi to suggest that solidaristic motives are as important as instrumental motives in determining union membership.

As Korpi's sample consisted of a relatively affluent and well-established section of the manual working class, this does question the assumption by Goldthorpe (1978) of a 'maturation of the working class' thesis. It seems that in Sweden, working-class communities rather than being 'instrumentalised' by affluence and technologically determined workplace deprivations, place considerable emphasis on intrinsic job satisfactions and class loyalty.

To be sure, the younger workers were more likely to express instrumental attitudes to union membership, but it seems reasonable to agree with Korpi's assessment that this reflects the long-term experience of work and union membership by the older employees rather than an inter-generational difference. Certainly one would expect that the LO's mode of wage bargaining coupled with its educational and political activities would have a gradual impact on its members' attitudes. In addition, as younger workers are more likely to be experiencing the financial problems associated with the expense of young families, it would not be surprising if they gave greater emphasis to the economic benefits of union membership.

One would expect that the long-term experience of high living standards in Sweden would have the sorts of effect indicated by Inglehart's Maslovian based thesis. Korpi's findings of relatively low economism equate well with Sweden's very high standing in the international league of per capita income (Table A.1, p. 219),

Further evidence for the relatively modest emphasis on economistic concerns can be easily found. We have already seen that the relative calm of Swedish industrial life was broken by a wave of unofficial strikes that began in 1969. Although many of these strikes were concerned with pay and earnings they also reflected dissatisfaction with the intrinsic aspects of work and particularly those of job satisfaction. Certainly, most commentators do not attribute anything like as high a proportion of the causes of Swedish unofficial strikes to economic factors as in Britain (Korpi, 1978b, Table 6, p. 364). In any case the rise in strike activity was one of the factors underlying the LO's increased concern with the quality of work experience.

In addition, the preceding years had seen the introduction by management of some schemes of worker participation. As these were designed to overcome some of the more alienating effects of modern technology that were believed to be increasing absenteeism and labour turnover, it suggests that at least management thought that economic factors by themselves were not sufficient to motivate the workforce. At all events, as we have seen, the consequence was a series of legislative reforms in the early and mid-1970s which broke the 'historic compromise' as managerial prerogatives were limited.

However, the interpretation of this development is not clear-cut. There is little evidence to suggest that the new legal changes were widely sought by manual workers. Indeed, they proved relatively unsuccessful in mobilising support for the SAP, as it lost the 1976 election, albeit by a small margin but with its lowest level of post-war support from manual workers (Korpi, 1983, Figure 5.3, p. 88).

The 1976 election also saw another issue come into prominence. It is quite clear that the SAP lost support because of its policy on nuclear energy. Indeed, Korpi (1978a; 1983, Ch. 6) claims that this became the dominant issue of the campaign. The SAP's former coalition partner, the Farmers Party, now known as the Centre Party, gained support because of its opposition to the development of nuclear energy. But again, the evidence is not clear-cut for poll data suggest that the issue was more salient for middle-class than working-class electors and had more effect on their electoral choice. However, it is remarkable that the issue attained such significance and certainly points to less emphasis on material issues than would be the norm in most western countries.

Support for the Environmental Party is small, reaching only 1.7 per cent in the 1982 election (Ersson and Lane, 1983, Table 1, p. 288) but this could reflect the concern with environmental matters shown by the main parties. Himmelstrand (1981, p. 168) refers to a survey by Ahrne in the mid-1970s that showed that people wanted to switch resources to solving environmental and social problems. Again, this is another indication that there is widespread concern with non-material factors.

The argument is not that economic issues are unimportant or that the bulk of the workforce is unconcerned with 'bread and butter' problems. However it is suggested that compared with many other western countries, and in particular with one of our other case studies, the UK, the level and intensity of economism is lower in Sweden. In relative terms, non-instrumental factors have greater weight in areas such as orientation to work, the causes of strikes and electoral politics. Doubtless this reflects the existence of high living standards and the expectation of further advance, but these were precisely the circumstances that were suggested in Chapter 2 as being likely to lead to economistic values being relatively muted.

NORMATIVE RESTRAINT

We have already seen that in Sweden the maturation of the working class does not seem to be associated with a rise in instrumental concerns. In addition, it is clear that there are important restraints on the way economic and material goals are pursued. Central to these has been the role of the LO in taking account of the potentially inflationary consequences of wage claims and seeking to control wage settlements so that the prices of Swedish exports rise in line with those of their international competitors.

The structure of centralised wage agreements provides the mechanism for restraining wages but it does not in itself provide the basis of the policy of wage restraint. That rests on other elements of which the most important are the egalitarian, meritocratic ideology promoted by the LO and the general awareness of how wage restraint by moderating inflation promotes employment, economic growth and enhanced living standards and social welfare expenditure.

We have already outlined the origins of the centralised wage agreements between the LO and the SAF in terms of an attempt to avoid the consequences of the widespread use of lockouts and strikes that had characterised Swedish industrial relations in the early part of the century. The institutionalisation of conflict through the 'peace obligation', the legal restraints on industrial action and the complex set of arbitration procedures had significant effects in reversing the Swedish record of industrial unrest. In addition the peak organisations, the LO and SAF, had considerable power over their constituent members particularly as regards the sanctioning of strikes and lockouts (Martin, 1984, pp. 197–9).

This might not in itself have led to a system of centralised wage agreements if the LO had not used the authority, gained through its alliance with the electorally popular SAP, to promote the solidaristic wage policy. This reflected the egalitarian ideology of the LO's leadership for it was based on the notion of equal pay for equal work, rather than allowing market forces to determine wages. This ideology in turn reflected the broad base of the LO unions, the fact that for accidental, historical reasons they had been organised along industrial rather than craft lines (Korpi and Shalev, 1979). Thus the sectionalism which characterised British industrial relations was not part of the Swedish heritage.

Centralised wage agreements, introduced in the 1950s,

were a logical outcome of the LO's concern to promote solidaristic wage increases and to take account of the inflationary impact of excessively high wage settlements. However, they could only be introduced because of the prior centralisation of the LO confederation with its associated control of its constituent unions and because the SAP government could be relied upon to pursue the Keynesian full employment policies which were a necessary backcloth to the policy of wage restraint.

The fact that the government could be relied on to pursue a policy of growth and full employment with consequential increases in living standards and social welfare expenditure helped legitimate the policy of wage restraint. It delivered practical benefits to the workforce. Swedish experience provides perhaps the best indication of Olson's argument about broadly based employer and employee federations being conducive to the pursuit of the collective goods of high growth, high employment and low inflation. However, strong peak associations by themselves were not enough to produce this effect, it also required the presence of a suitably sympathetic and responsive government.

The success of the post-war Swedish economy has been one factor enabling the LO to 'sell' its wage policy to its members. Another crucial factor lies in the nature of the policy itself. Its solidaristic form is designed to strengthen the cohesion and collectivism of the manual working class. It aims at avoiding the sectionalism that has characterised wage-determination in the UK and USA by strengthening the feeling of class solidarity.

Scase's work indicates the success of this policy for he demonstrates that intra-class comparisons are far less marked in Sweden than in the UK. Scase attributes this to the experience of the solidaristic wage policy and the promotion of a meritocratic, egalitarian ideology by the LO through its educational and cultural institutions. However, the centralisation of wage agreements is also important for if they were decentralised then the solidaristic wage increases could not be maintained. There would be a 'breakdown in working-class solidarity, a growth of narrow group egoism and the development of a dual labour market' (Stephens, 1979, p. 123).

Class solidarity is also maintained by promoting the concept of collective advance at the expense of a capitalist class, or its privileged managerial and professional employees. Again, this comes over very clearly in Scase's survey. It also forms a key element of the LO's policy for there is a repeated concern to squeeze profits, to make sure that they are sufficient for investment purposes but not such a surplus that there would be a significant increase in the wealth of capitalists. Indeed Meidner (1980), who was one of the LO's main economists, saw the introduction of wage-earners' funds as one of the principal ways of making sure that workers rather than capitalists benefited from any surplus. He also saw the development of these collective funds as a further breach in the principle of market forces determining the distribution of economic rewards.

As we have already seen, the maintenance of the solidaristic wage policy and the centralised wage agreements has not been without its difficulties. Working-class cohesion and unity has been threatened when the contractual wage increase has been too low thereby facilitating significant wage-drift through local bargaining. Conversely, if profits are squeezed too much by a high contractual wage increase, the investment process is jeopardised and very little wage-drift is possible. This, in turn, affects the support of more affluent workers.

The difficulties of the LO's economists in calculating the appropriate target, that is the appropriate wage fund which is then to be distributed amongst the various industrial sectors, are exacerbated if the government's economic planners cannot accurately calculate the precise set of monetary and fiscal policies necessary to maintain economic growth and full employment. This may result in the overall level of domestic demand being higher or lower than predicted with consequences for profits, investment and wage-drift. For example, too high a level of demand results in labour shortages and consequential high wage-drift as the price of scarce labour is bid up. At the same time profits are greater than expected. This both facilitates the high wage-drift and leads to an increase in the inequality of income and wealth distribution as shareowners benefit.

The difficulties of the government planners have in turn been exacerbated by the sharp changes in the international economy since the early 1970s. These changes make it far more difficult to calculate what would be a tolerable level of price increase in the competitive sector of the Swedish economy and the likely level of export demand for Swedish goods. In the circumstances it is not surprising that there have been several occasions since the late 1960s when the economy has had too much or too little slack. The result has been some increase in strike activity to apply pressure for increased wage-drift when this can be afforded, with corresponding strikes to try to narrow the newly-widened differentials, and acute problems of lack of finance for capital investment when the economy has experienced a recession (Martin, 1984, Part 4).

The LO has tried to maintain cohesion and meet the problem of capital accumulation through attempts to democratise workplace relationships and by introducting the wage-earner funds. Thus a more active and interventionary policy has evolved.

The recent rapid growth of the TCO and SACO–SR has posed additional problems as they have tried to make separate wage agreements. The LO have tried to bring them into the centralised wage agreements or, at least, make its own contractual agreements after they have settled thereby making sure that account can be taken of them. Again, this is indicative of the LO's attempt to find practical solutions to problems as they emerge.

More recently, the LO has had to face a fresh set of challenges. The SAF has tried to break the centralised bargaining system and return to market-based principles of remuneration. This reflects their concern with the various changes that the LO have introduced in the 1970s and early 1980s that have limited managerial prerogatives and threatened the system of private ownership. In addition some employers, particularly in the engineering industries, are concerned that differentials have become too narrow with consequential difficulties in recruiting and training skilled workers.

In 1983 the engineering sector withdrew from the centralised agreement. The Metalworkers Union which is also concerned about narrowing differentials was a willing accomplice. As Lash (1985) points out, this poses a cruel dilemma for the LO leadership. If they wish the engineering sector to return to the centralised system they will have to sacrifice elements of the solidaristic wage policy and allow for some widening of differentials. However, this will threaten the ideological unity of the labour movement and jeopardise the power base both of the LO and SAP. However, if it cannot bring this key sector back into the centralised system it will lose its ability to control the labour markets and implement effectively its policy.

It may be that a combination of the traditional appeal of labour solidarity and renewed economic growth will seal the breach. The metalworkers' concern must to some extent reflect the recent slowdown in Swedish economic growth (Table A.2, p. 220) and the enormous cost of job creation and training schemes that keep down the official unemployment figures but need to be financed by heavy taxation. This has significant effects on the real disposable income of wage-earners (Pontusson, 1984; Scharpf, 1984, pp. 266–8).

Whatever the future will hold, there can be no doubt of the effects of the wage policy in the past. There has been some wage restraint as Swedish unions have not exploited the tight labour market conditions but have held wage increases to levels comparable with other western countries (Table A.3, p. 222). Moreover, there have been the consequential real economic and social benefits that have already been described. In addition manual workers do attribute these benefits to the two arms of the labour movement, the LO and the SAP. Scase (1976, p. 298) cites a survey by Dahlstrom suggesting that half the manual workers 'attribute improvement [in living standards] to demands made by labour unions', and one by Segerstedt and Lundquist, that two-thirds of their respondents attributed improvements in working conditions to the working-class movement. Last and by no means least, it is clear that the existence of the solidaristic wage policy has led to a narrowing of differentials (Lash, 1985, Figure 1, p. 219). Thus strengthening the egalitarian effect of the LO's policies and, in general terms, increasing working-class cohesion and limiting the development of a sectional 'group egoism'.

POWER CONCENTRATION AND DISPERSION

The discussion in earlier sections of this chapter has already indicated that there are significant concentrations of power on both sides of industry and that the principal union confederation, the LO, has considerable political leverage with the SAP. There is no reason to repeat much of this material. However, as yet no data have been presented on the concentration of business power.

In 1963, the 100 largest private companies accounted for 40 per cent of private sector industrial employment and 46 per cent of the production of that sector (Commission on Industrial and Economic Concentration, 1976, p. 31). By 1975, the 200 largest companies employed 1.3 million out of about 2 million private sector employees. In addition, many of these companies are effectively linked together. The most significant case, the Wallenberg group, comprised some 21 companies in 1976, of which 11 were amongst the largest 50 companies. Lastly, 91 per cent of exports are accounted for by the largest 50 companies (Israel, 1978).

These data indicate how extensive aggregate concentration is in Sweden, even though because of the small size of the Swedish economy there are few really giant firms.[9] Market concentration is even more marked. In Chapter 4, we pointed out that Pryor's analysis of data from the early 1960s indicated that Swedish market concentration as measured by the four firms concentration ratio was on average some 50 per cent higher than that of the USA, and well above the levels in the UK and Germany. In addition we reported Kristensen as showing that by 1970 in 17 out of 21 sectors the largest four Swedish firms accounted for over 50 per cent of production. The clear implication of these data is that unless there is significant foreign competition Swedish firms are essentially price-makers rather than price-receivers. Hence the importance of the distinction made by the LO's economists between the 'competitive' and 'sheltered' or domestic sectors of the Swedish economy.

This extreme concentration of Swedish industry, coupled with the very high levels of unionisation, now in excess of 80 per cent, might in other circumstances prove to be ideal for stimulating wage–price spirals. However, this is to ignore two factors. First, as we have repeatedly pointed out, both employers and employees have strong, centralised federations. This means that the power fragmentation that characterises British industrial relations does not occur. It becomes at least feasible that the two main power blocs, the SAF and LO, will try to offset one another's power rather than letting distributional conflict run its anomic course through the decisions of individual firms and sectionalised unions acting autonomously.

Second, the visibility of these power relationships makes it more likely that the key actors, the SAF and the LO, will have to take account of the consequences of their behaviour for the economy as a whole, particularly because of the highly vulnerable position of the Swedish economy in world markets. Indeed, this appears to be the case as both blocs accepted the 'peace obligation' and then institutionalised voluntary centralised wage agreements. Thus the centralisation of power both gave the impetus and the means for regulating industrial conflict and wage settlements. In addition, as we have already seen, one of the main threats to the orderliness of this system has come with the growth of two other labour federations who were not part of the centralised system. This illustrates how power fragmentation threatens the stability of the Swedish system.

However, there is a further point of consideration. The industrial relations system has developed against the back-cloth of the political dominance of the political arm of the labour movement, the SAP. Again, we have discussed at some length how the LO has been able to influence and shape key legislative items as well as how the general expectation has developed that governments can and should maintain policies of growth and full employment. The symbiotic relationship between the LO and SAP has served both entities well. It has enabled the LO to sell wage restraint to its members through the pay-offs of full employment, higher living standards and enhanced welfare provision. The SAP has reaped the benefit of continued electoral success.

Yet the implications of labour's dominance are far greater. At one level the full employment policies of successive governments have greatly strengthened the hand of the LO in its centralised bargaining with the SAF. At another level the LO and SAP have been able to shape a 'dominant ideology' that is radically different from those of most other western countries. In particular, the expectation of full employment is so ingrained that any government has to give this priority. Hence, after 1976 the bourgeois coalition strove to keep unemployment down by a massive programme of subsidies and job creation schemes.

This means that it is not only capital that is able to impose constraints on the Swedish government's freedom of manoeuvre through the need to maintain the system of private capital accumulation that is the engine providing jobs, output, higher living standards and enhanced welfare. In addition, labour provides an important constraint, the expectation of full employment. Furthermore, as we have already discussed, organised labour in Sweden is seeking through the wage-earner funds to dilute further business power, in particular by altering the relationship between profits and private investment.

This suggests that Sweden stands as the mirror-image of the German case discussed in Chapter 5. There the 'social partnership' was underpinned by the dominance of capital interests. Organised labour in the form of the DGB, as well as its political ally, the Social Democrats, had accommodated to the 'social market' economy based on private accumulation. In Sweden, the reverse is true, the SAF and the bourgeois parties have had to accommodate themselves to the 'full employment' economy. Webber (1983a) quite specifically relates the modest increase in Swedish unemployment compared to that of Germany in the early 1980s to the political commitment to full employment rather than to any policy of wage moderation. Indeed wage rises have been far more restrained in Germany than in Sweden during this period (Table A.3, p. 222).

In addition, as in Germany, the successful running of the economy has strengthened the hand of the dominant partner. Thus the 'historic compromise', which is in a sense Sweden's equivalent of the 'social partnership', has been altered to take account of organised labour's changing demands as managerial prerogatives have been curtailed and the wage-earner funds introduced. In Sweden, organised labour has avoided incorporation by organised business through its ability to mobilise political support for its solutions to emergent problems and to set the agenda for developments in wage bargaining, workplace democracy and the financing of investment.

The SAF, as the weaker partner, has found it increasingly difficult to break out of these shackles. Even when it used the particular combination of circumstances of a bourgeois government in office and a world recession that affected Swedish production and employment prospects to try to free itself from the centralised wage determination system and impose a 'market solution' to the investment problem, it failed. The lockouts organised by the SAF in 1980 resulted in the loss of over 4 million working days, far in excess of the total number of days lost in recorded stoppages over the previous 30 years! Yet they failed to limit wage settlements to the low levels that the SAF felt were required to maintain price competitiveness, let alone to 'break' the centralised system (Martin, 1984, Part 4, and Table 3.4, p. 346).

THE SWEDISH VIRTUOUS CYCLE

We have spent some time discussing how the balance between the power concentrations of the SAF and LO led to the institutionalisation of industrial conflict and subsequently to the centralised wage-determination system. By implication, we have also seen some of its consequences for the development of the productive capacity of the Swedish economy.

In the first place the 'historic compromise', by leading to a very substantial decline in Swedish strikes and lockouts as in the German case, greatly facilitated production. In addition, the preservation of management workplace prerogatives removed from contention some of the issues that have bedevilled British industrial relations, where they have been used as an excuse for uncooperativeness and renewed bargaining. The ability of management to utilise the workforce's productive capabilities was reinforced by the LO's active labour policy, which, as we saw earlier, encouraged labour mobility and retraining. This mobility, aimed at moving labour to more productive concerns, was itself one of the micro-economic consequences of the solidaristic wage policy that facilitated a reallocation of resources from low-productivity to high-productivity firms.

Thus in a number of ways the developments that have been discussed are conducive to greater industrial harmony and a more effective use of productive resources. However, there are important counter-tendencies. The strike rate has shown some increase in recent years and the aforementioned lock-out in 1980 was the most disruptive event for a generation. Several companies have introduced participatory schemes in order to improve employee motivation. Managerial prerogatives have been curbed with possible implications for their ability to introduce new technologies and work processes.

These recent developments cannot be ignored. Certainly the Swedish growth rate and productivity increases have slowed in recent years (Tables A.2 and A.3, pp. 220–222). However they should not be exaggerated. The strike rate is still modest in comparison with most western societies (Table A.5, p. 224). The active labour policy is still operative, and although managerial autonomy has been limited the new legal changes are intended to improve the quality of working life and thereby increase motivation and commitment.

The Swedish system has been one of 'high trust' relationships. The legal changes do not terminate but strengthen the basis of 'high trust' by giving workers a greater involvement in their firms. Managers have to justify proposed changes either to the local union, or if they cannot reach agreement, to an outside arbitrator. As these changes of working practices or introductions of new technologies are not directly related to the wage-determination process they cannot be used by Swedish unions as bargaining tools. The new procedures should serve to re-legitimate managerial authority by making it more accountable. If this is the case they should enhance productive capacity by resolving some of the motivational problems that came into prominence in the 1960s.

A far greater threat to industrial harmony is posed by the renewed threat of the SAF to end the centralised bargaining arrangements and by those unions and federations such as the Metalworkers, TCO and SACO–SR who also wish to decentralise bargaining. This development will almost certainly involve more industrial stoppages, as evidenced by the 1980 lockouts, both in order to disrupt the current system and because decentralisation will facilitate sectionalism. Sectionalism is likely to increase industrial disputes as particular groups use their industrial muscle to further their own cause and exploit market opportunities.

However, should the Swedish economy show some improvement, the consequential rise in real wages coupled with the reduced cost of concealing unemployment may limit the pressures to decentralise bargaining. If this is the case then the Swedish virtuous cycle should reassert itself.

We have seen that the past success of the Swedish economy has to some extent muted economistic aspirations. These are in any case held back by the normative restraints embodied in the industrial relations and wage-bargaining systems. Two items are particularly important here. First, the 'peace obligation', for 'the essence of the Scandinavian law on industrial relations is the idea that the parties to the collective agreement have pledged to maintain industrial peace for a definite period of time' (Schmidt, 1974, p. 39). This by implication must limit the forcefulness with which claims are pursued confining most disputes to the period when (wage) contracts are to be renewed.

The second factor is the egalitarian ideology fostered by the LO's solidaristic wage policy. This maintains the unity and cohesion of the working class and largely avoids the sectional, distributional conflict that has characterised wage bargaining in the UK. It is reinforced by the educational and cultural institutions fostered by the LO and the widespread feeling that so much of the distinctively good things of Swedish life stem from the advances promoted by organised labour.

However, the industrial relations and wage-bargaining systems could not have been developed without the prior concentration of organised business and labour into two broad federations, the SAF and LO. It was their awareness of the damaging implications of their overt conflict that led to the institutionalisation of conflict and their powerful, centralised organisations that provided the means of developing the wage-bargaining system. In addition the LO's structure, a broad federation of industrial unions, helps explain its egalitarian ideology. Thus, this power balance had important implications for the development of normative restraints. But in turn the power structure was affected by the development of the industrial relations and wage-bargaining systems because the resultant enhanced unity and cohesion of the working class was reflected in increased unionisation and renewed political support for the SAP. As we have seen, LO membership increased significantly in the post-war period, whilst the SAP's success depended on increased support and higher turnout amongst its shrinking electoral base of manual workers. The maintained and enhanced strength of the two arms of the labour movement has facilitated the sustained Keynesian management of the economy and the fostering of the 'full employment' ideology. It has also enabled the LO to take the initiative in promoting legal changes that maintain working class unity, strengthen its egalitarian ideology and support the normative restraints embodied in the industrial relations and wage-bargaining systems.

The combination of the growth in the power of organised labour and the maintenance of industrial relations and wage-bargaining systems that curb the free play of market forces has also enhanced the production capacity of the socio-economic system. The most obvious factors here are the relative absence of industrial stoppages and the LO's active labour policy. In turn this has helped Sweden to reach its very high position in the economic league table, thereby completing the virtuous cycle.

The complex interplay of the set of normative restraints within the particular form of power relationships, that is, the initial concentrations of power in the SAF and LO and the subsequent growth of organised labour's power with the attendant 'full employment' ideology, suggest that the Swedish virtuous cycle takes the form depicted in Figure 6.1.

The virtuous cycle has clearly played a role in moderating the Swedish rate of inflation. It is not that inflation has been held at the low levels of the German economy but that for most of the post-war period it has been about or just below the average of the main western countries, despite the consistently low level of unemployment. That after all was the aim of the LO's economic strategy, to maintain full employment without undermining Sweden's international competitiveness. As productivity increases in the 'sheltered' domestic sector are likely to be lower than in the 'competitive' sector, a policy that held price increases in the latter to a 'world' average should have resulted in slightly higher than average price increases across the Swedish economy as a whole.

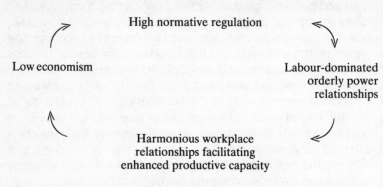

Figure 6.1: The Swedish 'virtuous cycle'

Kristensen (1981, Table 3.1, p. 27) shows that in the 1950s and 1960s wage rises were very similar in the 'competitive' and 'sheltered' sectors, but the difference in productivity increases meant that prices rose more quickly in the 'sheltered' sector. However, the key point is that the increase in wages was sufficiently modest for price inflation to be almost negligible in the 'competitive' sector. From 1952 to 1960, annual wage increases averaged 6.5 per cent in both sectors but prices rose by an annual average of only 0.9 per cent in the 'competitive' sector as opposed to 3.7 per cent in the sheltered sector, thus reflecting the differential changes in productivity. From 1960 to 1968, wage increases were slightly greater in the competitive sector – 10.2 per cent as opposed to 9.5 per cent – but price increases were still held to a modest 1.2 per cent as opposed to 4.7 per cent in the 'sheltered' sector.

From Table 1.1 (p. 3 above) it can be seen that in the late

1960s and through the 1970s price increases in Sweden were usually only just above the OECD average, suggesting that the 'competitive' sector inflation was in line with 'world' inflation. In addition, in 1974–75 Swedish price increases were clearly below the OECD average, suggesting that the virtuous cycle enabled Sweden to damp down rather than magnify the imported inflation triggered off by increased oil prices. However, the Swedish economy was not able to repeat this performance after the second major oil price increase, and in 1980–81 Swedish prices increased slightly faster than the OECD average. This reflects the increased difficulty and inflationary public expenditure the Swedes have had in maintaining full employment during the world recession.

None the less the Swedish performance in moderating inflation whilst keeping unemployment at such low levels for so long is quite remarkable. They appear to have reduced the 'natural rate' of unemployment, in monetarist terms, or shifted the trade-off between inflation and unemployment, in Keynesian or 'Phillips curve' terms. The active labour policy has played a part by increasing labour mobility but so has the solidaristic wage policy by restraining distributional conflict. The result has been that until the system has experienced its recent strains, the Swedes have had the best of both worlds: full employment and international price competitiveness.

7 The East European 'Social Contract'

Several writers have pointed recently to the existence of an East European variant of the 'social contract' or 'social compact' (Connor 1980, p. 16; 1981, pp. 165–6; Pravda, 1982, p. 194; Bunce, 1983, pp. 134–6). The 'contract' exists between the state and the working class, and is an informal and implicit agreement. Perhaps the most explicit outline of the terms of this arrangement is given by Connor (1981, p. 165):

> The 'people', but workers most specifically, will forswear political challenge and organised expression of discontent, will work (regularly if not always well), and generally remain quiet. The regime, in turn, undertakes to avoid broadscale terror or coercion in everyday administration, and promises to provide (and to take credit for) moderate but steady increases in the living standard, secure employment, and to shield workers from the psychological status consequences of a too-evidently different reward system which would underline the disadvantages of the 'leading class'.

Connor is careful to point out that the terms of this agreement vary from country to country and time to time. They are contingent on particular historical and cultural circumstances. Later in this chapter we shall discuss the Polish variant in some detail, but before doing so it is necessary to analyse the reasons underlying the creation of these 'contracts' and the functions they serve.

Formally at least, the East European states are workers' states, that is to say, they are to be run for and in the interests of the working class. The state apparatus exists for this purpose. However, in order to attain these goals, be they of material advance, rising welfare or national defence, the state apparatus needs the cooperation or at least the compliance of the workforce, that is the working class, in the fulfilment of its productive roles within the division of labour.

As in other societies, such cooperation or compliance is problematic. Bendix has pointed to the difficulties of using either moral factors, such as nationalism, or coercive measures, such as force or rigid supervision, to attain such ends. In particular he has indicated how even the most formally defined and closely supervised tasks still depend on some minimum degree of voluntary compliance by the role incumbents. All work roles have some discretionary components. The use of force and/or close supervision to engender compliance are both costly and impractical for ultimately it is only the individual worker who knows what to do (or what not to do) and can control his/her performance (Bendix, 1956, p. 204).

Moral mechanisms too are fallible, particularly, if as often is the case, the political regime is lacking in legitimacy. This can occur either because the regime has been imposed or maintained through the use of external force, Czechoslovakia provides the best example, or because the regime appears to be failing to achieve its stated ends. An obvious illustration of the latter point is Connor's allusion to the existence of widespread social and economic inequalities which are very much to the disadvantage of the allegedly 'leading class', the working class.

At one level the 'social contracts' may be seen as devices to facilitate a minimum level of work performance (and attendance) by the indispensable factor of production, the working class. In return for this cooperation or compliance, the state rules out the more excessive exercise of force which it controls and whose use would jeopardise support, and promotes various economic and welfare goals. Here the most obvious targets (or covenants to the contract) are the maintenance of full employment and steady if not spectacular rises in living and welfare standards. In terms of our earlier discussion the state undertakes to try to meet the working class's rising materialistic expectations.

The implicit contract is highly precarious. It can be 'blown off course' by exogenous factors such as rising world commodity prices that threaten the ability to expand economic production. It can be jeopardised by internal strains and in particular the widespread feeling that other groups are benefiting unduly through access to secondary (black) markets or party-based economic and social privileges. A further potential strain lies in the delicate balancing act the state planners have to perform when allocating scarce resources to competing ends such as consumption, welfare, investment and defence; a task made more difficult by the cumbersome bureaucratic nature of the planning process and the entrenched position of some corporate chieftains, such as agricultural and defence, in the decision-making process (Bunce, 1983).

At another level, the underlying issue is not that of economic role performance in particular but of the legitimacy of the state in general. As Connor hints, the 'social contracts' are also mechanisms for staving off widescale social and political unrest. Such disorder may have as a potential basis the underlying lack of legitimacy of state apparatuses that are remote from and not particularly responsive to the working class as a whole and, as indicated above, may have been imposed externally. Again, the use of force to defeat mass protest is both costly in itself and may further undermine the remaining shreds of legitimacy. 'Social contracts' can be seen as attempts to 'buy' legitimacy. They are responses not simply to problems of economic performance but to an underlying 'legitimation crisis'.

LEGITIMATION CRISES IN EAST EUROPEAN SOCIETIES

Habermas (1976) and Offe (1984, Chs. 1, 2 and 5) have developed a concept of 'legitimation crisis' for the analysis of problems of social and system integration in capitalist societies. However, their approach is directly applicable to the issues outlined above. In addition, it also lends itself to indicating how and why inflationary pressures arise and are coped with in East European societies.

Figure 7.1 depicts the key schema showing the relationship between the various sub-systems. In Habermas's analysis of western liberal-capitalist societies he argues that recurrent steering problems (by the state of the economy) threaten not only the performance of the economic (sub-)system but also the underlying patterns of legitimation of the state (sub-)system and the motivation necessary for effective participation.

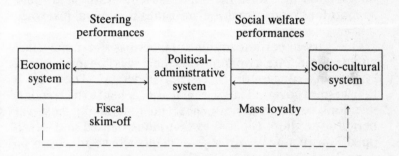

Figure 7.1: The Habermas–Offe systems model

Source: Habermas (1976), p. 5, taken from a working paper by Offe.

Habermas contends that western societies suffer periodic structural problems particularly concerning profitability, the ability to realise profit through actual sales, and associated difficulties in investment and capital accumulation.[1] As we have already seen, western governments are impelled to attempt to resolve these problems because their efficacy is assessed by the electorate in terms of their ability to manage or steer the economy. Successful management produced economic growth, rising living standards and high levels of employment. These outputs of the economic (sub-) system not only benefit directly the population but also provide the fiscal base for governments to maintain and enhance the scale of welfare services such as pensions, health and education that are typically provided by the state.

Failures to manage the economy successfully jeopardise the bases of support of the government and provoke a 'legitimation crisis'. Indeed, Habermas suggests that this crisis is one of the political-administrative (sub-)system as a whole rather than of any particular government for it throws into

doubt the ability of the system to produce desirable economic
and social welfare outcomes. As the 'legitimation crisis'
means that support is reduced or withdrawn this compounds
the underlying 'economic crisis'. Habermas argues that this is
because the recurrent and endemic economic crises of liberal-
capitalist societies require more rather than less government
intervention to resolve them at least temporarily and, thus,
support for 'tough', 'realistic' measures is minimal just when
it is most wanted.

One very important strand of Habermas's argument that
also occurs in Offe's work mirrors the discussion in Chapter 2
of Brittan's concept of 'excessive democracy'. The point is
that western governments are increasingly held to be responsible for economic performance and that in the post-war
period even those economies that industrialised and developed in a relatively *laissez-faire* manner have relied on an
overall governmental economic management, albeit sometimes only of a Keynesian sort. As in Brittan's argument, this
gives rise to heightened expectations about the ability of
governments to manage the economy and an increased likelihood that they will be judged in terms of the efficacy of their
'steering' performance.

Governments are caught in a trap of their own (or the
system's) making. They are forced into increasingly interventionary policies to resolve fundamental economic crises.
Each successive intervention is tantamount to a further
politicisation of the economy and increases the expectation
that governments are ultimately responsible for economic
prosperity and therefore must intervene to resolve future
crises. Successful 'steering' simply postpones the day of
reckoning and makes it more difficult to meet future expectations that have been consequentially enhanced. Even where
expectations are no greater, past success may make future
failure less tolerable because successful economic management
is a taken-for-granted result of the belief in the technocratic
powers of government – a belief that successive governments have encouraged as the main basis of their claims for
legitimation.

Of course, both Habermas and Offe, unlike Brittan, rest
their claims on the belief that liberal-capitalist economies will

be subject to endemic economic crises that cannot be easily resolved. Both writers put problems of capitalist accumulation at the centre of their analysis. This reflects their dependence on Marxian theory but also their focus on accumulation as the engine of growth, consumption and social welfare.[2] In addition, both writers contend that particularly in the light of the increased internationalisation of capital such crises are likely to increase in frequency and intensity.

Habermas extends the consequences of economic crisis not only to a legitimation crisis but also to a motivational crisis. It is not simply the question of support for the political system that is at stake but also the issue of motivation to participate within the economic system. In terms of Figure 7.1, deficiencies in inputs of economic goods and social welfare benefits to the socio-cultural (sub-)system threaten not only 'mass loyalty' but also the desire to participate in and comply with task requirements in the economic (sub-)system. Thus, the motivational crisis compounds the legitimation crisis by making it even more difficult for the economy to produce the appropriate output. Put very simply, the more difficulty the economic (sub-)system has in meeting the materialistic demands and expectations of the population, the more likely it is that participation in the economic (sub-)system will decline both quantitatively and qualitatively, thereby making economic success even less likely. Thus, both the economic problem and the legitimation problem will be compounded.

It should be apparent that the Habermas–Offe analysis of western liberal-capitalist economies leads to the very problems that have already been identified in the discussion of the bases of the East European 'social contracts' – work-role performance and the legitimacy of the state. However, in some respects their line of argument is even more applicable to the East European societies.

First, as has been outlined above, much of their analysis hinges on the assumption that western governments are judged primarily by the electorate in terms of their ability to manage the economy successfully. The two writers tend to put their emphases somewhat differently. Habermas stresses the basis of legitimation. He indicates that traditional forms of legitimation are undermined in capitalist market economies and are replaced by claims based on technical rationality. Offe tends to give greater emphasis to the outcomes of economic management and the extent to which consumer demands are met and welfare benefits generated by the expanding economy.[3] However, whereas in western capitalist societies, governments can attempt to distance themselves from accountability for economic and material success by pointing to the essentially private nature of market activities (Offe, 1984, Ch. 2), this cannot be done in East European societies.

There, economic relationships are politicised directly through the fusion of economic and political agencies. The state is formally responsible through its planning agencies for economic advancement. In addition, the state claims greater formal rationality than the liberal market equivalent for its ability to plan this development. This claim is itself divisible. It rests in part on the ability to industrialise and increase economic productivity, but it also depends on the ability to direct resources between contending claims such as those of consumption, investment and defence. The former point is easily transferable to crude measurements of economic growth as indicated by changes in national output or per capita national income. Success can then be measured by comparison with western capitalist countries in the international league of economic growth rates.

The latter point relates to issues of distribution. It is not just distribution between broad areas but also within those areas, particularly private consumption and social welfare. The state does not just have to meet expectations of rising living and welfare standards from the population as a whole but also from essential groups such as technocrats and skilled workers. The key point is not only that these issues mirror the distributional conflict of western societies but that the state is directly responsible for the outcome of these conflicting claims, for it has the power to distribute resources between different areas and to determine the real value of rewards going to different groups. The state cannot insulate itself from bearing the responsibility for these outcomes by attributing the results of distributional conflict to market processes for it has superseded market mechanisms.

The East European state apparatuses are caught in a double trap. They are directly responsible both for managing the economy and for meeting aspirations for higher living and welfare standards. Unsuccessful 'steering' of the economic (sub-)system suspends belief in the rationality of the planning mechanisms and makes it more difficult to meet consumer expectations. A failure to meet consumer demands either in general or for particular groups in comparison with one another, promotes a 'legitimation crisis'. It need hardly be added that a 'legitimation crisis' is also likely to lead to a 'motivation crisis'.

The typical response of the East European states to this situation has been twofold. First, virtually without exception, they have given a greater role to technocratic experts in the planning process. This is sometimes accompanied by greater decentralisation or by shifts in the distribution of resources between consumption and investment. However, it is always accompanied by an increased emphasis on consumerism and economism (Bunce, 1983; Woodall, 1982, pp. 33–50).

Neither reaction is surprising. If technical rationality is the basis of legitimation then one would expect an enhanced role for technocratic experts in the state apparatus, whilst consumerism is a logical way of 'buying' the support of the working class. In addition, economic rewards gained through the use of incentive schemes may be used directly to motivate work performance (Lane and O'Dell, 1978, pp. 79–81; Woodall, 1982, p. 45). Furthermore, the use of economic motivators may be consistent with the prognosis of some of the rising technocratic group, particularly if they favour the use of a pricing system that more closely relates the prices of goods and services to their costs of production.

So far, mention of inflation has been avoided in this discussion. As is well known, inflation is frequently suppressed in East European societies. Changes in prices of consumer goods can deviate sharply from underlying changes in costs because of the use of subsidies and indirect taxes by the central planners.

There are a number of reasons why governments may wish to limit overt price rises. Some are ideological and stem from direct application of Marxist-Leninism and, in particular, the desire to move away from market-based principles of allocation and distribution. Others are more pragmatic and relate directly to the preceding discussion. In particular, inflation is also something for which governments are held to be directly responsible. Prices are set by administrative fiat rather than by market forces. Under such circumstances it is not surprising that governments seek to avoid the opprobrium associated with inflation as, in addition, it also threatens the living standards of the masses. Particularly in Poland, there are clear signs that rises in prices of key goods such as meat trigger off widespread popular protest, whereas shortages of goods occasioned by a failure to let prices rise to 'clear markets' appear to be relatively more tolerable (Montias, 1981, p. 180).

A further reason for artificially restraining inflation lies in its legitimating function of demonstrating how much better socialism is than capitalism in resolving economic problems. Thus price stability shows both the skill of the state bureaucracy/technocratic élite and the underlying strength of Marxist-Leninism. Avoidance of inflation demonstrates how the working masses benefit in East European societies in contrast to their 'exploitation' in western capitalist societies. An inflation league table can be used to serve ideological purposes in the same way as an economic growth table.

By now it should be clear why 'social contracts' are widespread in East European societies. They embody the solutions outlined above to potential legitimation and motivation crises. They allow patterns of social integration to be maintained and thereby buy time whilst solutions to systemic problems of economic performance can be sought. Of course, whether such solutions are available is another matter. It is also clear why the 'social contracts' place such emphasis on economic factors such as rising living standards, enhanced social welfare and full employment. It is these factors that are most consonant with the growing consumerism and economism of the working masses that stem from the regimes' attempts to legitimate their role and performance.

PERFORMING THE SOCIAL CONTRACT

It is one matter for governments to have informal 'social contracts' with their working classes but quite another to deliver their side of the bargain. For a considerable period East European economies were able to provide the required economic advance but recently their capacity to do so has lessened, often at the very time that the emphasis on economic factors has increased. The high growth rates that are necessary for increased private and public consumption are now more difficult to attain.

Some of the reasons for this pertain to historical factors. For example, for a considerable period high growth rates could be obtained by adopting western industrial technologies and by shifting labour surpluses from the relatively low-productivity agrarian sector to the higher-productivity industrial sector. Thus industrial output could be raised substantially both because a higher proportion of the adult population was employed in industry and because of higher productivity per unit of labour.

Sadly, neither mechanism has been readily available in recent years. In several East European societies the proportion employed in the primary sector has shrunk to near western proportions, whilst in others the endemic low productivity of that sector makes it difficult to reduce labour there. The result is that the industrial labour supply is generally drying up (Johnson, 1981; Smith, 1983, p. 39). In addition, the jump in productivity engendered by imitating western industrial organisation and technology is also at an end. To be sure, it is still possible to avoid some of the costs of research and innovation by importing western technology through contractual arrangements that allow multinational companies direct production facilities, but the quantum leaps available to the relatively late industrialisers have been utilised already. In all events, the growth rate has slowed quite dramatically in recent years, particulary in the more industrialised countries such as Hungary, Czechoslovakia and the USSR (Ellman, 1982; Smith, 1983, Table 3.1, p. 40).

The consequences of this decline in the growth rate just when economism is rising are analogous to a western economy facing 'excess demand'. The increased demand for personal consumption and social welfare, coupled with the political priority of increasing defence expenditure, whilst still leaving resources free to expand investment as the seed corn of future prosperity, means that total demand exceeds available production. In the short term time may be bought by increasing imports, but this only postpones the day of reckoning unless in the interim economic growth can be greatly increased.

In a western economy the excess demand for goods and services would probably result in inflation being tolerated by a government as a relatively non-conflictual way of equilibriating supply and demand (Crouch, 1978, p. 228). In an East European economy this need not necessarily be the case. The ability, at least in theory, of the central planners to control prices and wages means that inflation may be choked off, hidden or repressed.

In the fomer case the central planners may equilibrate consumer demand to available production of consumer goods by limiting disposable incomes either through wage controls or by raising taxes on income. In this way consumer demand can be choked off without price increases. This policy is obviously incompatible with the 'social contract' approach outlined above.

However, inflation may be hidden or repressed. As Smith (1983, Ch. 6) points out, there is a distinction between 'open', 'hidden' and 'repressed' inflation. 'Open' inflation is that reflected in the official price index. However, the authorities may allow price increases in goods that are not included in the official index or in secondary (black) markets thereby facilitating 'hidden' inflation, that is, inflation that is not included in the official index. An additional possibility is that consumers may switch expenditure towards the higher-priced secondary markets as they try to purchase goods that are in scarce supply in the ordinary market. This increased demand will lead to higher prices in the secondary markets but again without this being reflected in the official price index.

The other possibility is that of 'repressed' inflation. In this case the volume of goods and services available in the shops is simply not sufficient to meet the volume of consumer demand. The authorities do not choke off the surplus spending power by raising prices. Instead, they allow the demand to remain unmet. This results in shortages, queues and the development of secondary markets that may be legal or illegal. People are forced either to dissipate some of their earning power in 'hidden' inflation or to save more than they originally intended because they cannot purchase goods they wished to buy.

These indicators of 'repressed' inflation may occur not just because of general shortages of goods but also because of shortages of particular products. These can result from inadequate planning or because production targets are set in quantitative rather than qualitative terms. However, in some cases, most notably in Poland, there have been clear signs of 'repressed' inflation – clear, not least of all, because the authorities have sometimes brought inflation into the open by sudden, sharp increases in key consumer goods such as food. In addition, as Smith indicates, the consequences of 'repressed' inflation may be cumulative as the unspent income of previous years that reflects the past gaps between planned-for consumption and actual consumption is available to augment the current gap between desired and actual expenditure.

'Hidden' and 'repressed' inflation, although not present in the official indices of inflation, represent breaches in the 'social contract'. Both amount to restraints on growth in living standards. Indeed, in some cases, they may threaten the maintenance of existing levels. They resolve distributional conflict by back door methods. However, although it appears to be the case that price increases are more resented than shortages or rationing through queueing, none the less 'hidden' and 'repressed' inflation threaten social cohesion and legitimation. This is particularly likely if it is widely thought that some groups are able to evade these problems. Thus the existence of 'coupon' stores or 'foreign currency' stores where those with coupons or foreign currency can obtain scare or high-quality consumer products further strains social cohesion, for it hardly need be pointed out that access to them is limited to an élite few, mainly comprising party and state officials (Smith, 1983, p. 98).

It is precisely under these circumstances that moral resentment is added to economic resentment and that commitment both to the state system and to work activity is likely to be reduced. Not surprisingly, the state authorities have sought other ways to avoid these problems. Clearly, the solution lies in raising production and by implication raising labour productivity. However, the available mechanisms seem either to threaten key elements of the 'social contract' and/or to place ever greater strains on it by heightening economistic expectations.

One potential solution is to increase capital investment with a view to raising labour productivity. The obvious difficulty here is that of freeing resources for the increased investment. If the initial problem is already one of resource shortage this solution is hardly tenable unless time can be bought by borrowing from abroad so that capital and consumer goods can be imported to augment domestic production. However, as the Polish case shows, this path is fraught with danger, for foreign borrowing brings with it the future difficulty of servicing the interest payments on the accrued debt. In addition, the borrowing must directly or indirectly finance investment that will enhance labour productivity. Yet, if this is used as a last resort when economic and social relationships are already in crisis, much of the borrowing is likely to be dissipated in higher consumption in order to buy social harmony. Even when this does not occur and investment is boosted, workplace relationships are not likely to be conducive to realising the potential gains in production and productivity.

If capital investment cannot be increased then the alternative lies in making better (that is, more efficient or effective) use of existing resources. Hence labour and capital, often both in relatively short supply, either must be switched to more productive activities or better utilised in existing ones. Concern with this normally leads to the rise of technocratic experts in the state system because, allegedly, they are better able to foster the required economic management, that is, to resolve the steering problem. In turn, the technocratic solution usually involves some decentralisation and a return to a reliance on market mechanisms. These include attempts to relate workers' earnings to their output through incentive schemes that try to motivate higher production.

The rise of the technocracy and the resistance to the growth of their influence and their reliance on decentralised market mechanisms by the old bureaucratic state *apparatchniks* whose claims to authority do not rest on technical expertise have already been well documented (Parkin, 1972). However, this development also has important implications for the 'social contracts' that have arisen in most East European societies.

First, one of the factors underlying the introduction of market mechanisms is the attempt to induce shifts in labour from low to high-productivity industries. However as they are not always located in the same area, this can produce strains within the traditional working-class communities that are tied to the older and declining industries. Whereas workers in the expanding areas can expect both good employment opportunities and higher real wages – the signalling device of the market to induce labour mobility – this is not true of the former group. The employment prospects and advance, if any, in real wages will be worse for workers in areas with a heavy economic concentration of traditional industries such as mining, steel and ship-building. As a consequence, feelings of deprivation will be heightened. In addition, the basis of support and legitimacy will be undermined because the implicit guarantees of the 'social contract' for full employment and egalitarian wage and living standard rises will be breached.

Thus support for the regime from its traditional base, the well-established mature working class, will be put in jeopardy. It is not surprising that frequently the technocrats with support from skilled workers find themselves opposed by an alliance of the old party *apparatchniks* and the traditional working class. To some extent political, economic and social interests will be superimposed on one another for the old party élite is also more likely to have been recruited from the traditional proletariat.

This resistance to reform may result in concessions being made to groups who are threatened or disadvantaged. Smith (1983, p. 122) points out that on grounds of fairness or equity they may win wage rises commensurate with those in the high-growth sectors. However, such wage rises if unbacked by productivity increases, generate inflationary pressures. In addition, as Woodall (1982, p. 50) indicates, the reformist technocrats may buy off resistance to change by increased emphasis on consumerism. If so this replicates the western model that applies in the UK and US, and did so until recently in Sweden, where managerial autonomy is preserved through privatising workers' interests.

Economism is also reinforced by the renewed emphasis in several East European countries on using piece-rate incentive schemes (Haraszti, 1977, pp. 21–41; Lane and O'Dell, 1978, pp. 79–81; Woodall, 1982, p. 45). The focus on material incentives as the primary motivation for working undermines other forms of motivation that have been stressed in state socialist ideology. The cash nexus is presented as the link between the individual and workplace activity. In addition, piece-rate schemes can be divisive and lead to a fragmentation of working-class solidarity. In so far as individual or group incentive schemes lead to wage differentials even for those performing the same sort of work they undermine the moral solidarity that is based on the notion of similarity of work activity leading to similarity of reward. Instead they reinforce economic individualism and sectionalism.

The attempts to decentralise economic control and utilise market mechanisms in order to enhance productive performance place an even greater stress on economistic considerations. At the very point when the economy is struggling to provide for the material and social advance expected by the workers in a workers' state, they are encouraged to emphasise even more their material rewards and to focus on questions of relative advantage. This too at a time when opportunities for individual advance occasioned through changes in the occupational structure are being reduced compared to an earlier period of industrialisation when administrative, managerial and professional positions were rapidly expanding.

Overall, the situation is tending to correspond to the 'vicious cycle' of our sociological model. The 'social contracts' that have been used to resolve legitimation and motivational problems have come under increasing strain as governments have struggled to meet their side of the agreements. Several East European countries show signs of excessive claims on available resources, though this may not always result in increases in overt inflation as it can also be 'hidden' or 'repressed'.[4] In addition, attempts at economic reform can exacerbate the underlying tension by raising still further the need for economic 'pay-offs' to satisfy the aspirations of an increasingly privatised and economistic workforce, as well as producing a more fragmented and sectionalised working class that is less likely to be restrained by feelings of moral solidarity. In turn, workplace relationships are hardly likely to be harmonious where commitment both to state and enterprise is so tenuous. Thus three elements of the 'vicious cycle' are present. The conditions are ripening for distributional conflict to produce its inflationary consequences. Only the state's formal monopoly of power stands as a key check on this process. Hence, as Runciman (1985) points out, the likelihood that if economic and ideological factors cannot control dissent, then force is the only effective form of power left.

INFLATIONARY PRESSURES IN POLAND

It has been pointed out already that the precise form of any 'social contract' depends on the particular historical and cultural circumstances of each country. In addition, the likelihood of any agreement being successfully maintained depends not only on these factors and the available economic resources but also on the skill and ability of those in leadership positions, particularly within the state system. This being so the choice of Poland as a case study should be seen as just that, and not necessarily as a prototype for other East European societies.

During the 1960s, Polish economic performance was disappointing. Output, consumption and investment consistently failed to meet targets. Woodall (1982, pp. 33–46) ascribes much of the problem to the rigidities of the planning process coupled with the decline in agricultural productivity. The latter meant that there could only be modest increases to the industrial labour force as it was impossible to release significant numbers from the agrarian sector. This in turn meant that the Polish growth strategy depended heavily on a massive investment programme designed to raise labour productivity.

However, as Woodall points out, this dependence on in-vestment squeezed resources available for increasing output of consumer goods, and thus for increasing real wages. Planned-for increases of real wages fell for each five-year period from 1951–55 through to 1966–70 from 40 to 30 to 22.5 per cent and finally 10 per cent. Yet actual performance was even worse, the increases being consecutively 4, 20, 8 and 8 per cent (Staniszkis, 1979, Table 3, p. 176). The restraints on real wages were most marked after 1968.

Not surprisingly the Polish authorities began to introduce economic reforms designed to improve labour productivity by better use of investment resources. One element in this programme was the introduction of an incentive scheme in 1970 intended to link wages more closely to actual increases in labour productivity. However, this resulted in wage increases being limited and 'many categories of worker actually experi-enced a reduction in income: real wage levels fell at a time when nearly 50 per cent of the average working-class family budget was spent on food' (Woodall, 1982, p. 45).

At the time there was no immediate opposition to the introduction of the new incentive scheme. However, the an-nouncement of 15–30 per cent increases in food and fuel prices in December 1970 triggered off widespread protest. This direct 'attack' on living standards was the cue for a series of riots, demonstrations and strikes that forced the authorities to offset the price increases by a 25 per cent wage increase early in 1971 (MacShane, 1981, pp. 36–7). The disturbances also provoked a change in political leadership, as in the earlier troubles of 1956, with on this occasion Gomulka being ousted in favour of Gierek. As Staniszkis (1979) has argued, the nature of the regime is such that economic crises tend to be transformed into political crises. Protest takes the form of an implicit challenge to the authority of the regime which is directly responsible for the 'attack' on workers' living stan-dards. A switch in party leadership may help to restore normality by providing a scapegoat and by opening the way to a change in policy, in this case a short-term boost to living standards.

The Gierek administration adopted a policy that in the West would be termed a 'dash for growth'. The new economic strategy tried to boost both consumption and investment. In 1971–75 real wages rose by 42 per cent, well in excess even of the planned target of 18 per cent. As investment rose at about double this rate there was a squeeze on available resources even though output rose strongly. The result was that the gap between input and demand was largely met by increasing imports, largely financed by borrowing from western banks (Tyson, 1981, pp. 120–2).

The policy clearly relates to the 'social contract'. The state was providing increases in living standards and because of the high level of demand, full employment was maintained. In addition steps were taken to remove differentials between manual and non-manual workers (de Weydenthal, 1981, p. 197). This was in accord with the relatively egalitarian ideology of Polish workers as exemplified by Malewski's (1958) survey of Warsaw workers. He found that two-thirds of his respondents favoured relatively equal incomes whilst only a fifth were opposed to this.[5]

In the short term the new strategy appeared to be succeeding. Output was strongly increased and dissent had been bought off. However difficulties were looming. First the new policy had given a strong boost to consumerist values. Kolankiewicz (1981, pp. 142–4) points out that the early 1970s saw a marked rise in the purchase of consumer durables. In addition, he suggests that the formal abolition of the manual/non-manual division heightened awareness of existing inequalities. Both developments indicated a rise in consumer aspirations which would only be met by further rises in output and real wages. Kolankiewicz (1981, pp. 134–42) also points out that by the mid–1970s there was no clear relationship between wages and productivity so that workers simply came to expect wage increases as the result of managerial decisions rather than as a reward for effort or skill. The structure of wage-earnings had become anomic.

Second, the increased dependence of the Polish economy on imports was leading to a foreign debt crisis. The share of imports in gross national income rose from 10 per cent in 1970/71 to well over 30 per cent by 1974/75. As this could not be offset by rising exports the trade deficit increased to 8 per cent of net national income (Samulewicz, 1984). This position could not be sustained, particularly as the prices of imported fuels were rising rapidly.

By the mid–1970s, the Polish economy showed all the symptoms of excess demand. Imports were high, queues and shortages were widespread, and even 'open' inflation was about 5 per cent per annum from 1974–76 (Wanless, 1985, Table 1, p. 408). The Polish authorities reacted by raising food prices by 60 per cent in June 1976. Again this provoked widespread demonstrations and strikes and, in a short time, the withdrawal of the price increases (MacShane, 1981, pp. 38–9). However, the underlying problems still remained. Claims on resources were still far in excess of actual output. The authorities were still allowing real incomes to rise in order to quieten dissent but growth was slowing because of the rigidities of the planning system. 'Open' inflation continued to rise towards double figures (Wanless, 1985, Table 1, p. 408); shortages and queues for basic goods became relatively widespread. In addition, Poland continued with a massive trade deficit and its western hard currency debt mounted from about $7\frac{1}{2}$ thousand million dollars in 1975 to just under 20,000 million dollars by 1979 (Tyson, 1981, Table 6.2, p. 120).

In some ways the underlying situation was even worse by the late 1970s than it had been earlier in the decade. A crucial factor had been the growth of secondary markets in the 1970s. The development of 'coupon' and 'foreign currency' shops to which the party élite and functionaries had privileged access, together with increases in bribery and corruption to gain possession of scarce goods, heightened working-class resentment. Also, the availability of social services was becoming more limited and more unequally distributed. In addition mobility opportunities were declining because of the relative rigidity of the occupational structure coupled with the inequality of access to educational qualifications necessary for recruitment to privileged positions. A further factor leading to disaffection among the working class was that job security was declining as the authorities tried to switch labour to more productive areas (Kolankiewicz, 1981, pp. 144–6; Woodall, 1982, pp. 191–2; Norgaard and Sampson, 1984).

Taken together, these developments amounted to a significant breach in the Polish 'social contract'. Expected rises in standards of living were not occurring, security of employment was declining and mobility opportunities were decreasing. Over and above this, perceptions and resentment of existing inequalities were mounting. In particular, by the late 1970s there was widespread frustration and anger that earnings did not seem to be related to the work that was actually done and that the normal methods of distribution of scarce and basic goods and services could be by-passed by those in privileged positions and through the use of corruption (Koralewicz-Zebik, 1984).

This underlying discontent was heightened by the remoteness of the political élite from the masses, and by the absence of effective representative channels whereby working-class feelings could be communicated upwards. At the workplace increased industrial concentration had undermined the already feeble instruments of participation and worker management, whilst the absence of an independent trade union movement limited the effectiveness of that potentially representative channel (Woodall, 1982, pp. 170–85). As regards the broader political system, 'participation in policy formulation was restricted to a small group of top party officials and their advisers. The workers' organisations were kept at the level of passive supporters and the working masses were simply ignored' (de Weydenthal, 1981, p. 193).

The reaction of workers during the late 1970s had been twofold. First, there had been the growth of a quasi-independent union movement voicing worker demands. This development reflected the maturation of the working class and its ability to learn from the past troubles of 1956, 1970 and 1976. It was also contingent on circumstances peculiar to Poland, in particular the ideological legacy of nationalism; the alternative source of power possessed by the (Catholic) Church; and the alliance between workers and intelligentsia forged by the creation in 1976 of the Committee for the Defence of Workers (KOR).

Second, the increasing disillusionment and resentment of the working classes had led to widespread disaffection at the workplace. Absenteeism and industrial sabotage had risen; and low morale and the generalised feeling of unfairness had weakened work discipline, with strikes and overtime bans increasing. These factors were hardly conducive to attaining the necessary increases in labour productivity that could have significantly increased output (Kolankiewicz, 1981, p. 145; Nuti, 1982, p. 49).

In 1980 the authorities again imposed food-price rises of 30 per cent this time by transferring meat to the higher-priced secondary shops. Again widespread strikes resulted. Worker demands for higher wages were now coupled with political demands for civil liberties and independent unions. The resultant Gdansk Agreement of August 1980 was in effect an explicit 'social contract'. It granted higher wages and a 'fairer' system of distributing goods and services, as well as acceding to a number of the more political demands (MacShane, 1981, pp. 46–7, 151–60).

The agreement represented another attempt to buy off dissent. However, as the underlying problems still existed it is difficult to see how it could have succeeded. Nuti (1982, pp. 48–9) points out that on the basis of past experiences the Polish people expect that the authorities will react to protest by reversing price increases and raising consumption. They are not prepared to accept the reality that output cannot cater for the consumption levels that they take for granted, nor for the fact that if output levels are to be increased in the short term, then labour effort must increase. Indeed, the economic basis of the Solidarity Movement was precisely to resist any erosion of living standards and intensification of work activity.

Under the circumstances, the Gdansk Agreement was unlikely to last long. The regime lacked the economic resources to meet its economic conditions nor, given the increased resentment of inequalities and the widespread feelings of unfairness about the structure of rewards, did it have the moral resources to appeal for a programme of reconstruction based on austerity and increased work effort. The military takeover of 1981 was almost a natural response to this situation. The policy of repression enabled a programme of economic austerity to be introduced. Per capita consumption was cut by 30 per cent and investment by 50 per cent. Attempts were made to introduce economic reforms which, by decentralising decision making, might encourage better use of resources even though this might increase inequality (Gomulka and Rostowski, 1984, pp. 387–8).

This brief economic and social history of Poland during recent years does not do justice to a number of factors, and in particular to the growth of Solidarity and the hamfistedness of the Polish authorities. It does, however, indicate how fragile were the Polish 'social contracts' and how they succumbed to the inability of the authorities to meet the material demand for higher living standards and social welfare that were their part of the agreements. It also indicates how problems of management and economic crises can be transformed into political crises which threaten both the legitimacy of the state and the motivation of people to perform their work roles.

It also corresponds to the 'vicious cycle' model of inflation. Economism has risen in Poland. The Polish people have expected that the regime will provide for increasing material prosperity and enhanced social welfare. There are some signs that a second-generation, urbanised, industrial workforce have developed new yardsticks of economic comparison and no longer judge their position with reference to their rural past. If so, this process has been accentuated by the gains in prosperity during the early 1970s and by increased contact with the West (Norgaard and Sampson, 1984, p. 780). Consumerism has also been affected by the increase in consumer durables during the early 1970s and by the spasmodic introduction of incentive schemes that have enhanced the significance of economic motivators at work.

At the same time moral restraints have weakened. This is partially because of the overt lack of fairness by which some privileged groups can gain access to scarce goods and services. It also reflects the disparity between actual inequalities and the formal abolition of the division between manual and non-manual workers. Both of these comparative factors are conducive to manual workers seeking higher rewards to which they feel they are entitled in order to counteract these unjust and undeserved differentials. In addition, the low level of participation by workers and their representatives in decision-making processes means that they are less likely to accept decisions that are harmful to their interests.

Heightened concern with material factors, be they the

absolute scarcity of some basic goods or the desire for higher living standards, coupled with a decline in normative restraints on their pursuit, suggest that Polish workers will press their demands wherever possible. Compared with workers in the West, their power resources are relatively modest. However, numerical strength and their indispensability in the production process do give a certain capacity for action (Connor, 1981, pp. 158–61). Indeed, Polish experience indicates four separate occasions when widespread riots, demonstrations and strikes could not easily be repressed by directly coercive measures. In 1956, 1970, 1976 and 1980 the authorities, despite their formal monopoly of power and the weak organisation of workers, were forced to back down from their economic policies and make concessions in order to buy off the widespread active dissent.

This dissent has also manifested itself in other ways. The increase in absenteeism, labour turnover and other aspects of work indiscipline such as theft lowered productive potential. In turn this has made it even more difficult for the authorities to expand output to meet material aspirations. It has also made it far more difficult to adjust to exogenous shocks. It is no accident that the Polish crises of 1976 and 1980 followed closely after the two explosive increases in oil prices. In addition, it looks as if the Polish 'vicious cycle' has steadily worsened with material concerns increasing and moral disillusionment rising. Certainly 'open' inflation has risen, becoming noticeable by the mid-1970s, reaching double figures by the end of the decade, and accelerating to over 100 per cent by 1982 (Wanless, 1985, Table 1, p. 408).

It remains to be seen whether other East European societies can avoid the 'Polish disease'. At least, they have the opportunity to learn from the Polish experience. In some cases there are clear signs that institutional mechanisms are being used that may regulate the pursuit of economic goals. The obvious examples are worker self-management in Yugoslavia and various pseudo-participation schemes in Romania. Another possibility is the Hungarian attempt to enhance economic performance by a rapid and coherent programme of decentralisation. However, more generally, the East European societies' economic performance has been declining. This does not augur well for their chance of avoiding at least a milder version of Poland's problems.

8 Prognosis

In Chapter 2 we outlined a sociological model of inflation. The aim of this model was not to suggest that sociological variables by themselves could explain or account for the pervasiveness of inflation in particular societies but rather to indicate how they could contribute to an understanding of international variations in inflation rates. Thus the sociological model was intended to complement rather than replace the models of other disciplines and in particular those of economics. By the same token, the model presented in Chapter 2 was also counterposed to earlier sociological and Marxian accounts that suggested that western capitalist societies almost inevitably tended to generate marked inflationary tendencies (Goldthorpe, 1978; O'Connor, 1973). Our model allowed explicitly for variation in inflationary tendencies and, in particular, suggested the possibility of directly opposite configurations of key variables described respectively as a 'virtuous cycle' and a 'vicious cycle'.

The sociological factors could affect the likelihood of relatively high or low inflation rates in a variety of ways. First, they could be more or less likely to generate inflationary pressures within a particular society or to magnify those produced exogenously. The obvious example here being their implications for the development of either a wage–price or a price–wage–price spiral. Another example would be their effect on exacerbating or mitigating pressures on governments to pursue budgetary policies where expenditures significantly exceeded income with consequences for the likelihood of 'excess demand'.

Next, they could make it more or less difficult for governments to introduce counter-inflation policies. To some extent this is simply the mirror-image of the first point with the difference that the emphasis is not on the generation of endogenous inflationary tendencies or the magnification of exogenous ones, but on the extent to which the government's freedom of manoeuvre may be more or less circumscribed or enhanced. Examples of this would be the extent to which institutional arrangements favour the introduction of prices and incomes policies, with or without statutory backing, and whether the combination of the political business cycle and the structure of pressures on the government facilitates the correction of budgetary deficits.[1]

Last, the sociological factors may affect not just the generation or magnification of inflationary tendencies, nor directly the likelihood of counter-inflationary policies being introduced, but the chances of success of such policies when they are introduced. In particular, resistance to these policies may cause them to be modified or abandoned particularly if they raise the costs of successful implementation. Crouch (1985) explicitly discusses how differences in the British and German industrial relations systems mean that the introduction of a tight monetary policy is less likely to result in high levels of unemployment in the latter case because the German trade unions are more likely to adjust their bargaining strategy and restrain wages in anticipation or acceptance of that policy. In Britain, on the other hand, trade unions may go on pressing for significantly higher wage increases until unemployment has risen to such high levels that their bargaining strength has been weakened. Thus the impact of the tight monetary policy is felt more in increasing unemployment than in restraining wages and prices.[2] This lengthens the time necessary for the policy to have its desired effect (of curbing inflation) and may increase pressure on the government to change its policy either because it does not appear to be working or because of the perceived electoral unpopularity of high unemployment.

Empirical variations in these sociological factors also act as a corrective to the view that inflation is inherent in western capitalist societies. There may be tendencies such as the maturation of the working class and the decline of the status order (Goldthorpe, 1978) or the increasing 'fiscal crisis of the state' (O'Connor, 1973) that can have inflationary implications. But the precise form that these developments take and their effects on inflationary tendencies are likely to be contingent on the particular historical, cultural and institutional circumstances of each society. Thus the sociological model suggests that other factors may determine whether significant inflation is more or less likely and, in particular, points to the possible existence of a 'virtuous cycle' where inflationary pressures are more or less contained as opposed to a 'vicious cycle' where they are exacerbated.

The utility of this model is borne out by the case studies. It is not simply that with the exception of the USA they do fit one or other of the two variants of the basic model, but also, as will be discussed shortly, that they indicate that similar developments associated with the maturation of capitalist economies in general can have very different consequences given the particular contingencies of each country.

THE CASE STUDIES ASSESSED

The UK, and the illustration of East European societies, Poland, exemplify the 'vicious cycle'; West Germany and Sweden in different ways offer examples of the 'virtuous cycle'. In each case the four variables of the model – economism, normative regulation, power concentration and dispersion, and workplace relationships – interlock. Only in the USA is there no close relationship between the different elements.

In the UK historical circumstances linked with the *laissez-faire* form of early industrial development have laid the roots of the post-war 'British disease' which has surfaced as the advantages of early industrialisation and empire have receded. The dual legacy of economism coupled with the pursuit of a narrow individual or sectional self-interest has augmented inflationary tendencies. It has facilitated the development of wage bargaining and industrial relations systems which are highly fragmented and lacking in normative regulation. Against this anomic backcloth the maturation of the British working class in terms of its increased organisational, political and market strength has resulted in greater pushfulness for economic and social rewards. These claims are pursued in covert or overt competition with those of other sectional groups more or less regardless of their effect on the economy as a whole. In addition, these claims have been prosecuted more vigorously just at the time when loss of empire coupled with increased international competition make it less rather than more likely that the British economy can meet these renewed demands.

It is the combination of the historical legacy, embodied in distinctive cultural values and institutional arrangements, with the post-war shifts in the concentration and dispersion of power and the relative decline of the British economy that have formed a 'vicious cycle'. A less economistic or sectionalised society might have seen a moderation of distributive conflict either because claims could have been diverted to less materialistic concerns or because a collective policy of regulation or restraint might have been pursued. Instead groups of income-receivers have competed for short-term advantages *vis-à-vis* one another. They have thereby generated and exacerbated inflationary pressures as well as making the introduction of counter-inflationary policies both politically more difficult and less likely to succeed.

Central to these processes have been the pursuit, if appropriate by industrial conflict, of sectional wage claims designed to improve living standards, maintain or restore a group's position in the wage league table, or to compensate for past or expected price increases. However they also include the repeated resistance to the introduction of new techniques and working procedures at the workplace, as well as pressures on governments to enhance the provision of social welfare and provide fiscal and monetary conditions favourable for the maintenance of growth and full employment. All of these factors generate, or magnify at least in the short term, inflationary pressures. They also make the introduction of counter-inflationary initiatives such as prices and incomes policies, attempts to raise productivity, or deflationary fiscal and monetary policies more difficult to sustain.[3] This reflects the direct opposition to their introduction and the resistance to the consequences of their introduction. Thus it is not just that it is relatively difficult for UK governments to introduce these policies but the costs of enforcement are relatively high. This is most marked in the case of prices and incomes policies which are antithetical to the fragmented, sectional nature of the wage bargaining and industrial relations systems.

On the surface, Poland appears to show similarities to the UK. During the 1970s Poland was characterised by high economism and increased sectionalism. The moral authority of the regime weakened thereby lessening the potential restraints of normative regulation. Workers increasingly used what power they had to disrupt work procedures, thereby reducing the productive capacity of the economy. The one radical difference was that the Polish workers increasingly used direct action to threaten the maintenance of the state regime as a whole. Thus, unlike in the UK, their behaviour came to have overt political aims.

However, the origins of the Polish 'vicious cycle' appear to be radically different. First, the state regime which had been imposed by external force appears to have sought to have legitimated itself by providing economic advance. Hence the repeated 'social contracts' rewritten after periods of unrest whereby the state withdraws or offsets price increases and promises prosperity, employment and social welfare for the future. Thus the state has directly fuelled economistic and materialistic claims. This has made it particularly difficult for the Polish authorities to introduce programmes of economic reform and decentralisation because in the short-term these threaten the real wages and employment prospects of key groups of the traditional working class.

The loyalty of these groups is further jeopardised by the fact that various signs of social and economic inequality have become more overt with the growth of secondary markets and corruption. This further weakens the moral strength of the regime as it undermines the collectivist egalitarian ideology which is fairly widespread. In addition, sectionalist tendencies are directly encouraged by the introduction of piece-rate schemes as part of the economic reforms.

The net result has been a spiral in which the inflationary elements of the 'vicious cycle' are enhanced in each circuit. Economism becomes more entrenched, normative regulation declines as collectivism is replaced by sectionalism, the state's moral resources are depleted and resistance to economic reform rises whilst disruptive workplace practices increase. As in the UK case, the Polish experience demonstrates that the sociological variables help to explain not only how inflationary tendencies may be generated or magnified but also the limitations on the introduction of counter-inflationary policies. Arguably, it has only been the imposition of military rule and directly coercive measures that has enabled the suspension of the Polish 'vicious cycle' and a very sharp reduction in Poland's inflation rate (Gomulka and Rostowski, 1984).[4]

West Germany and Sweden provide examples of the 'virtuous cycle'. The similarities between them are important. In both cases there are signs that economistic values have been to some extent sated by a sustained rise in economic prosperity. In addition the pursuit of materialistic values has been restrained by systems of normative regulation based on two elements. First, the structure of wage determination gives an important role to broadly-based employers' and employees' federations. This limits the sectional nature of wage bargaining compared to the UK, and facilitates account being taken of the macro-economic consequences of wage bargaining for factors such as prices, international competitiveness, investment, employment and growth. Second, there is an implicit 'social contract' between government and organised labour so that full employment, economic growth and rising living and social welfare standards are exchanged for wage moderation and relative industrial harmony. As a consequence wage claims are not pursued in the short term as vigorously as might otherwise be the case and workplace relationships are relatively harmonious with favourable consequences both for maintaining production without industrial disruption and for the introduction of new technologies and processes that enhance productivity.

However, there are also important differences in the underlying mechanisms buttressing the respective 'virtuous cycles'. In Germany organised labour is relatively weak compared to Sweden. Union density is far lower. The representative institutions of co-partnership and co-determination to some extent fragment the power of organised labour and act as a safety valve relieving potential strains whilst diverting (worker) attention from more fundamental issues. The widespread use of migrant labour further segments the labour market whilst generally increasing the potential labour supply. In addition, the post-war German 'economic miracle' developed with a Christian Democrat rather than a Social Democrat party in power. As a result union and Social Democrat leaders have accommodated themselves to a socio-economic system which gives primacy to business values and particularly those that emphasise the role of private accumulation as the engine of social and economic advance. In so far as German cultural values stress collective goals and the subordination of individual or group aims to some higher authority (Fox, 1978; Currie, 1979), then this authority resides in the dominance of capital's interests. The form and substance of the system of normative regulation reflects this dominance.[5]

In Sweden, on the other hand, the systems of normative regulation have developed over an extensive period of political dominance by the Social Democratic Party (SAP), during which union density has become very high. This has enabled the main Swedish union federation, the LO, to augment its industrial position through its ability to influence the broad thrust of economic policy and to initiate developments in industrial and economic democracy. The ideological framework within which Swedish economic decision-making takes place has been shaped by this relative dominance of the industrial and political wings of organised labour. As a result high prominence has been given to the Keynesian goals of economic growth and full employment. In turn pursuit of these goals has secured support both for the SAP and LO, and enhanced their authority. This has been crucial for wage restraint embodied in the solidaristic wage policy, the promotion of an egalitarian ideology, and for relative industrial harmony. These in turn have helped moderate inflation to levels comparable with Sweden's international competitors whilst facilitating sustained economic growth and high levels of employment. Thus the core of the Swedish 'virtuous cycle' is the mutual reinforcement of the relative dominance of organised labour and the system of normative regulation.

In Sweden the 'virtuous cycle' results not in very low rates of inflation but inflation which until recently maintained international competitiveness (the main aim of their counter-inflationary policies) and is accompanied by a very low rate of unemployment. In recent years the Swedish system has shown increasing signs of strain. These stem from the slow-down in the rate of growth of the Swedish economy. This makes it more difficult to meet the material aspirations of the population. In turn, this poses a threat to the wage-bargaining system as it makes it more likely that particular groups will try to utilise their market strength to attain the rewards to which they aspire. Thus the collectivism of the wage determination system may be replaced by a sectionalism more akin to that of the UK.[6]

At the same time Swedish employers have tried to use the decline in Swedish economic growth and its attendant problems as a lever to place greater emphasis on the role of private capital accumulation as the engine of economic and social advance. By doing so they hope to shift the parameters of economic and political decision-makers towards their own priorities and thus reduce the dominance of organised labour. The LO's counter-strategy has been to stress the role of the wage-earner funds not just as an instrument of engendering economic democracy and reducing social and economic inequality, but also as a non-inflationary collectivist solution to the problem of financing private (i.e. non-state) economic investment. If this strategy is successful it will help to generate greater economic growth without sacrificing the egalitarian and collectivist nature of the system of normative regulation. In turn, this will help combat the incipient sectionalism of the Swedish workforce whilst maintaining the industrial and political dominance of organised labour.

In Germany, strains are appearing for somewhat different reasons. The recent loss of political office by the Social Democrats poses a serious threat to the system of normative regulation. The leaders of the unions may be less willing to cooperate with the more conservative regime now in office, particularly as they are less likely to be assured of the policy side-payments that have helped cement the 'social partnership' that has characterised much of the post-war period. In any case this partnership was under considerable strain during the late 1970s as the union leaders withdrew from the 'concerted action' programme in protest at the Social Democrat government's tightening of macro-economic policy and the business leaders' resistance to the introduction of extensions of co-partnership and co-determination at the workplace.

The Christian Democrat government is showing itself less inclined to pursue economic and social welfare policies that are favourable to the union leaders and their members and, to say the least, is unlikely to extend the institutions of industrial democracy. Rather, it may be more susceptible to business pressures to use the shifts in the balance of industrial power occasioned by recession and the new international division of labour to reassert the dominance of capital interests. Market and political power would be used more openly to subjugate organised labour with less dependence than hitherto on normative regulation as embodied in the concept and institutions of 'social partnership'.[7]

This development would bring Germany more into line with the situation in the USA, where, we saw in Chapter 4, there is no cycle either of the 'virtuous' or 'vicious' variety. Instead, the relatively unrestrained economistic values of the population are held in check by the power structure. The key elements are the responsiveness in the medium term of the political system to pressures to control inflation and the relatively low power of organised labour both at the workplace and over the polity. In particular, the marked dualism of the American economy is an important factor in restraining inflationary pressures. The weakness of large sectors of the workforce in terms of their low unionisation, employment in competitive sectors of the economy and easy replacement by other workers substantially reduces their bargaining position. In addition the sheer scale of the American economy coupled with its geographical spread has allowed producers the possibility of switching production and investment internally without waiting for the development of multinational production and the new international division of labour. Thus, the possibility of significant wage–price or price–wage–price spirals are confined to relatively small sectors of the economy where market competition is limited and workers are well organised.

THE SOCIAL CONDITIONS FOR MODERATING INFLATION

The analysis of the case studies gives little support to the contention that social factors are inevitably conducive to inflationary strains in western societies. Clearly, this version of the 'convergence' thesis has little empirical support. Instead it would appear that the likelihood of inflationary pressures becoming paramount is contingent on a variety of historical, cultural and institutional factors. Thus developments that might occur in a variety of countries, including those of Eastern Europe, may have an inflationary impact in some contexts but not in others.

An obvious example of this is the role that maturation of the working class might play in generating and exacerbating inflationary pressures. It will be recalled from the discussion in Chapter 2 that Goldthorpe (1978) placed great emphasis on this factor together with the decline of the old status order and the promotion of general citizenship rights in accounting for the rise in inflation in the UK. However, the development of a mature, stable and organised working class does not necessarily play the same role elsewhere even when the traditional status order has little force and citizenship rights are widespread.

Certainly, in Poland the maturation of the working class has contributed to the development of inflationary forces as it has been an important factor in the effectiveness of resistance to successive governments and, in particular, in allowing for the prosecution of the workforce's material claims. However, in Germany and Sweden this has not been the case. In the former country working-class maturation has been accommodated within the institutions of 'social partnership' because of the culture's collectivist traditions and because of the ideological and political dominance of business interests. It is, of course, arguable that had German unionisation been at the UK level this would not have been the case. This claim cannot be made in the Swedish case where unionisation is considerably higher than in the UK and expectations about social and economic entitlements embodied in the notion of citizenship rights are also greater. On the contrary, in Sweden, working-class maturation appears to have been an important factor in the development of a centralised, corporatist strategy for avoiding rates of inflation that would have undermined international competitiveness.

This in turn raises the question of whether the key to moderating inflationary pressures lies in the ability to centralise bargaining arrangements. The argument is that such mechanisms enable narrow sectional interests to be transcended and account to be taken of the overall implications of wage determination for the development of the economy in general and for inflation in particular. Of course the circumstances whereby such mechanisms evolve may reflect particular historical conditions such as the presence or absence of collectivist as opposed to individualist values during the industrialisation process and whether unions were organised on an industrial as opposed to a craft basis. However, the import of our analysis is that centralisation of bargaining is neither a necessary nor a sufficient condition for moderation of inflationary pressures.

First, the US experience suggests that inflationary strains may be relatively modest even when the role of centralised employer and employee federations in wage determination is fairly limited. As we have already discussed, this reflects the structure of power both at the macro level of pressures on the political system and at the micro level of the individual enterprise. In addition, as noted above, Germany may be moving more towards the US example, with a decline in the significance of centralised bargaining and greater use of market and political dominance to hold potentially inflationary pressure in check. Though in the German case these factors are still likely to be supplemented by normative restraints stemming from the workplace institutions of social partnership and the attempt to foster an identity of interests between workers and their enterprise.

Second, Swedish, German and, to a lesser extent, Polish experience suggests that although centralised bargaining arrangements facilitate normative regulation and thereby the moderation of inflationary pressures they do not ensure this outcome. In all these cases restraint in the pursuit of wage claims depends on an explicit or implicit agreement in which the government of the day holds out the prospect of sustained advances in economic prosperity and social welfare benefits, and business interests too agree or, at least, are thought to be likely to facilitate these outcomes through the pursuit of appropriate programmes of capital investment.[8] Failure by another party to the agreement to honour its part of the 'contract' almost certainly results in a weakening of the regulative system. Thus in Sweden it is no coincidence that the centralised bargaining system has come under threat during recession not only from employers seeking a return to market criteria for allocating resources and rewards but also from the Metalworkers Union who also seek to utilise their market strength. In Poland, the strongest challenges to the system have occurred when economic failure has been most overt, when large price increases in food have been made.

It seems then that for short-term restraints to be operative there must be a feeling that there are longer-term economic and social advantages to be gained. This must be so, because otherwise it would be difficult for the leaders of centralised employees' federations to ensure the support of their constituent unions and members. However, normative regulation can also be influenced by factors other than whether practical benefits appear to follow from restraint. Commitment to the regulative mechanism can be engendered by more directly normative means. One such method is participation or at least the feeling of participation in decision-making either directly or through representative channels. Such participation can occur either in the enterprise or in national economic fora. The German and Swedish 'virtuous cycles' have been bolstered by this sense of participation. Conversely, in Poland the absence of effective participatory mechanisms, despite the promise of their introduction by successive governments, has been an important factor in undermining support.

The content of wage policies can also be important for engendering normative commitment. Here the obvious contrast is between Sweden and Poland. The Swedish solidaristic wage policy with its strongly egalitarian values has helped to maintain the cohesion of the manual working class and thereby the centralised bargaining system. Conversely, in

Poland, the overt and covert manifestations of breaches in the fairly widespread egalitarian ideology occasioned, in particular, by the development of secondary (black) markets and corruption have again undermined support for the regime and the possibility of voluntary continued restraint.

In the UK and the USA the voluntarist tradition has affected the development of the industrial relations and wage-determination systems. The sturdy independence of individual unions and enterprises makes it unlikely that they will be drawn into centralised arrangements for any substantial period of time. Where there is a power imbalance that substantially favours business interests, as in the USA, inflationary pressures can be restrained in the medium to long term. Where this is not the case, as in the UK, inflation is likely to be endemic.

This suggests that unless the structure of power is such that capital interests are able to restrain inflationary pressures at the micro level of the enterprise and at the macro level of governmental monetary and fiscal policy some system of normative regulation is necessary. Implicitly or explicitly this must involve some sort of incomes policy. Centralised bargaining arrangements and participation by broadly-based employer and employee federations in national economic fora facilitate the development of such policies. However, they need to be bolstered by the feeling, backed by experience, that they do contribute to economic success which feeds back in the form of sustained growth, higher real wages, high employment and higher social welfare benefits. The functioning of these policies also needs normative underpinning either in the form of commitment engendered by the development of participatory mechanisms and/or the collectivist substance of the policies themselves.

Although the agreements have important micro-economic consequences in terms of their effects on the growth of wages they have to be related to macro-economic policies. Indeed, as in the Swedish case, the support of union leaders may be conditional on the government adopting policies that are likely to provide the long-term benefits desired by them. Macro-economic policies must supplement the 'contracts' reached between the corporate partners both by avoiding overloading the capacity of the economy – the 'excess demand' problem – and by providing a generally expansionary stimulus. The difference between the German and Swedish experience shows that there are radically different ways of achieving this end that reflect the different power structures of the two countries. In Germany the emphasis has been on incorporating union leadership into accepting the 'social market' economy, such acceptance being sweetened by economic prosperity and enhanced social welfare. In Sweden, on the other hand, the union leadership has steered the political leadership towards Keynesian economic management policies which, because they work, bolster support for both the industrial and political wings of the labour movement.

The import of this discussion is that the piecemeal transference to countries such as the UK which suffer from a 'vicious cycle' of particular institutional mechanisms such as an incomes policy, a reform of wage-bargaining structures or a national economic forum is unlikely to have much effect. These devices are only likely to be of significance where they are consonant with the cultural traditions and with other institutional arrangements. In particular, although centralised, collectivist bargaining arrangements may facilitate normative regulation of the rewards of groups of income-receivers they cannot perform this task by themselves. Thus the establishment of a 'virtuous cycle' may involve the wholesale transformation of a set of institutions which may be a near-impossible task if, as in the UK, these go against voluntarist and individualist traditions.

However, the alternative solution of re-establishing the dominance of capital interests may also be difficult to effect in countries such as the UK. As noted above the imposition of tight monetary and fiscal policies may be resisted strongly where organised labour is relatively well-entrenched and where expectations about state provision of basic social benefits are significant and widespread. In such circumstances the attempt to impose counter-inflationary policies through market and political dominance may be both costly and ultimately impossible: costly because unemployment may have to be raised to high levels until market power can be asserted; ultimately impossible because the workings of the political business cycle will probably lead to the electoral defeat of any government that tried to pursue consistently such a policy before it succeeded.

Appendix

Table A.1 *Per capita gross domestic product of twenty OECD countries in $US, 1960–80[a]*

1960		1970		1975		1980	
USA	2804	USA	4789	Sweden	8845	Switzerland	15904
Canada	2229	Sweden	4107	Switzerland	8472	Sweden	14938
Sweden	1865	Canada	3884	Denmark	7438	Norway	14111
Luxembourg	1652	Switzerland	3349	Canada	7223	Germany	13236
Switzerland	1594	Denmark	3220	USA	7141	Denmark	12953
Australia	1580	Luxembourg	3159	Norway	7094	Luxembourg	12843
New Zealand	1576	Germany	3055	Australia	6875	Iceland	12542
Iceland	1385	Australia	2964	Germany	6749	France	12183
UK	1358	Norway	2882	Luxembourg	6543	Belgium	12154
France	1315	France	2775	Belgium	6424	Netherlands	11979
Germany	1301	Belgium	2652	France	6419	USA	11448
Denmark	1289	Iceland	2432	Netherlands	6066	Canada	10781
Norway	1277	Netherlands	2429	Finland	5880	Finland	10480
Belgium	1232	Finland	2305	Iceland	5869	Austria	10261
Finland	1116	New Zealand	2235	Austria	5009	Australia	10244
Netherlands	971	US	2199	New Zealand	4603	UK	9404
Austria	891	Japan	1961	Japan	4470	Japan	8910
Italy	695	Austria	1945	UK	4179	New Zealand	7658
Ireland	624	Italy	1727	Italy	3480	Italy	7011
Japan	458	Ireland	1317	Ireland	2605	Ireland	5366

Note:

a. Greece, Portugal, Spain and Turkey have been excluded from this table. With the exception of Spain in 1975 and 1980 they have consistently had lower per capita GDP than all the other OECD countries. Until 1970 the leading OECD countries had higher per capita incomes than any other country. Since then some of the oil-based Third World economies, such as Qatar, the United Arab Emirates and Brunei, have moved to the head of this league table.

Sources: UN (1980), Table 1A; UN (1985), Table 1.

Table A.2: Growth of real GDP for OECD countries, 1961–83

| | Percentage change | | | | | | | | | | | |
	1961	1962	1963	1964	1965	1966	1967	1968	1969	1970	1971	1972
Australia	−0.1	6.4	6.6	6.3	5.5	2.8	6.9	6.0	6.4	6.2	5.8	3.7
Austria	5.6	2.6	4.2	6.0	2.9	5.6	3.0	4.5	6.3	7.1	5.1	6.2
Belgium	5.0	5.2	4.4	7.0	3.6	3.2	3.9	4.2	6.6	6.4	3.7	5.3
Canada	3.1	6.8	5.5	6.4	6.8	7.0	3.4	5.6	5.2	2.6	7.0	5.8
Denmark	6.4	5.7	0.6	9.3	4.6	2.7	3.4	4.0	6.3	2.0	2.7	5.3
Finland	7.6	2.7	3.3	5.2	5.3	2.4	2.2	2.3	9.6	7.5	2.1	7.6
France	5.5	6.7	5.3	6.5	4.8	5.2	4.7	4.3	7.0	5.7	5.4	5.9
Germany	5.1	4.4	3.1	6.7	5.5	2.6	−0.1	5.9	7.5	5.1	3.1	4.2
Greece	11.1	1.5	10.1	8.3	9.4	6.1	5.5	6.7	9.9	8.0	7.1	8.9
Iceland	0.7	7.5	9.4	8.5	6.6	8.5	−1.7	−5.7	3.1	7.8	12.7	6.5
Ireland	4.7	3.7	4.8	4.2	2.0	1.0	5.1	8.1	6.1	3.5	3.4	6.4
Italy	8.2	6.2	5.6	2.8	3.3	6.0	7.2	6.5	6.1	5.3	1.6	3.2
Japan	14.6	7.1	10.5	13.2	5.1	10.6	10.8	12.8	12.3	9.8	4.6	8.8
Luxem-bourg	4.4	1.2	2.6	7.5	1.7	1.7	1.6	4.2	8.9	2.2	4.3	6.2
Nether-lands	3.1	4.0	3.6	8.3	5.2	2.7	5.3	6.4	6.4	6.3	4.3	3.4
New Zealand	3.3	3.1	4.8	4.9	4.7	3.1	−0.9	1.0	8.2	1.5	4.0	3.9
Norway	5.1	4.7	3.8	5.0	5.3	3.8	6.3	2.3	4.5	2.0	4.6	5.2
Portugal	5.5	6.7	5.9	6.6	7.5	4.1	7.5	8.9	2.1	9.1	6.6	8.0
Spain	11.8	9.3	8.8	6.2	6.3	7.1	4.3	6.8	8.9	4.1	5.0	8.1
Sweden	5.7	4.3	5.2	6.8	3.8	2.1	3.4	3.6	5.0	6.5	0.9	2.3
Switzer-land	8.1	4.8	4.9	5.3	3.2	2.5	3.1	3.6	5.6	6.4	4.1	3.2
Turkey	1.7	6.1	9.4	4.1	2.6	11.7	4.5	6.7	5.3	4.9	9.1	6.6
UK	3.3	1.0	4.2	5.2	2.3	1.9	2.8	4.2	1.3	2.2	2.7	2.3
USA	2.3	5.6	4.1	5.0	6.2	5.8	2.8	4.0	2.9	−0.2	3.1	5.4
Average OECD	4.8	5.3	4.9	6.1	5.4	5.4	3.8	5.4	5.1	3.1	3.7	5.4

Sources: OECD (July 1981), Table H.1, p. 132; OECD (June 1985), Table R.1, p. 156

A.2: continued

			Percentage change						*Average % change*			
1975	1976	1977	1978	1979	1980	1981	1982	1983	1961–65	1966–70	1971–75	1974–80
2.4	3.2	1.0	2.8	4.5	1.7	4.0	0.0	1.0	4.9	5.7	3.9	2.6
−0.4	4.6	4.4	0.5	4.7	3.0	−0.1	1.0	2.1	4.3	5.3	3.9	3.4
−1.5	5.2	0.4	3.0	2.0	3.5	−1.3	1.1	0.4	5.0	4.9	3.5	2.8
1.1	6.1	2.2	3.9	3.4	1.0	4.0	−4.3	2.8	5.7	4.7	5.0	3.3
−0.7	6.5	1.6	1.5	3.5	−0.4	−0.9	3.0	2.0	5.3	3.7	2.0	2.5
1.2	0.3	0.2	2.6	7.4	5.6	1.9	2.8	2.9	4.8	4.8	4.1	3.2
0.2	5.2	3.1	3.8	3.3	1.1	0.2	2.0	1.0	5.8	5.4	4.0	3.3
−1.7	5.5	3.1	3.1	4.2	1.8	0.0	−1.0	1.0	4.9	4.2	2.1	3.5
6.1	6.4	3.4	6.7	3.7	1.8	−0.3	−0.1	0.3	8.1	7.2	5.2	4.4
−0.5	3.5	5.8	3.9	4.1	4.1	2.2	−0.9	−4.7	6.5	2.4	6.1	4.3
3.7	1.4	8.2	7.2	2.8	3.3	2.9	1.9	0.6	3.9	4.8	4.5	4.6
−3.6	5.9	1.9	2.7	4.9	3.9	0.2	−0.4	−1.2	5.2	6.2	2.5	3.9
2.3	5.3	5.3	5.0	5.1	4.9	4.2	3.1	3.3	11.0	11.3	4.7	5.1
−6.1	1.9	0.6	4.5	4.0	1.7	−1.8	−1.1	−2.4	3.5	3.7	3.8	2.5
−1.0	5.3	2.4	2.5	2.4	0.9	−0.7	−1.7	0.6	4.8	5.4	3.2	2.6
−1.1	3.0	−5.0	−0.6	−0.7	2.0	3.6	−0.8	3.7	4.2	2.6	4.3	−0.3
4.2	6.8	3.6	4.5	5.1	4.2	0.9	1.0	3.2	4.8	3.8	4.7	4.8
−4.3	6.9	5.6	3.4	6.2	4.1	0.8	3.2	−0.1	6.4	6.3	4.5	5.3
1.1	3.0	3.3	1.8	0.2	1.5	0.4	0.9	2.1	8.5	6.2	5.6	2.0
2.6	1.1	−1.6	1.8	3.8	1.7	−0.3	0.8	2.5	5.2	5.1	2.6	1.4
−7.3	−1.4	2.4	0.4	2.5	4.6	1.5	−1.1	0.7	5.3	4.2	0.9	1.7
10.1	10.8	5.1	3.2	−1.7	−0.3	4.5	5.7	3.7	4.8	6.6	8.1	3.4
−0.7	3.8	1.0	3.6	2.1	−2.2	−1.1	1.9	3.3	3.2	2.5	2.2	1.7
−0.8	4.7	5.5	4.7	2.6	−0.4	3.4	−3.0	2.9	4.6	3.1	2.5	3.4
−0.3	4.8	4.0	4.0	3.3	1.1	2.3	−0.8	2.3	5.3	4.6	3.1	3.4

Table A.3: Annual percentage changes in manufacturing productivity, hou
compensation in manufacturing and unit labour costs in manufacturing for f
case-study countries, 1960–82

| | Output per hour | | | | | Hourly compe | |
	Germany	Sweden	UK	US	UK rank out of 12 countries[a]	Germany	S\
1960–82	5.1	4.8	3.6	2.6	10	10.0	
1960–73	5.7	6.6	4.4	3.0	11	9.6	
1973–82	3.6	2.2	1.8	1.7	10	8.5	
1973–79	4.5	2.0	1.6	2.0	12	9.2	
1980	1.4	1.6	−1.0	0.2	11	8.8	
1981	2.3	0.4	6.7	3.5	2	7.6	
1982	1.7	1.3	3.8	1.2	4	5.5	

Note:

a The other countries were Belgium, Canada, Denmark, France, Italy, Japan, Neth
and Norway.

Source: Alvarez and Cooper (1984), Table 1, p. 53, and Table 4, p. 55.

Table A.4: Standardised unemployment rates in fifteen OECD countries, 1965–84[a]   (% Total labour force)

	1965	1966	1967	1968	1969	1970	1971	1972	1973	1974	197
Australia	1.5	1.7	1.9	1.8	1.8	1.6	1.9	2.6	2.3	2.6	4.
Austria	1.9	1.8	1.9	2.0	2.0	1.4	1.3	1.2	1.1	1.4	1.
Belgium	1.8	2.0	2.6	3.1	2.3	2.1	2.1	2.7	2.7	3.0	5.
Canada	3.6	3.3	3.8	4.4	4.4	5.6	6.1	6.2	5.5	5.3	6.
Finland	1.4	1.5	2.9	3.8	2.8	1.9	2.2	2.5	2.3	1.7	2.
France	1.5	1.8	1.9	2.6	2.3	2.4	2.6	2.7	2.6	2.8	4.
Germany	0.3	0.2	1.3	1.5	0.9	0.8	0.9	0.8	0.8	1.6	3.
Italy	5.3	5.7	5.3	5.6	5.6	5.3	5.3	6.3	6.2	5.3	5.
Japan	1.2	1.3	1.3	1.2	1.1	1.1	1.2	1.4	1.3	1.4	1.
Netherlands	0.6	0.8	1.6	1.5	1.0	1.0	1.3	2.2	2.2	2.7	5.
Norway	1.8	1.6	1.5	2.1	2.0	1.6	1.5	1.7	1.5	1.5	2.
Spain	2.5	2.1	2.5	3.0	2.6	2.4	3.1	3.1	2.5	2.6	3.
Sweden	1.2	1.6	2.1	2.2	1.9	1.5	2.5	2.7	2.5	2.0	1.
UK	2.3	2.3	3.4	3.4	3.0	3.1	3.9	4.3	3.3	3.1	4.
USA	4.4	3.6	3.7	3.4	3.4	4.8	5.8	5.5	4.8	5.5	8.

Note: The OECD only gives data over this period for 15 of the 24 OECD countries.
standardisation is designed 'to adjust "registered" unemployment with a view
including unemployed persons not covered on the register and to excluding em
persons still carried on the register.' Its main effects are on the data for Germany
and the UK.

Sources: OECD (July 1981), Table H12, p. 142; OECD (June 1985), Table R12, p. 1

A.3: Continued

Hourly compensation			Unit labour costs				
K	US	UK rank out of 12 countries	Germany	Sweden	UK	US	UK rank out of 12 countries
.4	7.0	3	4.7	6.8	9.5	4.3	2
.7	5.0	10	3.7	3.5	4.1	1.9	5
.8	9.5	1	4.7	10.0	15.7	7.7	1
.0	9.3	2	4.6	12.1	17.1	7.2	1
.6	11.7	1	7.3	9.3	22.9	11.5	1
.2	9.9	2	5.1	10.4	9.9	6.1	6
.1	8.5	6	3.8	5.8	5.1	7.2	8

A.4: Continued

7	1978	1979	1980	1981	1982	1983	1984	Average 1965–69	Average 1970–74	Average 1975–79	Average 1980–84
6	6.2	6.2	6.0	5.7	7.1	9.9	8.9	1.7	2.2	5.5	7.5
6	2.1	2.1	1.9	2.5	3.5	4.1	–	1.9	1.3	1.9	–
4	7.9	8.2	8.8	10.8	12.6	13.9	14.0	2.4	2.5	7.0	12.0
0	8.3	7.4	7.4	7.5	10.9	11.8	11.2	3.9	5.7	7.5	9.8
8	7.2	5.9	4.6	5.1	5.8	6.1	6.1	2.5	2.1	5.0	5.5
9	5.3	6.0	6.4	7.3	8.1	8.3	9.7	2.0	2.6	4.9	8.0
6	3.5	3.2	3.0	4.4	6.1	8.0	8.6	0.8	1.0	3.5	6.0
0	7.1	7.5	7.5	8.3	9.0	9.8	10.2	5.5	5.7	6.8	8.9
0	2.2	2.1	2.0	2.2	2.4	2.6	2.7	1.2	1.3	2.0	2.4
3	5.3	5.4	6.0	8.6	11.4	13.7	14.0	1.1	1.9	5.3	10.7
5	1.8	2.0	1.7	2.0	2.6	3.3	3.0	1.8	1.6	1.9	2.5
2	6.9	8.5	11.2	14.0	15.9	17.4	20.1	2.5	2.7	5.8	15.7
8	2.2	2.1	2.0	2.5	3.1	3.5	3.1	1.8	2.2	1.9	2.8
4	6.3	5.6	6.9	10.6	12.3	13.1	13.2	2.9	3.5	5.8	11.2
9	6.0	5.8	7.0	7.5	9.5	9.5	7.4	3.7	5.3	6.9	8.2

Table A.5: *Industrial stoppages: working days lost per thousand employee industries and services, 1971–83*

	1971	1972	1973	1974	1975	1976	1977
Australia	670	430	550	1250	700	760	330
Austria	. .	. .	. .	–	–	–	–
Belgium	410	120	280	180	200	290	220
Canada	400	1040	730	1120	1300	1360	380
Denmark[a]	10	10	2010	100	50	110	120
Finland	1670	290	1440	230	160	680	1310
France	270	230	230	200	230	290	210
Germany	210	–	30	50	–	30	–
Ireland	380	290	280	730	390	1030	570
Italy	1000	1320	1550	1430	1970	1810	1160
Japan	180	150	130	270	220	90	40
Netherlands	30	40	150	–	–	–	60
New Zealand	130	110	210	180	210	480	430
Norway	10	10	10	230	10	90	20
Spain	110	70	130	200	210	1470	1940
Sweden	310	–	–	20	100	10	20
Switzerland	. .	. .	. .	–	–	10	–
UK	610	1080	320	650	270	150	450
USA[b]	670	370	360	610	410	480	460

Notes: Data are rounded to nearest 10 less than 5.
      a. Danish data excludes stoppages involving less than 100 people
      b. The method of data collection for the USA was changed in 1982 re
      coverage.

Sources: Department of Employment (1982), February, Table 1, p. 69.
      Department of Employment (1985), April, Table 1, p. 150.

.5: *continued*

	1980	1981	1982	1983	Average 1971–74	Average 1975–78	Average 1979–83
	640	780	410	320	720	550	590
	10	–	–	–	. .	–	–
	70	. .	. .	. .	250	260	. .
	930	890	610	460	820	970	750
	90	320	50	40	530	90	110
	840	340	110	360	910	550	360
	100	90	130	90	230	220	120
	10	–	–	–	70	60	10
	480	510	510	400	420	690	730
	1120	720	1270	960	1320	1410	1190
	30	10	10	10	180	100	20
	10	10	50	30	60	20	30
	360	360	300	350	160	420	350
	60	20	170	–	60	40	50
	790	680	370	590	130	1250	970
	1150	50	–	10	80	40	250
	–	–	–	–	. .	–	–
	520	200	250	180	660	320	480
	360	250	. .	. .	500	430	. .

Notes

CHAPTER 1

1. In this study inflation is used to refer simply to increases in the average level of prices of goods and services in an economy and not to increases in the supply of money as in some definitions. This avoids confusing description of a phenomenon with a particular explanation of its cause.
2. The term 'organised labour' rather than 'trade union' is used because it includes reference not only to official union activity but also to the collective action of groups of workers 'on the shop-floor' which might take place quite independently of the formal union structure and, indeed, be practised by groups who are not members of a union.
3. This can result in stagflation as, on the one hand, prices and wages rise in an inflationary spiral, whilst on the other, the original effects of the devaluation are so offset that domestic prices become even less competitive internationally with a resultant fall in sales.
4. These issues are discussed at length by Wood (1978). He argues for what he terms 'direct relativity bargaining', that is, bargaining which takes place not in money terms but directly over relativities between different groups, thereby confronting at first hand the conflict inherent in sectional bargaining. In order for this to be successful, Wood argues that bargaining units could not remain as fragmented and decentralised as at present.
5. Again the institutional framework is important. A more centralised and coordinated bargaining system will alter the frame of reference within which individual and group demands are made because more information will be available about the claims and awards of other groups. See the discussion of rational bargaining strategies under conditions of uncertainty by Laver (1980).
6. The 'free-rider' argument can be derived directly from the discussion by Olson (1965) of collective goods. The point is that if everyone else shows restraint then inflation is moderated. Lower inflation is a 'collective good' because its benefits are experienced by everybody. Thus there is a temptation for any individual or group to accept the benefit without paying the cost with their own restraint, for their own action has virtually no direct effect on whether lower inflation can be attained.

7. Of course, there are counter-strategies available to employers. Deskilling occupational tasks reduces the monopoly power of skilled workers because other workers can be substituted for them. Additionally, it has become relatively common for large manufacturers to develop alternative sources of supply of components both from outside suppliers to whom they sub-contract and from their internal divisions. Outside suppliers are often highly dependent on the large firm and have a weak bargaining position whilst multiple internal suppliers, often from divisions located in different countries, weaken the position of any one group of workers unless they can surmount the problems of organising international industrial action. This is discussed further in the following chapters.

8. Effectively this is another version of the Prisoner's Dilemma. No individual firm can be sure of its optimal response unless it knows what the responses of its competitors are. To take on a long strike whilst competitors buy off their own workforce is not a happy prospect!

9. Control of profits or dividends may also be included if only to legitimate the wage controls.

10. See the discussion by Crouch (1977, Part II).

11. The first (1979) Thatcher administration adopted most of these policies. As Holmes (1985) points out, they did not result in the predicted rise in overt industrial unrest and wage claims were reduced. However, whether this was because of the success of the legal measures, as Holmes claims, or because the high level of unemployment sapped union strength is debateable. Certainly, after 1983 wage claims increased in both the private and public sectors; in the former as production picked up and in the latter as successive cuts in real incomes in the public services, such as education, had their effect. Furthermore, industrial action has less overt forms than strikes and it is likely that informal mechanisms of non-cooperation increased. These issues are discussed at greater length in Chapter 3.

12. The 'natural rate' of unemployment is taken to be that level of unemployment at which the rate of wage inflation will be equal to the rate of growth of productivity and hence (price) inflation will not occur. Apart from the rate of growth of productivity it is determined by the degree of structural unemployment, i.e. unemployment caused by a misfit between the supply and demand for labour because of occupational, skill or geographical discrepancies, and the functioning of labour markets in terms of how adequately vacancies can be filled from the stock of unemployed people. If unemployment falls below this 'natural rate' then labour shortages will occur with resultant wage inflation.

13. This involves trying to trade off unemployment against inflation as shown by the famous Phillips curve which apparently demonstrated an inverse relationship between the rate of unemployment and the rate of wage and thereby price increases. Lower demand weakens the bargaining position of labour, hence lowering the rate of wage increase. Monetarists, of course, would suggest that this means simply an end to the attempt to lower unemployment below the 'natural rate'.

14. This is almost the converse of arguments by earlier writers such as Lipset (1960, Ch. 3) who relate the political legitimacy and stability of a regime to its efficacy mainly in achieving economic goals. In particular, whereas Lipset sees political parties as ensuring continued electoral success by presiding over economic prosperity, an early theory of the political business cycle, Brittan sees this as being likely to lead to a long-term problem of meeting newly-created higher aspirations.

15. During the 1983 British general election it was noticeable that the Conservative Party emphasised the 'resolute approach' in espousing its economic and social policies. This was a clear reference to the government's determination, and in particular that of Mrs Thatcher during the Falklands War. In so far as the electorate were prepared to transfer this leadership characteristic from the international to the domestic sphere (and there were signs that they were), this contributed to the Conservative Party's electoral success.

16. Opinion poll data show that for some years unemployment has most often been identified as the major problem facing the nation, but to a much lesser extent as the major problem from the respondent's personal point of view.

17. This is not dissimilar to the systems analysis approach to legitimation of Habermas (1976). He also focuses on the way governments are held accountable for economic management and the promotion of prosperity with corresponding implications for support if expectations are not met. This approach will be discussed more fully in Chapter 7.

18. See the exchange between Brittan, Goldthorpe and Peacock in Hirsch and Goldthorpe (1978), pp. 214–16.

19. Gough (1979, Chs. 3, 4) provides a useful corrective to the teleological approach by stressing the distinction between the origins and functions of policies.

20. Cross-sectional national studies have become quite common in recent years. Unfortunately, not all the writers have been as sensitive to the conceptual and methodological problems as Crouch (1985) who supplements his work with two case studies. Although the cross-sectional method is not utilised here, advantage will be taken of the findings of some studies when they show a clear correlation between relevant variables.

CHAPTER 2

1. This claim has been subject to an acrimonious debate between Smith (1982, 1985) and Goldthorpe (1983). Smith claims that both high employment and inflation resulted from world pressures and do not correlate with variations in union strength. However, this is not particularly relevant to the model developed in this chapter because it does not explain why Britain's experience of inflation was worse than most other western countries; that is, it deals only with the generation of inflation, not why its impact is more or less severe or prolonged.

2. Subsequent experience does not seem to support Goldthorpe. Several years' experience of high levels of unemployment has not resulted in a united working-class challenge to the government. Indeed, although there have been spasms of social unrest as in the urban riots of 1981, these have been relatively isolated. Unified class action has not occurred, instead the working class is fragmented, not least between those who are employed and the unemployed. Goldthorpe (1984) has significantly revised his earlier argument to show how organised labour has become weaker.

3. Crouch's use of the 'high trust' dynamic owes much to Fox (1974).

4. This relates directly to the structure of shareholding interests. Managers are more likely to be accountable to shareholder interests where ownership has not been divorced from control, that is where the Board of Directors, or equivalent body, contains representatives of those with large shareholding interests. Representation of financial institutions provides a case in point. When such interests are present they may discipline management who do not make profitability the prime consideration.

5. The gist of this argument is not that well-off people do not have material concerns, rather that they may be 'satisficers' as opposed to 'maximisers'.

6. It is also similar to the distinction between the culturally given goals of action and the culturally approved means of achieving them used in his discussion of anomie by Merton (1949, Chs. 4, 5).

7. How limited these options are may depend on the strength of capitalist interests, particularly those of financial interests. Where these are very strong, as in the UK, and bolstered by the way national prosperity is said to depend on financial probity or the fear of capital movements overseas, a left-wing government may have very few options. Elsewhere, as in Sweden, where capital is not so international in nature, a left-wing government may have more freedom of manoeuvre.

8. The relationships between effectiveness and legitimation are discussed by Lipset (1960, Ch. 3) and Fox (1971, Ch. 2).

9. This may seem paradoxical as the discussion is about which system reduces inflation: but the point is that inflation will be lower than it otherwise would be for that level of demand and unemployment if wage moderation occurs. It improves the trade-off between inflation and unemployment. Furthermore, it shows that governments who value both employment and price stability may be rational to adopt this policy mix rather than a more deflationary stance. It is only if one believes that unemployment cannot be lowered below a pre-set 'natural rate' that these policies would appear irrational.

CHAPTER 3

1. In some surveys the precise elements vary or respondents were asked to choose from a greater number of factors. In his first study in this

area, Inglehart (1971) refers not to materialist and post- materialist but to acquisitive and post-bourgeois values.

2. By 1984, Belgium and France had slipped below Britain when the ratio of post-materialists to materialists is considered. This could reflect immediate economic exigencies. The Belgium growth rate has been almost negligible in recent years whilst its unemployment rate has been the highest of the western advanced industrial societies (Tables A.2, p. 220, and A.4, p. 222). In 1984 the French were experiencing the severe deflationary policies of the Mitterand government. As the discussion in Chapter 2 pointed out, Inglehart does suggest that short-term changes in economic circumstances can cause short-term value shifts.

3. In all countries the younger cohorts are more post-materialist and less materialist than the older cohorts. Inglehart argues that this is accounted for by their socialisation at a time of greater economic prosperity, but it could also reflect that those without family responsibilities simply have fewer economic concerns.

4. The other nine factors were 'maintain order', 'fight crime' and 'strong defence forces', reflecting safety needs; 'more say on job', 'less impersonal society' and 'more say in government', indicating the need for belonging; and 'protect free speech', 'more beautiful cities' and 'ideas count', reflecting self-actualisation.

5. This is a particularly controversial area. The difficulty is that if workers have had their legitimate aspirations channelled into areas of economic concern they are hardly like to voice interest in lack of intrinsic job-satisfaction or participation in decision-making. Thus their responses to survey questionnaires may reflect a fatalistic view of what they regard as inevitable features of working life. However, in Chapters 5 and 6 we shall see that German and Swedish workers do give more priority to these factors.

6. Scase and Gallie are primarily concerned with manual workers. However, there is not reason to suppose that these attitudes are confined to that category. Runciman's white-collar respondents also tend to make intra-class comparisons. Moreover, the recent increase in unionisation amongst white-collar, administrative, professional and managerial employees is part of a defensive strategy designed to maintain or restore pay differentials that they have customarily held. This suggests again that their root cause is comparisons with other occupational groups that hold adjacent positions in the income league table.

7. The policy collapsed in the winter of 1978–79 when there were widespread strikes, particularly in the public sector, for pay settlements above the government's target norm. This pressure reflected a number of elements. The narrowing of differentials in the previous three years was certainly an important factor, particulary as an egalitarian ideology has never been significant in British trade unionism. The squeeze on living standards during the previous three years was also important, particularly as during 1976–77 it had been coupled with significant cutbacks in welfare expenditure. It signified to many workers that the policy of restraint embodied in the social contract was not working,

bargained corporatism was not producing desirable consequences. However, a particularly important factor was the private sector pay award by the Ford Motor Company to its employees which clearly breached the target norm. As was noted in Chapter 2, deviant cases can prove highly damaging to attempts to restrain wages.

8. This factor highlights the limitations of using strikes as an indicator of the strength and cohesion of organised labour. From some points of view actually striking may be a sign of weakness as it indicates that muscles cannot just be flexed but have to be put into operation as well. In addition, strike statistics measure only one aspect of industrial militancy: on occasions they may be just the tip of the iceberg.

9. It is somewhat paradoxical that critics of corporatist arrangements make precisely the same criticism of the growth of union power. They claim that each successive bargain or arrangement requires new policy commitments by the government in return for the same commitment to restraint by organised labour and that accordingly the government pays a higher and higher price for the cooperation of organised labour. In addition, they sometimes claim that organised labour requires legal changes that strengthen their position, for example, in industrial relations as part of the 'side-payment'. Holmes (1985) is perhaps the clearest advocate of this ratchet effect. However, in practice organised labour has only obtained legal changes that restore the original position, that is reverse what they consider to be adverse legislation. In addition, the bargain of restraint in exchange for policies of full employment, growth and a higher 'social wage' involve both sides making the same commitment each time the bargain or contract is renewed.

10. In this context it should be mentioned that the formation of the CBI by the merger of three separate employer organisations in the early 1960s was itself promoted by the government who wished to have one representative organ of industry which could participate in tripartite agencies such as the NEDC (Grant and Marsh, 1977, Ch. 2).

11. The last stage of the 1970–74 Heath government's pay policy allowed for threshold elements to be built into wage agreements. These meant that price increases above a certain level would trigger off automatically a wage increase. Thus, the unexpected oil price explosion of 1973–74 set in train a price–wage–price spiral in 1974 as successive thresholds were reached. The consolidation of these rises into basic wage rates in 1974–75 gave the appearance of a wage explosion. It is remarkable how many commentators ignore the threshold agreements when discussing the cause of inflation in 1974–75.

12. The government's choice of restraining PSBR reflects its own ideological preference of favouring private rather than public production and consumption of goods and services. Apart from cutting public expenditure in order to limit aggregate demand, it frees resources for the private sector. As there is no direct relationship between the PSBR and the money supply, the government has to use other policy instruments. High interest rates have been the most significant of these tools as they restrain the private sector's demand for credit.

13. The official figures almost certainly underestimate the real extent of unemployment. These figures reflect those who are out of work and claiming benefit. They exclude important categories such as female (ex-)workers who are not eligible for benefit. Young people are also under-represented, either because they too are not eligible for benefit or because they participate in the government-sponsored Youth Training Scheme.
14. This is the 'supply-side' aspect of Thatcherism. It also places great emphasis on the role of new small enterprises, particularly in the service sector, who are said to be more flexible and responsive to consumer needs.
15. Beckerman does acknowledge that international as opposed to purely national deflations may affect inflation. This is because of their impact on world commodity prices and hence import costs.

CHAPTER 4

1. State regulation is intended to enforce 'competitive' behaviour on these monopolies. The recent British zest for privatisation or denationalisation seems to ignore the need for regulatory bodies when public monopolies are transformed into private monopolies. This reflects the political rather than the economic reason for the change. In the same way the initial British preference for nationalisation often reflected political pressures to socialise the ownership of key elements of the economy.
2. The development of industrial unions during the middle third of the twentieth century should not be ignored. They too were drawn into these processes. More generally, the extent of collective bargaining should not be exaggerated. Even in manufacturing industry unionisation has never been more than about 50 per cent although it must have reached higher levels amongst the large-scale firms (Estey, 1981, Ch. 1).
3. These conclusions are both tentative and involve considerable generalisations. As noted in earlier chapters some of the analysis depends on very small sub-samples and often differences are not statistically significant. In addition, not all sectors of American society have shared to the same extent in American prosperity. In particular, there have been marked regional variations in the experience of prosperity at different times, and ethnic groups have had radically different exposure to the advantages of freedom from economic scarcities.
4. The AFL–CIO also regulates and attempts to resolve inter-union disputes over matters such as jurisdiction and demarcation. In a sense this indicates its weakness for it reduces it to the role of manager of disputes between its constituents.
5. The discussion here also mirrors the earlier accounts of the Prisoners' Dilemma. Again, not only is there the prospect that individual legislators are unlikely to show restraint unless they can be sure of the moderation of others, but also even then they may be 'free-riders' on

the backs of other people's restraint. However, there is one important difference: they can, if they are so minded, join together to restrain expenditure and/or balance the budget. The relatively small numbers (100 Senators and 435 Representatives) leave open the possibility of the collective pursuit of generally restrictive budgetary policies which would then act as the framework within which they could attempt to attain their sectional targets.

The approval by Congress in December 1985 of the Gramm-Rudman-Hollings budget reform plan provides such a framework. This sets out a programme to eliminate the budget deficit by 1991. However, there is considerable scepticism about whether this programme will be adhered to.

6. It should not be supposed that all Republican administrations will place control of inflation at the top of the agenda, or, even if they do, that they will be able to curb inflationary pressures by resolving the fiscal crisis of the state. The first Nixon administration was not able to offset the higher expenditures of the Vietnam War by raising taxes or cutting significantly other areas of expenditure. The resultant price inflation led directly to the 1971 price and wage controls. The Reagan administration as not been able to offset its tax-cutting programme with corresponding expenditure cuts. This is partially because of the pressures to which it is ideologically susceptible to maintain or expand military expenditures. It also reflects the fact that the Democratic controlled House of Representatives will not make deep cuts in welfare expenditure because this would affect the basis of their electoral support. So far the Reagan budgetary deficits have not resulted in an inflationary surge. This is because the preceding recession allowed for a substantial recovery before excess demand could manifest itself. In addition, a tight monetary policy conducted through high interest rates has led to an inflow of money which until recently meant that the value of the dollar was very high. This has beneficial effects on the prices of imported goods and commodities, hence helping to restrain inflation (Beckerman, 1985).

7. One reason why the USA performance was not better than average may be because American producers of goods that are traded internationally would have experienced less competitive conditions because their rivals were affected more severely. Hence they could have allowed profit margins to rise whilst taking the higher prices. By the same token they would have been less resistant to domestic wage claims. Other domestic producers would have come under strong pressure to grant similar wage claims thereby generating higher prices. This process assumes the validity of the Swedish model whereby prices in the competitive (international) sector are set by world forces and then transmit inflationary consequences to the sheltered (domestic) sector (Edgren, Faxén and Odhner, 1973). This will be more fully discussed in Chapter 6.

8. The difficulties in raising American productivity should not be underestimated. As the USA has been the most advanced industrial country it has been operating nearer the frontiers of technological knowledge. It

cannot perform the trick of boosting productivity and growth by imitating its competitors. It has to generate its own improvements. In addition, the development of multinational companies has facilitated 'technological transfer'. This may make it more likely that the mother-countries of multinational companies will bear the costs of technological development whilst the benefits are increasingly realised elsewhere. In this context, the USA as the mother country of most of the major multinationals is not in an enviable position.

CHAPTER 5

1. The processes described here are very similar to those discussed by Scott (1979). In his discussion of interlocking directorships, he places great emphasis on how they build channels of communication that have implications for the harmonisation of strategic rather than operational decisions.
2. Elsewhere large-scale business is likely to tolerate modest rates of inflation as the price of engineering expansion. This will be particularly so if the price inflation is relatively predictable and can be allowed for in long-term projects. High rates of inflation or sharp rises are not desired. They threaten the value of company savings as well as personal savings. In the German case, the presence of the banks' representatives means that the 'tolerable' level of inflation will be lower than elsewhere.
3. Monissen (1977) provides a detailed account of the origins of the legal system as well as the particulars of the legislation itself. The critical legislation by the Christian Democrats smacks strongly of an attempt to buy the support or compliance of organised labour with the minimum concessions at a time when business was weak. This is supported by the more general argument of Ramsay (1977). Subsequent legislation owes much to the Social Democrats seeking to strengthen their ties with their union allies.
4. In practice the unions dominated membership of the Works Councils and greatly influenced the choice of worker representatives on super-visory boards (Furstenberg, 1978).
5. Pahl and Winkler (1974) discuss similar mechanisms in their account of the functioning of British Boards of Directors. Again, their emphasis is on manipulation of information and informal meetings prior to meetings of the full Board.
6. It need scarcely be pointed out that although many of these limitations apply equally to the employers' use of lockouts this does not have an equivalent impact, for whereas unions use strikes to gain something they otherwise cannot get, employers by virtue of their control of management positions need only use the lockout as a counter to a strike.
7. The actual question forms the basis of the distinction between 'materialists' and 'post-materialists'. The respondents were asked: 'Which of the four Freedoms do you personally consider most import-

ant – Freedom of Speech, Freedom of Worship, Freedom from Fears, or Freedom from Want?'

8. It may be unwise to generalise too much on the basis of this limited study. Cable and Fitzroy's findings are based on analysis of the economic performance of those firms who exceed the statutory requirements. Therefore, they do not tell us anything directly about the great majority of German firms who simply follow those requirements. However, it would be surprising if participation only enhanced productive performance in these 'high-participation' companies and had absolutely no effect elsewhere, particularly as there is independent evidence about the popularity of the universal schemes.

CHAPTER 6

1. The LO's pre-eminence in the bargaining system does not simply rest on this heavy representation of manual workers but also on the consideration that its constituent unions organise a clear majority of Sweden's trade unionists. In recent years the white-collar and salaried unions have been growing rapidly, but even by 1980 the LO still represented over 60 per cent of union members (Martin, 1984, Table 3.3, p. 345).

2. Although there is no formal link between the LO and the SAP there are frequent meetings between their leaders, some 30 per cent of LO members are also members of SAP and many Members of Parliament have been drawn from the ranks of LO (van Otter, 1975, pp. 199–200; Martin, 1984, p. 191).

3. Edgren, Faxén and Odhner (1973) outline the main arguments that underpin the policy.

4. State-owned industries only account for about 5 per cent of industrial production, a remarkably small proportion in comparison to most West European countries (Skold, 1976, p. 25).

5. Martin (1984, p. 249) shows that in the second year of the 1969–70 wage agreement, wage-drift rose to 7.2 per cent, over twice the level of the contractual increase of 3.4 per cent. He suggests that this reflects the fruits of strike activity. This is disputed by Korpi. He claims that as the strikes were concentrated in firms paying less than their regional average they were not against the solidaristic wage policy. He interprets them more as a reaction to an inflationary surge with workers seeking to maintain their living standards (Korpi, 1981, pp. 79–81).

6. The funds have now been introduced in an experimental form to operate from 1984 to 1990. In order to meet the objection that they would give too much power to the LO's leadership, they have been decentralised into five regional funds. The government will appoint independent nine-member Managing Boards with five of the members representing 'employee interests'. The funds will receive their income from a proportion of the employers' pension contribution and from a 20 per cent tax on each company's profits after allowance for inflation (Gill, 1984).

7. There have been independent studies of materialism and post-materialism carried out in Sweden using the same questionnaires as those of the Eurobarometer surveys. However, their findings are not available to the author.

8. It is possible that Scase's findings may have been influenced to a modest extent by a difference in the two samples. Although they were matched carefully in terms of a number of important characteristics such as income, occupation and workplace technology, there were some differences in the community setting in which the English and Swedish factories were embedded.

9. Dunning and Pearce (1981, Part II) record only 25 Swedish firms amongst the 831 who in 1978 had a turnover in excess of $2.25 billion.

CHAPTER 7

1. Habermas's observations are particularly relevant to the Swedish case discussed in Chapter 6. There we saw how the LO's attempts to squeeze profits in pursuit of their solidaristic wage policy faced difficulties through the possible decline in private investment from which future employment and production would stem. One of the attractions of the wage-earners funds' proposal was that it could facilitate private investment without profits or the concentration of wealth increasing.

2. Both Habermas and Offe are particularly likely to be influenced by developments in their own country, Germany. Notice the similarity of their approach with the views of Brandt and Schmidt discussed in Chapter 5.

3. This is a simplification. Habermas draws heavily on Offe's earlier work, much of which was published in English after a delay of several years. Thus in Offe (1984), Chapter 1 was originally published in Germany in 1973 and not translated until 1976; whilst Chapter 2 appeared in Germany in 1979.

4. Smith (1983, Ch. 7) provides a variety of data. In Czechoslovakia 'open' inflation was 3.6 per cent in 1979; in Romania in 1983 he estimates that state retail prices rose by 25–30 per cent; in Bulgaria retail prices rose by 13.9 per cent in 1980; in Hungary 'open' inflation was 8.9 per cent in 1979. Data on changes in the USSR price index are notably difficult to obtain. Ellman (1982, pp. 134–5) points out that from 1977 to 1982 there were a series of significant price increases in a variety of goods. Polish inflation will be referred to in detail in the last section of this chapter.

5. The survey had a relatively low response rate which may indicate that the findings are not reliable.

CHAPTER 8

1. Prices and incomes policies as used in this context may take a multiplicity of forms. They include not just formal policies with specific rules

and guidelines for allowable price and wage increases (including the zero norm of a freeze) but also the less specific norms and restraints implicit in social contracts and in centralised bargaining between broadly-based union and employer federations that explicitly take into account the macro-economic implications of wage-bargaining.

Resistance to the correction of budgetary deficits may occur because some groups may suffer material losses through such corrective policies (Gordon, 1975; Crouch, 1978, pp. 228–9). Hence the power and capacity for political organisation of such groups becomes critical *vis-à-vis* the power of groups who might benefit.

2. The restrictive money supply cannot accommodate both a substantial rise in the level of wages and prices and the maintenance of the existing level of output and production. If higher than budgeted-for wages and prices occur, then output and production will be lower than anticipated with resultant lower employment. More precisely, individual firms may not be able to finance both higher wages and existing levels of employment, the obvious case in point being public sector enterprises and services subject to strict 'cash limits' on their financing.

3. In the case of deflationary policies, we indicated in Chapter 3 that financial interests, particularly as manifested in the City, have been successful in gaining their introduction. However, counter-pressures from organised labour and (industrial) business, coupled with fears about the political business cycle, have normally meant that they have not been maintained for lengthy periods. This has meant that the UK has had the worst of all possible macro-economic worlds, a series of 'stop–go' policies that have neither generated the long-term growth that could have helped to meet economistic demands, nor provided the long-term financial rectitude that might have forced competitive behaviour on businesses and a change in bargaining strategy on organised labour.

4. Blazyca (1985, p. 435) points out that Polish inflation fell from over 100 per cent in 1982 to 22.1 per cent in 1983 and probably about 16 per cent in 1984.

5. One other critical cultural factor is the German fear of inflation. In Chapter 5 we presented some modest evidence that the hyper-inflation of the inter-war period still has an effect on contemporary values. This cultural legacy alters the nature of the political business cycle. It means that governments will be rewarded for giving priority to curbing inflation and that counter-inflation policies are more likely to be supported both by the electorate and by organised labour. Hence the lower costs in unemployment of restrictive monetary policies as noted above.

6. This likelihood has been enhanced by the recent rapid growth of two other labour federations, TCO and SACO–SR, who represent different interests from those of the LO.

7. As Streeck (1984) has suggested this would mark a shift from centralised agreements over wage determination to more localised company specific procedures. This fragmentation of wage determination need

not result in the anomic British situation if employers can use their superior market power to hold wage increases in check. Streeck tends to underplay the element of market power by stressing how the institutions of co-determination and co-partnership could foster the identification of workers with their enterprises with resultant wage restraint to accord with corporate interests. However, this mechanism is only likely to be successful if the company can reproduce a 'virtuous cycle' at the level of the enterprise, that is, to produce obvious advantages in terms of higher wages and fringe benefits. In addition, it is not necessary where workers are in a weak bargaining position. Thus company incorporation may only be necessary as an employer strategy for relatively small sections of the workforce.

8. In the Polish case business interests and the government are not separate entities.

Bibliography

Aberg, R. (1984), 'Market-Independent Income Distribution: Efficiency and Legitimacy', in *Order and Conflict in Contemporary Capitalism*, ed. J. H. Goldthorpe (Oxford University Press, Oxford).

Adams, R. L. and Rummel, C. H. (1977), 'Workers' Participation in Management in West Germany', *Industrial Relations Journal*, 8.

Albrecht, S.L. and Deutsch, S. (1983), 'The Challenge of Economic Democracy: The Case of Sweden', *Economic and Industrial Democracy*, 4.

Alvarez, D. and Cooper, B. (1984), 'Productivity Trends in Manufacturing at Home and Abroad', *Monthly Labour Review*, 107.

Anderson, M. (1978), 'Power and Inflation', in *The Political Economy of Inflation*, ed. F. Hirsch and J. H. Goldthorpe (Martin Robertson, London).

Ashenfelter, O. C. (1978), 'Union Relative Wage Effects: New Evidence and a Survey of Their Implications for Inflation', in *Economic Contributions to Public Policy*, ed. R. Stone and W. Peterson (Macmillan, London).

Ashenfelter, O. C., Johnson, G. E. and Pencaval, J. H. (1972), 'Trade Unions and the Rate of Change of Money Wages in United States Manufacturing Industry', *Review of Economic Studies*, 39.

Bauman, Z. (1972), *Between Class and Elite* (Manchester University Press, Manchester).

—— (1982), *Memories of Class: The Pre-History and After-Life of Class* (Routledge & Kegan Paul, London).

Baxter, J. L. (1973), 'Inflation in the Context of Relative Deprivation and Social Justice', *Scottish Journal of Political Economy*, 12.

Beckerman, W. (1985), 'How the Battle Against Inflation Was Really Won', *Lloyds Bank Review*, 155.

Behrend, H. (1973), *Incomes Policy, Equity and Pay Increase Differentials* (Scottish Academic Press, Edinburgh).

Bendix, R. (1956), *Work and Authority in Industry* (John Wiley & Sons, New York).

Biedenkopf, K. (1976), *Co-Determination in the Company: The Biedenkopf Report*, trans. D. O'Neill (Legal Research Committee, Faculty of Law, Queen's University, Belfast).

Blazyca, G. (1985), 'The Polish Economy under Martial Law – a Dissenting View', *Soviet Studies*, 37.

Blumberg, P. (1968), *Industrial Democracy: The Sociology of Participation* (Constable, London).

Brittan, S. (1977), 'The Politics of Excessive Expectations', in *The Economic Consequences of Democracy* (Temple Smith, London).

—— (1978), 'Inflation and Democracy', in *The Political Economy of Inflation*, ed. F. Hirsch and J. H. Goldthorpe (Martin Robertson, London).

Brody, D. (1980), *Workers in Industrial America: Essays on the Twentieth-Century Struggle* (Oxford University Press, Oxford).

Brown, W. and Terry, M. (1978), 'The Changing Nature of National Wage Agreements', *Scottish Journal of Political Economy*, 25.

Buchanan, J. M. and Tullock, K. (1962), *The Calculation of Consent: Logical Foundations of Constitutional Democracy* (Michigan University Press, Ann Arbor).

Budde, A., Child, J., Francis, A. and Kieser, A. (1982), 'Corporate Goals, Managerial Objectives and Organisational Structures in British and West German Companies', *Organisation Studies*, 3.

Bunce, V. (1983), 'The Political Economy of the Brezhnev Era: The Rise and Fall of Corporatism', *British Journal of Political Science*, 13.

Burawoy, M. (1979), *Manufacturing Consent* (University of Chicago, Chicago).

Cable, J. A. and Fitzroy, F. R. (1980), 'Productive Efficiency, Incentives and Employee Participation: Some Preliminary Results for West Germany', *Kyklos*. 33.

Cameron, D. R. (1984), 'Social Democracy, Corporatism, Labour Quiescence, and the Representation of Economic Interest in Advanced Capitalist Society', in *Order and Conflict in Contemporary Capitalism*, ed. J. H. Goldthorpe (Oxford University Press, Oxford).

Cantril, H. (1965), *The Pattern of Human Concerns* (Rutgers University Press, New Brunswick, N. J.).

Castles, F. G. and McKinlay, R. D. (1979), 'Public Welfare Provision, Scandinavia, and the Sheer Futility of the Sociological Approach to Politics', *British Journal of Political Science*, 9.

Chandler, A. D. (1976), 'The Development of Modern Management Structure in the US and UK', in *Management Strategy and Business Development: An Historical and Comparative Study*, ed. L. Hannah (Macmillan, London).

—— (1977), *The Visible Hand: The Managerial Revolution in American Business* (Harvard Unversity Press, Cambridge, Mass.).

Clark, J. (1979), 'Concerted Action in the Federal Republic of Germany', *British Journal of Industrial Relations*, 17.

Clegg, H. (1971), *How to Run an Incomes Policy* (Heinemann, London).

Commission on Industrial and Economic Concentration (1976), 'Ownership and Influence in the Company', in *Readings in the Swedish Class Structure*, ed. R. Scase (Pergamon, Oxford).

Connor, W. D. (1980), 'Dissent in Eastern Europe: A New Coalition?', *Problems of Communism*, 29.

—— (1981), 'Workers and Power', in *Blue-Collar Workers in Eastern Europe*, ed. J. F. Triska and C. Gati (George Allen & Unwin, London).

Crenson, M. A. (1971), *The Unpolitics of Air Pollution: A Study of Non-Decision Making in the City* (Johns Hopkins Press, Baltimore).

Crouch, C. (1977), *Class Conflict and the Industrial Relations Crisis* (Heinemann, London).

—— (1978), 'Inflation and the Political Organisation of Economic Interests', in *The Political Economy of Inflation*, ed. F. Hirsch and J. H. Goldthorpe (Martin Robertson, London).

—— (1980), 'Varieties of Trade Union Weakness: Organised Labour and Capital Formation in Britain, Federal Germany and Sweden', *West European Politics*, 3.

—— (1985), 'Conditions for Trade Union Wage Restraint', in *The Politics of Inflation and Economic Stagnation*, ed. L. N. Lindberg and C. S. Maier (Brookings Institution, Washington).

Currie, R. (1979), *Industrial Politics* (Oxford University Press, Oxford).

Dalton, R. (1977), 'Was There a Revolution? A Note on Generational versus Life-Cycle Explanations of Value Difference', *Comparative Political Studies*, 9.

Daniel, W. W. (1975), *The PEP Survey on Inflation* (PEP, London).

Daubler, W. (1975), 'Co-Determination: The German Experience', *The Industrial Law Journal*, 4.

Davis, E. and Dilnot, A. (1985), 'The IFS Tax and Benefit Model', Institute of Fiscal Studies Working Paper No. 58 (IFS, London).

de Weydenthal, J. B. (1981), 'Poland: Workers and Politics', in *Blue-Collar Workers in Eastern Europe*, ed. J. F. Triska and C. Gati (George Allen & Unwin, London).

Department of Employment (1982), *Employment Gazette*, 90.

—— (1985), *Employment Gazette*, 93.

Dohse, K. (1984), 'Foreign Workers and Workforce Management in West Germany', *Economic and Industrial Democracy*, 5.

Domberger, S. (1983), *Industrial Structure, Pricing and Inflation* (Martin Robertson, Oxford).

Domhoff, G. W. (1975), 'Social Clubs, Policy-Planning Groups, and Corporations: A Network Study of Ruling-Class Cohesiveness', in *New Directions in Power Structure Research*, ed. G. W. Domhoff (The Insurgent Sociologist, Oregon).

Dore, R. (1983), 'Introduction', in *Japan in the Passing Lane*, S. Kamata, trans. T. Akimoto (George Allen & Unwin, London).

Downs, A. (1957), *An Economic Theory of Democracy* (Harper Brothers, New York).

Dunning, J. H. and Pearce, R. D. (1981), *The World's Largest Industrial Enterprises* (Gower, Farnborough).

Dyson, K. (1981), 'The Politics of Economic Management in West Germany', *West European Politics*, 4.

—— (1983), 'The Cultural, Ideological and Structural Context', in *Industrial Crisis*, ed. K. Dyson and S. Wilks (Martin Robertson, Oxford).

—— (1984) 'The Politics of Corporate Crisis in West Germany', *West European Politics*, 7.

Edgren, G., Faxén, K.-O. and Odhner C.-E. (1973), *Wage Formation and the Economy*, trans. M. Eklof (George Allen & Unwin, London).

Edwards, R. (1979), *Contested Terrain: The Transformation of the Workplace in the Twentieth Century* (Heinemann, London).

Elliott, J. (1978), *Conflict or Co-operation?: The Growth of Industrial Democracy* (Kogan Page, London).

Ellman, M. (1982), 'Did Soviet Economic Growth End in 1978?', in *Crisis in the East European Economy: The Spread of the Polish Disease*, ed. J. Drewnowski (Croom Helm, London).

Elvander, N. (1974), 'Collective Bargaining and Incomes Policy in the Nordic Countries: A Comparative Analysis', *British Journal of Industrial Relations*, 12.

Ersson, S. and Lane, J.-E. (1983), 'Polarisation and Political Economy Crisis: The 1982 Swedish Election', *West European Politics*, 6.

Esping-Andersen, G. and Korpi, W. (1984), 'Social Policy as Class Politics in Post-War Capitalism: Scandinavia, Austria and Germany', in *Order and Conflict in Contemporary Capitalism*, ed. J. H. Goldthorpe (Oxford University Press, Oxford).

Esser, J., Fach, W. with Dyson, K. (1983), '"Social Market" and Modernization Policy: West Germany', in *Industrial Crisis*, ed. K. Dyson and S. Wilks (Martin Robertson, London).

Estey, M. (1981), *The Unions: Structure, Development and Management* (3rd edn, Harcourt, Brace, Jovanovich, New York).

Foster, J. (1974), *Class Struggle and the Industrial Revolution* (Weidenfeld & Nicholson, London).

Fox, A. (1971), *A Sociology of Work in Industry* (Collier-Macmillan, London).

—— (1974), *Beyond Contract: Work, Power and Trust Relations* (Faber & Faber, London).

—— (1978), 'Corporatism and Industrial Democracy: The Social Origins of Present Forms and Methods in Britain and Germany', *Industrial Democracy: International Views*, Papers given at the International Conference on Industrial Democracy, Cambridge, 1977 (SSRC, Industrial Research Unit, Coventry).

—— (1983), 'British Management and Industrial Relations: The Social Origins of a System', in *Perspectives on Management: A Multi-Disciplinary Analysis*, ed. M. J. Earl (Oxford University Press, Oxford).

Fox, A. and Flanders, A. (1969), 'The Reform of Collective Bargaining: From Donovan to Durkheim', *British Journal of Industrial Relations*, 7.

Frobel, F., Heinrich, J. and Kreye, O. (1980), *The New International Division of Labour* (Cambridge University Press, Cambridge).

Furstenberg, F. (1978), *Workers' Participation in Management in the Federal Republic of Germany* (International Institute for Labour Studies, Geneva).

Galbraith, J. K. (1969), *The New Industrial State* (Penguin Books, Harmondsworth).

—— (1974), *Economics and the Public Purpose* (André Deutsch, London).

Gallie, D. (1983), *Social Inequality and Class Radicalism in France and Britain* (Cambridge University Press, Cambridge).

Gennard, J., Dunn, S. and Wright, M. (1980), 'The Extent of Closed Shop Arrangements in British Industry', *Employment Gazette*, 88.

George, K. D. and Joll, C. (1981), *Industrial Organisation: Competition, Growth and Structural Change* (3rd edn, George Allen & Unwin, London).

Geroski, P. A., Hamlin, A. P. and Knight, K. G. (1982), 'Wages, Strikes and Market Structure', *Oxford Economic Papers*, 34.

Gilbert, M. (1978), 'Neo-Durkheimian Analyses of Economic Life and Strife: From Durkheim to the Social Contract', *Sociological Review*, 26.

—— (1981), 'A Sociological Model of Inflation', *Sociology*, 15.

Gill, C. G. (1984), 'Swedish Wage-Earner Funds: The Road to Economic Democracy?', *Journal of General Management*, 9.

Goldthorpe, J. H. (1974), 'Social Inequality and Social Integration in Modern Britain', in *Poverty, Inequality and Class Structure*, ed. D. Wedderburn (Cambridge University Press, Cambridge).

—— (1978), 'The Current Inflation: Towards A Sociological Account', in *The Political Economy of Inflation*, ed. F. Hirsch and J. H. Goldthorpe (Martin Robertson, London).

—— (1983), 'Sociology of Inflation: A Comment', *British Journal of Sociology*, 34.

—— (1984), 'The End of Convergence: Corporatist and Dualist Tendencies in Modern Western Societies', in *Order and Conflict in Contemporary Capitalism*, ed. J. H. Goldthorpe (Oxford University Press, Oxford).

Gomulka, S. and Rostowski, J. (1984), 'The Reformed Polish Economic System 1982–3', *Soviet Studies*, 36.

Gordon, R. J. (1975), 'The Demand for and Supply of Inflation', *Journal of Law and Economics*, 18.

Gough, I. (1979), *The Political Economy of the Welfare State* (Macmillan, London).

Grant, W. and Marsh, D. (1977), *The CBI* (Hodder & Stoughton, London).

Habermas, J. (1976), *Legitimation Crisis*, trans. T. McCarthy (Heinemann, London).

Hannah, L. (1983), *The Rise of the Corporate Economy* (2nd edn, Methuen, London).

Haraszti, M. (1977), *A Worker in a Worker's State*, trans. M. Wright (Penguin Books, Harmondsworth).

Heidensohn, K. (1971), 'Industrial Democracy: The German Experience', *Social and Economic Administration*, 5.

Henry, S. G. B. (1981), 'Incomes Policy and Aggregate Pay', in *Incomes Policies, Inflation and Relative Pay*, ed. J. L. Fallick and R. F. Elliott (George Allen & Unwin, London).

Henry, S. G. B. and Ormerod, P. A. (1978), 'Incomes Policy and Wage Inflation', *National Institute Economic Review*, 85.

Hibbs, D. A. (1979), 'The Mass Public and Macroeconomic Performance: The Dynamics of Public Opinion Toward Unemployment and Inflation', *American Journal of Political Science*, 23.

Himmelstrand, U. (1981), *Beyond Welfare Capitalism* (Heinemann, London).

Hirsch, F. and Goldthorpe, J. H. (eds) (1978), *The Political Economy of Inflation* (Martin Robertson, London).

Hobsbawn, E. J. (1964), *Labouring Men* (Weidenfeld & Nicolson, London).

Holmes, M. (1982), *Political Pressure and Economic Policy: British Government 1970–74* (Butterworth, London).

—— (1985), *The First Thatcher Government 1979–83* (Wheatsheaf Books, Brighton).

Howe, M. (1971), 'Anti-Trust Policy: Rules or Discretionary Intervention', *Moorgate and Wall Street*, Spring.

Hudson, J. (1982), *Inflation: A Theoretical Survey and Analysis* (George Allen & Unwin, London).

Hughes, A. and Kumar, M. (1984), 'Recent Trends in Aggregate Concentration in the UK Economy', *Cambridge Journal of Economics*, 8.

Huhne, C. (1985), 'The Rich Push the Poor out of Work', *The Guardian*, 11 April.

Husbands, C. (1985), 'Government Popularity and the Unemployment Issue, 1966–83', *Sociology*, 19.

Ingham, G. K. (1974), *Strikes and Industrial Conflict: Britain and Scandinavia* (Macmillan, London).

—— (1984), *Capitalism Divided?: The City and Industry in British Social Development* (Macmillan Educational, Basingstoke).

Inglehart, R. (1971), 'The Silent Revolution in Europe: Intergenerational Change in Post-Industrial Societies', *American Political Science Review*, 65.

—— (1977), *The Silent Revolution: Changing Values and Political Styles Among Western Publics* (Princeton University Press, Princeton, N.J.).

—— (1981), 'Post-Materialism in an Environment of Insecurity', *American Political Science Review*, 75.

—— (1985), 'New Perspectives on Value Change: Response to Lafferty and Knutsen, Savage and Boltken and Jagodzinski', *Comparative Political Studies*, 17.

Israel, J. (1978), 'Swedish Socialism and Big Business', *Acta Sociologica*, 21.

Jackson, D., Turner, H. A. and Wilkinson, F. (1972), *Do Trade Unions Cause Inflation?* (Cambridge University Press Cambridge).

Jay, P. (1976), *Employment, Inflation and Politics: 6th Wincott Memorial Lecture* (Institute for Economic Affairs, London).

Jenkins, C. and Sherman, B. (1979), *White-Collar Unionism: The Rebellious Salariat* (Routledge & Kegan Paul, London).

Jenkins, D. (1985), 'A Theology for the Liberation of Tomorrow's Britain', edited version of 1985 Hibbert Lecture, *The Guardian*, 15 April.

Johnson, P. M. (1981), 'Changing Social Structure and the Political Role of Manual Workers', in *Blue-Collar Workers in Eastern Europe* ed. J. F. Triska and C. Gati (George Allen & Unwin, London).

Jones, A. (1973), *The New Inflation: The Politics of Prices and Incomes* (Penguin Books, Harmondsworth).

Jowett, P. (1985), 'The Second European Elections', *West European Politics*, 8.

Keohane, R. O. (1984), 'The World Political Economy and the Crisis of Embedded Liberalism', in *Order and Conflict in Contemporary Capitalism*, ed. J. H. Goldthorpe (Oxford University Press, Oxford).

Kolankiewicz, G. (1981), 'Poland, 1980: The Working Class under "Anomic Socialism"', in *Blue-Collar Workers in Eastern Europe*, ed. J. F. Triska and C. Gati (George Allen & Unwin, London).

Koralewicz-Zebik, J. (1984), 'The Perception of Inequality in Poland 1956–80', *Sociology*, 18.

Korpi, W. (1978a), 'Social Democracy in Welfare Capitalism – Structural Erosion, Welfare Backlash and Incorporation', *Acta Sociologica*, supplement, 21.

—— (1978b), 'Workplace Bargaining, the Law and Unofficial Strikes: The Case of Sweden', *British Journal of Industrial Relations*, 16.

—— (1978c), *The Working Class in Welfare Capitalism* (Routledge & Kegan Paul, London).

—— (1981), 'Unofficial Strikes in Sweden', *British Journal of Industrial Relations*, 19.

—— (1983), *The Democratic Class Struggle* (Routledge & Kegan Paul, London).

Korpi, W. and Shalev, M. (1979), 'Strikes, Industrial Relations and Class Conflict in Capitalist Societies', *British Journal of Sociology*, 30.

Krejci, J. (1976), *Social Structure in Divided Germany* (Croom Helm, London).

Kristensen, T. (1981), *Inflation and Unemployment* (Praeger, New York).

Kuster, G. H. (1974), 'Germany', in *Big Business and the State: Changing Relations in Western Europe*, ed. R. Vernon (Macmillan, London).

Lane, D. and O'Dell, F. (1978), *The Soviet Industrial Worker: Social Class, Education and Control* (Martin Robertson, Oxford).

Lange, P. (1984), 'Unions, Workers and Wage Regulation: The Rational Bases of Consent', in *Order and Conflict in Contemporary Capitalism*, ed. J. H. Goldthorpe (Oxford University Press, Oxford).

Lash, S. (1985), 'The End of Neo-Corporatism? The Breakdown of Centralised Bargaining in Sweden', *British Journal of Industrial Relations*, 23.

Laver, M. (1980), 'The Great British Wage Game', *New Society*, 51, 6 March.

Lawrence, P. (1980), *Managers and Management in West Germany* (Croom Helm, London).

Layard, R., Metcalf, D. and Nickell, S. (1978), 'The Effect of Collective Bargaining on Relative and Absolute Wages', *British Journal of Industrial Relations*, 16.

Layard, R. and Nickell, S. (1985), 'The Causes of British Unemployment', *National Institute Economic Review*, 111.

Lindberg, L. (1982), 'Inflation, Recession and the Political Process: Challenges to Theory and Practice', in *The Politics of Inflation: A Comparative Analysis*, ed. R. Medley (Pergamon, Oxford).

Lindberg, L. N. and Maier, C. S. (eds) (1985), *The Politics of Inflation and Economic Stagnation* (Brookings Institution, Washington).

Lipset, S. M. (1960), *Political Man* (Heinemann, London).

Lupton, T. and Wilson, C. S. (1959), 'The Social Background and Connections of "Top Decision Makers"', *Manchester School*, 27.

Mackenzie, G. (1973), *The Aristocracy of Labor: The Position of Skilled Craftsmen in the American Class Structure* (Cambridge University Press, Cambridge).

MacPherson, C. B. (1962), *The Political Theory of Possessive Individualism* (Oxford University Press, Oxford).

MacShane, D. (1981), *Solidarity: Poland's Independent Trade Union* (Spokesman, Nottingham).

McQuaid, K. (1982), *Big Business and Presidential Power* (William Morrow, New York).

Malewski, A. (1971), 'Attitudes of the Employees from Warsaw Enterprises Towards the Differentiation of Wages and the Social System in May 1958', *Polish Sociological Bulletin*, 24.

Markovits, A. S. and Allen, C. S. (1984), 'Trade Unions and the Economic Crises: The West German Case', in *Unions and Economic Crisis: Britain, West Germany and Sweden*, P. Gourevitch *et al*. (George Allen & Unwin, London).

Marsh, A. (1975), 'The "Silent Revolution", Value Priorities and the Quality of Life in Britain', *American Political Science Review*, 69.

Marsh, D. and Locksley, G. (1983), 'Capital in Britain: its Structural Power and Influence over Policy', *West European Politics*, 6.

Marshall, G. (1983), 'Some Remarks on the Study of Working-Class Consciousness', *Politics and Society*, 12.

Marshall, G., Rose, D., Vogler, C. and Newby, H. (1985), 'Class, Citizenship and Distributional Conflict in Modern Britain', *British Journal of Sociology*, 36.

Martin, A. (1977), 'Sweden: Industrial Democracy and Social Democratic Strategy', in *Worker Self-Management in Industry: The West European Experience*, ed. G. D. Garson (Praeger, New York).

—— (1984), 'Trade Unions in Sweden: Strategic Responses to Change and Crisis', in *Unions and Economic Crisis: Britain, West Germany and Sweden*, P. Gourevitch *et al*. (George Allen & Unwin, London).

Maslow, A. H. (1943), 'A Theory of Human Motivation', *Psychological Review*, 50.

Maurice, M. and Sellier, F. (1979), 'Societal Analysis of Industrial Relations: A Comparison between France and West Germany', *British Journal of Industrial Relations*, 17.

Medley, R. (ed.) (1982), *The Politics of Inflation: A Comparative Analysis* (Pergamon Press, Oxford).

Meidner, R. (1980), 'Our Concept of the Third Way', *Economic and Industrial Democracy*, 1.

Merton, R. K. (1949), *Social Theory and Social Structure* (Free Press, Glencoe).

Metcalf, D. (1982), 'Can Any Incomes Policy be Made to Work?', *New Society*, 71, 24 June.

Mills, C. W. (1956), *The Power Elite* (Oxford University Press, New York).

Mintz, B. (1975), 'The President's Cabinet 1897–1972: A Contribution to the Power Structure Debate', in *New Directions in Power Structure Research*, ed. G. W. Domhoff (The Insurgent Sociologist, Oregon).

Monissen, H. G. (1977), 'The Current Status of Labor Participation in the Management of Business Firms in Germany', in *The*

Co-Determination Movement in the West, ed. S. Pejovich (Lexington Books, Lexington).

Montias, J. M. (1981), 'Observations on Strikes, Riots and Other Disturbances', in *Blue-Collar Workers in Eastern Europe*, ed. J. F. Triska and C. Gati (George Allen & Unwin, London).

Moynihan, D. M. (1973), *The Politics of a Guaranteed Income* (Random House, New York).

Mroczkowski, T. (1984), 'Is the American Labour–Management Relationship Changing?', *British Journal of Industrial Relations*, 22.

Muller, G. M. (1974), 'Strikes, Lockouts and the West German Industrial Court', in *Industrial Conflicts and Their Place in Modern Society: An International Symposium*, ed. R. H. Preston (SCM Press, London).

Muller-Jentsch, W. and Sperling, H.-J. (1978), 'Economic Development, Labour Conflicts and the Industrial Relations System in West Germany', in *The Resurgence of Class Conflict in Western Europe since 1968*, vol. 1, *National Studies*, ed. C. Crouch and A. Pizzorno (Macmillan, London).

Mumper, M. J. and Uslaner, E. M. (1982), 'The Buck Stops Here: The Politics of Inflation in the United States', in *The Politics of Inflation: A Comparative Analysis*, ed. R. Medley (Pergamon Press, Oxford).

Noble, T. (1985), 'Inflation and Earnings Relativities in Britain After 1970', *British Journal of Sociology*, 36.

Nordhaus, W. D. (1975), 'The Political Business Cycle', *Review of Economic Studies*, 42.

Norgaard, D. and Sampson, S. L. (1984), 'Poland's Crisis and East European Socialism', *Theory and Society*, 13.

Nuti, D. M. (1982), 'The Polish Crisis: Economic Factors and Constraints', in *Crisis in the East European Economies: The Spread of the Polish Disease*, ed. J. Drewnowski (Croom Helm, London).

O'Connor, J. (1973), *The Fiscal Crisis of the State* (St Martin's Press, New York).

OECD (1981), *Economic Outlook*, 29.

—— (1984), *Economic Outlook*, 35.

—— (1985), *Economic Outlook*, 37.

Offe, C. (1975), 'Introduction to Part III', in *Stress and Contradiction in Modern Capitalism*, ed. L. N. Lindberg *et al*. (Lexington Books, Lexington).

—— (1984), *Contradictions of the Welfare State*, ed. and trans. J. Keane (Hutchinson, London).

Olson, M. (1965), *The Logic of Collective Action* (Harvard University Press, Cambridge, Mass.).

—— (1975), 'Comment', *Journal of Law and Economics*, 18.

—— (1982), *The Rise and Decline of Nations* (Yale University Press, New Haven, Conn.).

Oswald, A. J. (1982), 'Trade Unions, Wages and Unemployment: What Can Simple Models Tell Us?', *Oxford Economic Papers*, 34.

Pahl, R. E. and Winkler, J. (1974), 'The Economic Elite: Theory and Practice', in *Elites and Power in British Society*, ed. P. Stanworth and A. Giddens (Cambridge University Press, London).

Paloheimo, H. (1984), 'Pluralism, Corporatism and the Distributive Conflict in Developed Capitalist Countries', *Scandinavian Political Studies*, 7.

Parkin, F. (1972), 'System Contradiction and Political Transformation', *European Journal of Sociology*, 13.

Pencavel, J. H. (1981), 'The American Experience With Incomes Policies', in *Incomes Policies, Inflation and Relative Pay*, ed. J. L. Fallick and R. F. Elliott (George Allen & Unwin, London).

Pliatsky, L. (1982), *Getting and Spending* (Blackwell, Oxford).

Pontusson, G. (1984), 'Behind and Beyond Social Democracy in Sweden', *New Left Review*, 143.

Pravda, A. (1982), 'Poland 1980: From "Premature Consumerism" to Labour Solidarity', *Soviet Studies*, 34.

Price, R. and Bain, G. S. (1976), 'Union Growth Revisited: 1948–74 in Perspective', *British Journal of Industrial Relations*, 14.

Pryor, F. L. (1973), *Property and Industrial Organisation in Communist and Capitalist Nations* (Indiana University Press, Bloomington).

Ramsay, H. (1977), 'Cycles of Control', *Sociology*, 11.

Rosen, S. (1975), 'The United States: A Time for Reassessment', in *Worker Militancy and its Consequences, 1965–75*, ed. S. Barkin (Praeger, New York).

Rosenberg, S. and Weisskopf, T. E. (1981), 'A Conflict Theory Approach to Inflation in the Post-war US Economy', *American Economic Review*, Papers and Proceedings, 71.

Rothacker, A. (1984), 'The Green Party in German Politics', *West European Politics*, 7.

Rowthorn, R. E. (1977), 'Conflict, Inflation and Money', *Cambridge Journal of Economics*, 1.

Roy, D. (1952), 'Quota Restriction and Goldbricking in a Machine Shop', *American Journal of Sociology*, 67.

Runciman, W. G. (1966), *Relative Deprivation and Social Justice* (Routledge & Kegan Paul, London).

—— (1985), 'Contradictions of State Socialism: The Case of Poland', *Sociological Review*, 33.

Ryden, R. (1977), 'Labor Participation in the Management of Business Firms in Sweden', in *The Co-Determination Movement in the West*, ed. S. Pejovich (Lexington Books, Lexington).

Sabel, C. F. (1982), *Work and Politics: The Division of Labour in Industry* (Cambridge University Press, Cambridge).

Salzman, H. and Domhoff, G. W. (1980), 'The Corporate Community and Government: Do They Interlock?', in *Power Structure Research*, ed. G. W. Domhoff (Sage, Beverly Hills).

Samulewicz, W. W. (1984), 'Possibilities and Limitations of an Onward-Looking Growth Strategy in a Traditionally Centrally-Planned Economy: The Case of Poland', *East European Quarterly*, 18.

Scase, R. (1972), '"Industrial Man": A Reassessment with English and Swedish Data', *British Journal of Sociology*, 23.

—— (1976), 'Inequality in Two Industrial Societies: Class, Status and Power in Britain and Sweden', in *Readings in the Swedish Class Structure*, ed. R. Scase (Pergamon, Oxford).

—— (1977), *Social Democracy in Capitalist Society* (Croom Helm, London).

Scharpf, F. W. (1984), 'Economic and Institutional Constraints of Full-Employment Strategies: Sweden, Austria and West Germany, 1973–82', in *Order and Conflict in Contemporary Capitalism*, ed. J. H. Goldthorpe (Oxford University Press, Oxford).

Schmidt, F. (1974), 'Law on Industrial Conflict in Modern Society', in *Industrial Conflicts and their Place in Modern Society: An International Symposium*, ed. R. H. Preston (SCM Press, London).

Schmidt, M. G. (1984), 'The Politics of Unemployment: Rates of Unemployment and Labour Market Policy', *West European Politics*, 7.

Scitovsky, T. (1978), 'Market Power and Inflation', *Economica*, 45.

Scott, J. (1979), *Corporations, Classes and Capitalism* (Hutchinson, London).

Shonfield, A. (1965), *Modern Capitalism: The Changing Balance of Public and Private Power* (Oxford University Press, Oxford).

Shoup, L. H. (1975), 'Shaping the Post-War World: The Council of Foreign Relations and United States War Aims During World War Two', in *New Directions in Power Structure Research*, ed. G. W. Domhoff (The Insurgent Sociologist, Oregon).

Skold, P. (1976), 'NEB–Swedish Style', *Confederation of British Industry Review*, 20.

Smith, A. H. (1983), *The Planned Economies of Eastern Europe* (Croom Helm, London).

Smith, M. R. (1982), 'Accounting for Inflation in Britain', *British Journal of Sociology*, 33.

—— (1985), 'Accounting for Inflation (Again)', *British Journal of Sociology*, 36.

Soskice, D. (1978), 'Strike Waves and Wage Explosions, 1968–70: An Economic Interpretation', in *The Resurgence of Class Conflict in Western Europe Since 1968*, vol. II: *Comparative Analyses*, ed. C. Crouch and A. Pizzorno (Macmillan, London).

Staniszkis, J. (1979), 'On Some Contradictions of Socialist Society: The Case of Poland', *Soviet Studies*, 31.

Stephens, J. D. (1979), *The Transition from Capitalism to Socialism* (Humanities Press, Atlantic Highlands).

Story, J. (1981), 'The Federal Republic – A Conservative Revisionist', *West European Politics*, 4.

Streeck, W. (1981), 'Qualitative Demands and the Neo-Corporatist Manageability of Industrial Relations in West Germany at the Beginning of the Eighties', *British Journal of Industrial Relations*, 19.

—— (1982), 'Organisational Consequences of Neo-Corporatist Co-operation in West German Labour Unions', in *Patterns of Corporatist Policy-Making*, ed. G. Lehmbruch and P. Schmitter (Sage, Beverly Hills).

—— (1984), 'Neo-Corporatist Industrial Relations and the Economic Crisis in West Germany', in *Order and Conflict in Contemporary Capitalism*, ed. J. H. Goldthorpe (Oxford University Press, Oxford).

Sturmthal, A. (1982), 'Unemployment, Inflation and "Guest Workers": Comparative Study of Three European Countries', *Relations Industrielles*, 37.

Taylor, Richard (1985), 'Green Politics and the Peace Movement', in *A Socialist Anatomy of Britain*, ed. D. Coates, G. Johnston and R. Bush (Quality Press, Cambridge).

Taylor, Robert (1982), *Workers and the New Depression* (Macmillan, London).

Taylor-Gooby, P. (1983), 'Legitimation Deficit, Public Opinion and the Welfare State', *Sociology*, 17.

Thompson, E. P. (1967), 'Time, Work-Discipline and Industrial Capitalism', *Past and Present*, 38.

Tylecote, A. (1981), *The Causes of the Present Inflation* (Macmillan, London).

Tyson, L. D. (1981), 'Aggregate Economic Difficulties and Workers'

Welfare', in *Blue-Collar Workers in Eastern Europe*, ed. J. F. Triska and C. Gati (George Allen & Unwin, London).

UN (1980), 1979 *Yearbook of National Account Statistics*, vol. II. *International Tables* (UN, New York).

—— (1985), *National Account Statistics: Analysis of Main Aggregates 1982* (UN, New York).

Useem, M. (1980), 'Which Business Leaders Help Govern?', in *Power Structure Research*, ed. G. W. Domhoff (Sage, Beverly Hills).

van Otter, C. (1975), 'Sweden: Labor Reformism Reshapes the System', in *Worker Militancy and its Consequences, 1965–75*. ed. S. Barkin (Praeger, New York).

Vogel, D. (1982), 'The Power of Business in America: A Re-Appraisal', *British Journal of Political Science*, 13.

Wachtel, H. and Adelsheim, P. (1978), 'Inflation and Unemployment: Or "Which Came First the Chicken or ... "', in *The Federal Budget and Social Reconstruction: The People and the State*, ed. M. G. Raskin (Transaction Books, New Brunswick).

Wanless, P. T. (1985), 'Inflation in the Consumer Goods Market in Poland 1971–82', *Soviet Studies*, 37.

Webber, D. (1983a) 'Combatting and Acquiescing in Unemployment? Economic Crisis Management in Sweden and West Germany', *West European Politics*, 6.

—— (1983b), 'A Relationship of "Critical Partnership": Capital and the Social–Liberal Coalition in West Germany', *West European Politics*, 6.

Whitley, R. (1973), 'Commonalities and Connections among Directors of Large Financial Institutions', *Sociological Review*, 21.

Willman, P. (1982), *Fairness, Collective Bargaining and Incomes Policy* (Oxford University Press, Oxford).

Wilson, G. K. (1982), 'Why Is There no Corporatism in the United States?', in *Patterns of Corporatist Policy-Making*, ed. G. Lehmbruch and P. Schmitter (Sage, Beverly Hills).

Wood, A. (1978), *A Theory of Pay* (Cambridge University Press, Cambridge).

Woodall, J. (1982), *Socialist Corporation and Technocratic Power: The Polish United Workers' Policy, Industrial Organisation and Workforce Control 1958–80* (Cambridge University Press, Cambridge).

Wootton, Baroness (1954), *The Social Foundations of Wages Policy* (George Allen & Unwin, London).

—— 1974), *Fair Play, Relativities and a Policy for Incomes*, 20th Fawley Lecture (Camelot Press, Southampton).

Zweigenhaft, R. (1975), 'Who Represents America?', in *New Directions in Power Structure Research*, ed. G. W. Domhoff (The Insurgent Sociologist, Oregon).

Index

254